The Politics
of
American
Foreign Policy

The Politics
of
American
Foreign Policy

THE SOCIAL CONTEXT OF DECISIONS

MORTON BERKOWITZ
Brooklyn College, City University of New York

P.G. BOCK
University of Illinois at Urbana

VINCENT J. FUCCILLO
Brooklyn College, City University of New York

PRENTICE-HALL, INC., ENGLEWOOD CLIFFS, NEW JERSEY

Library of Congress Cataloging in Publication Data

Berkowitz, Morton. (date)
    The politics of American foreign policy.

    Includes bibliographies and index.
    1.–United States—Foreign relations—1945–
2.–World politics–1945–   I. Bock, P. G. (date), joint
author.   II.–Fuccillo, Vincent J. (date), joint author.
III.–Title.
JX1417.B46   327.73   76-14967
ISBN 0-13-685073-1

Printed in the United States of America

10 9 8 7 6 5 4 3 2 1

PRENTICE-HALL INTERNATIONAL, INC., *London*
PRENTICE-HALL OF AUSTRALIA PTY. LIMITED, *Sydney*
PRENTICE-HALL OF CANADA, LTD., *Toronto*
PRENTICE-HALL OF INDIA PRIVATE LIMITED, *New Delhi*
PRENTICE-HALL OF JAPAN, INC., *Tokyo*
PRENTICE-HALL OF SOUTHEAST ASIA PTE. LTD., *Singapore*

Contents

Preface

Despite heightened public concern, there continues to be a wide-spread ignorance about foreign policy. The public is largely uninformed about the nature of American foreign policy, the decision-making process by which it is formulated, and the principal objectives which it is designed to achieve. Students also appear ill-equipped to make sense of the foreign policy process, to view it in a meaningful historical perspective, or to relate it to the general literature of political and social science. In this volume we offer the student the means by which to begin to think more clearly, coherently, and systematically about foreign policy.

We start with the simple assertion that foreign policy is, by definition, a form of public policy, and must, therefore, be examined within the general social and political context that shapes all policy. All too often, however, books about foreign policy choose to approach the subject as if a special logic governed the formulation and execution of this type of policy and portray what appears to be a unique and distinct process by which a nation conducts its external affairs. This approach which, in its extreme form, is reflected in the saying "politics stops at the water's edge," focuses on the external forces and events that provide the stimuli for a nation's actions and on the impact of these actions abroad. It thus suggests that foreign policy is somehow removed from the political arena in which domestic policies are hammered out. And yet even a casual inspection of recent American foreign policy shows that major decisions regarding our interaction with the rest of the world are, in fact, strongly influenced by domestic political considerations—national elections being a most prominent example. In brief, then, the domestic sources and consequences of foreign policy are as important as the foreign ones.

This book is an attempt to illustrate that basic point, not by ignoring the important foreign elements of foreign policy, but by highlighting the domestic ones, and by showing how the two sets of elements interact to produce contemporary American foreign policy. In order to avoid an overly-abstract theoretical treatment or a detailed history of the United States' relations with other countries, we have chosen to achieve this aim by examining a number of significant episodes in the post-World War II era.

Initially we considered collecting a series of previously published case studies of foreign policy decisions and adding to them an extensive analysis and commentary. After a careful search of the literature, however, we were unable to find a group of cases suited to our purpose. Although there exist various excellent studies of individual decisions, the great variations among them in length, approach, and emphasis make it impossible to place any adequate number within a common framework for comparison and generalization. As a result, we decided to present a selection of original studies of various foreign policy decisions following a common design. The principal elements of this framework are presented in Chapter 1, where we define the nature of foreign policy, explain the selection of the cases, and introduce the broader social context within which foreign policy operates.

We then examine eleven major post-World War II foreign policy decisions spanning Democratic and Republican administrations and covering a wide range of substantive issues, decisional modes, and desired outcomes. In other words, we chose cases that variously illustrate the diplomatic, economic, and military dimensions of foreign policy, where the decisions had to be reached in crisis as well as non-crisis situations, and where the aim was to assist or frustrate other nations and to exercise or refrain from exercising American national power.

Each analysis of a foreign policy decision contains the following elements:

1. *The definition of the situation*—the external and internal stimuli that created the recognition that some change in policy was needed.
2. *The chronology*—the series of events leading to the decision.
3. *The participants*—the major individual and institutional actors involved in the decision, in particular the role of the president and his closest advisers.
4. *The process*—the manner in which the participants interacted using their strategies of communication and influence to achieve their goals.
5. *The outcome*—the decision reached and its translation into policy.

The cases are based primarily on four types of sources: public documents (e.g., State Department releases, congressional hearings and debates); memoirs of major participants (e.g., President Truman, Secretary of State Acheson); contemporary newspaper accounts; and secondary sources in the form of scholarly works.

In the two final chapters we describe the basic features of our interpretative framework, display the interrelationships of these elements, and show how this framework can be applied to illuminate our case studies and thus to enhance our understanding of the foreign policy process. These chapters also demonstrate how our work relates to the major scholarly contributions and controversies in foreign policy research and how it illuminates three principal issues in the field: the interaction between internal and external forces; the interplay between individuals and institutions; and the relationship between ideology, interests, and national objectives in the making of American foreign policy.

To the extent that our effort has succeeded, we believe that students will come to realize that foreign policy is made through a political process which, despite certain unique features, nevertheless forms an integral part of American politics, and that any understanding of the meaning and evolution of American foreign policy requires an understanding of American society.

Over the years we have acquired many intellectual debts, both individually and collectively, which we are happy to acknowledge here. Eugene Green provided perceptive research assistance at an early stage of this work. Joseph LaPalombara read the entire manuscript and made extensive comments and suggestions. Richard Merritt read and commented on portions of the manuscript, and A. F. K. Organski offered useful advice on the project. Our students in many foreign policy courses and seminars will probably recognize much here that was first "floated" before them. Their discussions, comments, and criticisms greatly influenced the structure of this book. We thank them all and absolve them of any errors and shortcomings.

The production of a book is as much a technical as an intellectual endeavor, and we were fortunate indeed in having the assistance of Frances Woodley who typed so much of the manuscript and helped improve its style. We are also grateful for the labors of Doris Glassman, Rose Lazar, and Lee Provitola of the Brooklyn College Department of Political Science. Our editors at Prentice-Hall, Roger Emblen, Stan Wakefield, and Marina Harrison provided the encouragement, patience, and expertise which much facilitated this joint venture and cleared the path to its successful completion.

Finally, we would like to thank colleagues and friends who offered personal support and exhortation: Albert Gorvine, Joel and Amy Kassiola, Ethel Sheffer, and Irving Fisher. To our wives, Linda and Mildred, we owe a special debt of gratitude for putting up with all those extended phone calls, postponed holidays, and altered plans which accompanied the writing of this book.

M.B.
P.G.B.
V.J.F.

1

Studying the Foreign Policy Process

Our purpose in this book is to examine the nature and structure of the political process by which foreign policy is made. More specifically, we shall attempt to explain the interplay between the structure of power and the patterns of interest and ideology in the development of American foreign policy. In order to meet these ends, we shall examine a number of major foreign-policy decisions in the post–World War II era, decisions that display a wide range of decisional modes and encompass a variety of substantive issues. In this way, we believe we can not only shed light on the manner in which the political system makes foreign policy, but be in a better position to assess several broad explanations that have been offered

1

in recent years for the particular orientation and direction of U.S. foreign policy during this period.

A nation's foreign policy may be defined as *the principles and practices used by that nation to govern its relations with the world outside its borders, especially other nations*. It might therefore seem that in order to describe any nation's foreign policy, one need only identify the relevant "principles and practices"; in order to explain it, one need only analyze their origins and formulation; and in order to evaluate it, one need only examine the extent to which they actually govern foreign relations. Furthermore, one might expect to find a considerable consensus, at least among informed and perceptive observers, about the major elements of any nation's foreign policy. And yet, shelves full of books demonstrate that even for the United States, whose international behavior has been submitted to constant and intensive scrutiny, this is not the case.

The reason is not hard to find. Once we leave the abstract realm of our definition and ask a slightly more specific question, such as "What was United States foreign policy in the 1960s?" great difficulties immediately appear. What were the principles and practices in that era? Were they specific to the 1960s, or were they common to the entire post–World War II era? Did they differ by geographic region, ideological bloc, or functional area (economic, military, cultural, and so on)? It soon becomes clear that only a detailed history of American relations with the rest of the world might provide a starting point for answering such questions. This history would then have to be supplemented by—or better yet, grounded in—a valid general theory of national and international politics before one could reach definitive conclusions about foreign policy.

Since a task of such magnitude is clearly beyond the capabilities of any single scholar, it is quite natural that one finds a large number of studies devoted to small segments of the field of American foreign policy. Some books deal with a given period in American foreign relations, others are devoted to American policy toward a region of the world or even one country, and still others cover particular aspects of foreign policy, such as military strategy, foreign aid, cultural exchange, or propaganda. The range of approaches, analytical frameworks, and methodologies employed in these studies is at least as diverse as the topics. Consequently, it would be surprising if scholars did not present a vast range of often conflicting interpretations of foreign policy.

Even where there is a widespread consensus, specifically in regard to the central role of the president in foreign-policy making, the range of views on the extent of presidential power and its dependence on support from other political and social institutions is very wide, as the following summary suggests.

1. By virtue of the information and expertise available to the president, which is quantitatively and qualitatively superior to that available to anyone else in the country, he, and only he, can make rational policy.
   Or:
On the contrary, precisely because the president is so dependent on information, he is severely constrained. He cannot absorb all the available information and is thus dependent upon interpreters, processers, and summarizers, who inevitably introduce some bias into the information reaching him, and thereby limit his options. In addition, some information reaches other parts of the polity, through other channels—in particular, the news media —and that information, especially if it contradicts presidential statements, may be sufficient to mobilize the opposition and further curtail the president's freedom of action.

2. The president as commander in chief has complete control over the military establishment and can therefore determine military policy—a crucial component of foreign policy.
   Or:
His power even in this area is limited, because the military establishment holds a strong independent position by virtue of the long careers of the top professional officers and by virtue of their ties with Congressional committees, industry, and other interest groups within the polity.

3. The cabinet is completely dependent upon the president, since its members serve at his pleasure. Therefore, individual secretaries act only as advisers to the president and implementers of his decisions.

Or:

Individual cabinet members can and do oppose the president, in part because they have their own political ambitions and their own constituencies outside the government, and in part because they represent the special perspectives and interests of their departments.

4. A major component of the president's power and freedom of action is his control over a large civilian bureaucracy that provides information, helps formulate policy, and implements it. This bureaucracy usually obeys and supports the president.

Or:

The bureaucracy is, in fact, entrenched, divided, dilatory, and composed of a number of almost independent subbureaucracies, each of which has its own goals, standard operating procedures, and, most important, alliances with the outside world—for instance, with congressional committees. As a result, the president cannot rely on this institution for much help in policy formulation, and must work very hard to have his policies carried out to his satisfaction.

5. Congress, recognizing the supreme importance of foreign policy, the serious national issues involved, and the president's constitutional rights, his access to secret information, and his expertise in this area, supports most of his policies most of the time. When it does disagree, it does so on a nonpartisan basis—that is, individual members act out of their own concern for national security, regardless of their party affiliations.

Or:

Bipartisanship in foreign policy may have worked at certain periods in American history and with certain issues that had great public support, but in many instances, particularly when large sums of money are involved or when there is no widespread public consensus but, rather, public controversy, Congress behaves in the foreign policy sphere much as it does in the domestic policy area.

6. The role of interest groups in foreign policy is largely irrelevant, since the powerful groups are domestically oriented, share the prevailing consensus on foreign policy, and are not interested in or capable of making major inputs into the foreign

policy process. The groups that are interested in foreign issues and oppose official policy are ephemeral, badly organized, and ineffective. Thus, the overall impact of interest groups is to strengthen the president's hand.

Or:

In many specific situations, certain interest groups have been highly effective both in promoting policies for example, the Marshall Plan, the recognition of Israel, military spending and the development of new weapons systems, and even in changing policy directions, as in the case of the Vietnam War and certain instances of foreign aid and international trade.

7. Public opinion is unimportant in foreign policy. The president's actions are almost always supported by large majorities of the people polled, and in any event, foreign policy has low salience for most citizens.

Or:

Public opinion is highly significant in special situations, such as election years, and on specific issues that have become "great debates," such as Vietnam, and if we look at segments of public opinion, we find that the opinions of an "attentive public" or of "opinion leaders" have considerable weight. Furthermore, public opinion is significant in establishing certain policy limits beyond which the president should not go, limits that he recognizes and does not exceed.

These differences in perceptions and interpretations, which demonstrate the difficulty of reaching consensus regarding both the nature and the role of foreign policy as well as the behavior of institutions in that domain of policy making, are not attributable solely to the magnitude of the topic and the conflicting approaches and values of the observers; they are due in no small part to the very nature of the phenomenon. Defined as "a set of principles and practices," foreign policy is, after all, the result of a complex, multidimensional political process. Such questions as "What is nation X's foreign policy?" or even "What was nation X's foreign policy in period Y?" cannot be answered by providing a list of coherent principles and a series of well-integrated practices flowing directly from them. True, enunciated principles may sometimes be identified, and we hope to be able to do so on the basis of our investigation. In the case of the United States, "no entangling alliances," "containment of Communism," or "the avoidance of nuclear war" might qualify. But whether these principles led to specific practices can be determined only by a careful study of the entire process that underlay the formation and execution of specific foreign policy actions. The reverse—whether such "practices" as neutrality acts, embargoes, nuclear-weapons-control treaties, or the suspension of economic aid flowed from officially announced "principles," or whether they resulted from other, less explicit but nonetheless powerful political considerations—depends equally on such a study of the foreign-policy-making process.

Some of the elements of this process are readily identifiable since they are common to all policy making. In the simplest terms, public policy is a response to events (stimuli), a response that is produced by the interaction of (1) the needs, interests, and motivations of individual decision makers, (2) the functioning of governmental institutions, and (3) basic societal structures and value systems. The nature of the response—that is, the specific policy adopted by a political system in a given situation—depends on the characteristics of these three elements and the relationships among them. Unfortunately, the identification of the relevant elements and the definition of the relationships among them has proved to be an extremely difficult task, one that is bedeviled by three basic problems.

The first problem is that of *rationality* versus *politics* in public policy making. On the one hand, policy making is supposed to be a rational, problem-solving process by which a government tackles issues of national concern. This approach stipulates a need to make an accurate assessment of the situation calling for a policy by using the best and most comprehensive information available, to identify alternate courses of action and carefully weigh their consequences, and, finally, to implement the policy that is most likely to succeed. On the other hand, the political context of policy making dictates a need to overcome some vested interests and serve others, to reconcile conflicting ideological positions, and to mobilize forces that resist change in existing policy. In other words, a need to produce results in a political environment in which different actors may all behave rationally from their individual perspectives, but, because their goals are so diverse, the resulting public policy is a politically acceptable compromise rather than a single rational policy. (For a detailed exploration of these problems, see Halperin and Kanter, 1973.)

Another problem arises from the recognition that policy cannot be made in a vacuum. Almost invariably, existing policy must be taken into account, so that what is called *policy making* is, as often as not, *policy changing*, and the process by which it occurs is severely constrained by past decisions and actions. It is for this reason that the notion of incrementalism has gained so much currency in discussions of domestic policy making. This approach asserts that policy changes very slowly, often by small increments, and that the safest prediction about next year's policy is that it will be only slightly different from this year's. This is not to say that innovation, or even radical change, can never occur, but rather that there is a predisposition in political systems to make the smallest possible changes in the face of new stimuli or changing circumstances, and that radical departures require truly important and lasting changes in the policy-making environment. As a result of this problem, students are confronted with two other interconnected issues. First, they must discover when a particular policy started. Second, they must determine at what point a change in existing policy is sufficiently marked to constitute a radical shift or "new" policy. For example, it is debatable whether the Alliance for Progress marked a fundamental departure in American policy toward Latin America, since the basic outlines of the program had already been developed within the Eisenhower administration before President Kennedy elevated it into an issue for his legislative agenda. A similar continuity characterized American trade policy as late as 1962 (see Chapter 7 for further clarification). We may, in fact, find that what appears to be simply incremental change is a reflection of a much greater degree of continuity in the basic orientation and thrust of post–World War II American foreign policy than is commonly assumed. (For a further discussion of incrementalism, see Lindblom, 1968.)

The second problem of policy-making analysis has a further dimension. It is tempting to think of the policy-making process as culminating in one major *decision*, preferably by a major political actor (for instance, the president of the United States), which is then implemented by other actors. The resulting feedback produces yet another decision, and thus determines future policy. The reality is, unfortunately, far more complex. As many observers have pointed out, it is far more common to find policy made by a series of small decisions, and even nondecisions, at many levels and in several branches of government. The analyst is therefore faced, in many cases, with the difficult task of determining which subset of these myriad governmental actions and inactions constitutes the policy that interests him.

A third problem of policy analysis arises from the need of any political system to make a large variety of specific public policies. The issue here concerns the relationship between the *substance* of the policy and the *process* by which it is made. Does the political system function in the same way regardless of the type of policy formulated, or do different processes—that is, different interactions among political institutions—characterize, say, agricultural, welfare, and defense policies?

Theodore Lowi (1964) pioneered this area of investigation, arguing that there are three distinct subsystems of the American polity and that these subsystems govern three basic types of public policy making in the domestic sphere: a pluralist subsystem for dealing with policies that are intended to *regulate* the use of resources, an elitist subsystem for policies meant to *redistribute* existing resources, and a log-rolling (or fragmented) subsystem for policies attempting to *distribute* new resources. Lowi implies that these three subsystems explain the full range of domestic policy making in the United States (1967, p. 298).

The question that comes immediately to mind is whether foreign policy is also determined by one or more of these subsystems, or whether it is a totally different phenomenon, accounted for by a fourth subsystem or set of processes. The traditional answer to this question has been to emphasize the distinctness of foreign policy, both on substantive and processual grounds. According to this view, foreign policy is made in response to external (foreign) stimuli, and its impact is external (on other nations). It deals with more important matters than those of domestic policy, specifically with issues of national security and national interest that affect the survival of the state and its progress in the world. These are matters on which all citizens could ideally agree, and whatever disagreements might exist certainly transcend narrow regional, economic or social interests and conflicts. For this reason, central political institutions function differently when foreign policy is considered and formulated. (For instance, it is assumed that Congress must act in a bipartisan manner in dealing with foreign affairs.) Moreover, special institutions, free from domestic political interference, are established to handle foreign policy. (A good illustration of this is the call for appointing only professional diplomats to ambassadorial posts instead of using these positions as rewards for domestic political support.) The core of this argument is perhaps best summarized by the old saying, "Politics stops at the water's edge."

In recent years, however, both scholars and practitioners have begun to challenge this position and its underlying assumptions. The most extreme form of this challenge is represented by Senator Fulbright's assertion in 1959 that "the line between domestic and foreign affairs . . . is wholly erased" (quoted in Rosenau, 1967, p. 21). The argument proceeds as follows: as a direct result of the growing interdependence among the countries of the world, particularly American involvement with an increasing number of countries in a large variety of military, political, economic, social, and cultural relationships, an ever growing number of public policy issues have acquired both domestic and foreign dimensions, and actions taken in one sphere inevitably affect actions taken in the other. Consequently, central political institutions do not handle foreign issues in a special manner; instead, as they become increasingly aware of the domestic implications of these issues, they treat them as de facto domestic issues and permit a large number of ostensibly domestic agencies to encroach on the domain of the specialized foreign policy institutions. Two striking recent examples are the American-Soviet wheat deal of 1972 and the American responses to the Arab oil embargo and price hikes of 1973. Trade expansion and foreign aid also illustrate this process, as we shall see in Chapters 7 and 11. (An older example, harking back to the Great Depression, is reflected in the saying, "When the United States sneezes, Europe catches pneumonia.")

The problem of determining the nature of foreign policy is, of course, more complicated than merely choosing between these two extreme positions. Even those who seem to argue for the uniqueness of foreign policy concede that since it is formulated by *national* institutions, it is at least affected by domestic considerations. Henry Kissinger spelled out this impact when he argued that the domestic structure of nations ultimately determines their perception of the international environment, their allocation of resources to foreign policy, and their elaboration and selection of foreign policy goals (1974, pp. 13–14). He went on to state that in the American context, "meaningful consultation with other nations becomes very difficult when the internal process of decision-making already has some of the characteristics of compacts between semisovereign entities" (*Ibid.*, p. 24).

By the same token, scholars who focus on the common elements of all public policy are aware of certain unique features of foreign policy. Since it is the external environment (for example, famine in Africa or civil war in Asia) that often produces the need for policy responses, and since the intended impact of the policy is also in the outside world, different instruments (for instance, foreign aid or military intervention) may be needed to implement it. Thus, James Rosenau, the first scholar to address this problem systematically, concludes that there is a distinct foreign policy "issue-area," which is distinguishable from domestic issue-areas by differences in the motives, roles, and interactions of government officials and agencies on the one hand, and of private citizens and groups on the other (1967; see p. 46 for a summary table). Similarly, Spanier and Uslaner argue that despite obvious and intimate connections between foreign and domestic policy, the process by which the former is made is basically different because it occurs exclusively at the national level, is concentrated in the executive branch, and is "therefore clearly hierarchical" (1974, p. 55). Even Lowi, whose tripartite typology of public policies was intended to synthesize different approaches to policy making, initially excluded foreign policy, regarding it as "obviously a fourth category" (1964,

p. 689). In a later article, he attempted to incorporate foreign policy into the three original categories, concluding that there are "three predictable subsystems of foreign policy, although they are not identical to the three domestic ones" (1967, p. 324). These are: (1) an elitist subsystem, which governs crisis situations and non-crisis situations in which no internal resources are involved; (2) a log-rolling subsystem, in which internal resources are to be distributed abroad; and (3) a pluralistic subsystem, in which internal resources are to be coercively regulated.

We need not worry about the differences between the two typologies, or even about their applicability to concrete situations. What is significant is, first, Lowi's important point that foreign policy crises are not necessarily unique policy-making situations (a point we shall return to below), and, second, the realization that it may be difficult, if not impossible, to distinguish clearly between foreign and domestic policies on the basis of the processes by which they are formulated.

Rosenau states this problem in the form of a provocative hypothesis: "The more an issue encompasses a society's resources and relationships, the more will it be drawn into the society's domestic political system, and the less will it be processed through the society's foreign policy system" (1967, p. 49). But even this formulation overemphasizes the differences between foreign and domestic policy in the contemporary American context. As we suggested above, the number of policy issues that do not have both domestic and foreign implications is shrinking rapidly, and there may no longer be much need to talk of separate political systems, or even subsystems, for each sphere. Rather, the fundamental issue is *the composition of the "mix" of foreign and domestic elements within a single policy-making process*, and the effects of this mix on the interaction of political institutions in specific cases.

In the following chapters we shall attempt to address this issue and, more broadly, to shed light on the basic problems of rationality and politics, policy making and policy changing, and substance and process, as these apply to foreign policy. We shall examine the political processes that culminated in eleven American foreign policy decisions in the post-1945 period (Chapters 2–12) and analyze the broader context within which policy is made with the aid of insights provided by these cases (Chapters 13 and 14). In order to understand why we chose this approach, it is important to remember what we are *not* trying to do. We are not attempting to describe all American relations with other nations since 1945; to do so, a much more detailed historical approach would be needed. We are also not concerned with evaluating the success or failure of any particular American action or general policy toward a specific nation or in a given problem area; this would require us to develop criteria for measuring the impact of the actions and for assessing whether that impact corresponded to the intentions of the policy makers. Instead, we are interested in probing the process by which U.S. foreign policy was formulated during this period, showing how that process led to certain decisions, and discovering what these decisions reveal about general patterns of American foreign policy behavior—that is, about this nation's interactions with the rest of the world.

The first part of our analysis might be termed a variant of the decision-making approach to foreign-policy making (see Snyder et al., 1962). It can perhaps be delineated best in a series of questions:

> 1. What were the *stimuli* that brought about a recognition of the need for a policy decision? Did they originate abroad or at home? What was the relative weight given to the foreign and domestic stimuli?
>
> 2. Who were the major *participants* in the decision-making process, and how did they perceive the stimuli and the action alternatives?
>
> 3. What were the major governmental and nongovernmental *agencies* involved in the decision, and how did their qualities or their modes of activity influence the process?
>
> 4. What was the structure of the *decision-making process* in each case? That is, what strategies of influence were used by the participants working through the institutions to achieve their goals, and how were their differences reconciled?
>
> 5. What was the *intended impact* of the decision? Was it to have primarily foreign or primarily domestic consequences? (Note that this is a matter completely different from the actual impact of a decision, which can be known only after the policy has been implemented and its results evaluated.)

One of the major criticisms of the decision-making approach is that is leads so often to single case studies, because only through case studies can the different complex relationships in the process be fully presented and understood. Entire books have been devoted to such foreign policy decisions as Korea (Paige, 1968), the Cuban missile crisis (Allison, 1971), and the Nuclear Test Ban Treaty (Lepper, 1971). The major drawback to single case studies, claim the critics, is that although they may illuminate a particular decision, they do not enable us to generalize to the political process operating in other decisions, since we cannot be certain that what was true in one case also applies in a set of cases or in all cases. In short, we do not know what the individual case represents. Supporters of the individual case study often respond to this charge by arguing that they are essentially interested in generating hypotheses, that on the basis of their intimate knowledge of a particular case such hypotheses are likely to be rich in theoretical content, plausible, and testable, and that when enough cases are examined their hypotheses will be proved or disproved.

Our decision to select a number of case studies and examine them within a common analytical framework is an attempt to benefit from both sides of this argument. We are mindful of the old saying, "For example is no proof," and we realize that even a series of examples may not constitute proof of any general assertion. However, if the examples are chosen carefully, if the relationships between them are made explicit and if they are analyzed within the same framework and presented in the same format, then we have, at the least, a more powerful method for examining the foreign policy process, and we can have at least some confidence in whatever general characteristics seem to emerge.

In this book, the selection of the cases flowed naturally from our desire to understand the interplay of domestic and foreign factors in the policy-making process and our conviction that this can only be done by analyzing a broad range of substantive issues, a variety of decisional modes, and a considerable length of time. Our cases as a group, therefore, were chosen to meet these three criteria.

First, we wanted to cover decisions that spanned a spectrum of perceived problems, intended outcomes, and required resources or instruments. Thus, we chose cases in which the issues were military intervention or disengagement (Indochina, 1954;

Lebanon, 1958; Dominican Republic, 1965; Vietnam, 1968), direct confrontation between the superpowers (Berlin, 1948; Cuba, 1962), increase in military security (Nuclear Test Ban Treaty, 1963), provision or withholding of economic assistance (Marshall Plan, 1948; Aswan Dam, 1956; Foreign Assistance Act, 1967), and encouragement of economic competition (Trade Expansion Act, 1962). We believe that such a range of issues is necessary in order for us to determine whether and to what extent the substance of policy affects the process by which a decision is reached. For example, we might discover whether Congress plays a larger role in cases involving high expenditures of public funds than in those calling for fewer resources; whether the State Department dominates cases involving diplomatic actions alone and plays a secondary role in those requiring military action; whether public opinion is more significant in cases that seem to threaten national survival or in cases that merely involve the prestige of the United States.

Second, we deliberately selected some cases that are generally defined as "crisis" decisions (the Berlin blockade and the Cuban missile affair) and others that are usually thought of as "noncrisis" decisions (the Marshall Plan and the Nuclear Test Ban Treaty). As we noted above, it is often assumed that crisis decisions differ profoundly from "normal" or noncrisis ones, and that even if the line between foreign and domestic policy is becoming blurred, a totally different process functions in crisis situations. A crisis situation has been defined as a situation displaying the following characteristics: (1) extreme threat to high-priority national goals, (2) surprise (unexpected external events), and (3) urgency—that is, a short time in which a response must be formulated (Hermann, 1971). In such situations, it is asserted, the policy process shifts into high gear, operates smoothly and rationally, and involves a select few participants who discard their institutional affiliations and ranks to act as high-minded, equal participants in a search for the best solution on the basis of a full consideration of possible action alternatives and their consequences. The role of other participants in the normal policy process (such as governmental bureaucracies, Congress, and interest groups) is negligible, and the president has a free hand acting as the commander in chief of the policy machine. By analyzing individual crisis decisions (see, for instance, Allison 1971), and even by comparing only such decisions (as did Halper, 1971, and Hermann, 1971), observers have found support for the uniqueness of crisis situations.

However, by comparing crisis and noncrisis decisions in a broader context we may begin to question this scenario on two grounds. First, what actually defines a crisis situation? Hermann's definition implies that a crisis situation includes objective indicators of a serious threat to high-priority goals. And yet it is at least arguable that in many, if not most, so-called crisis situations there has been disagreement on this issue. (For example, was there really such a threat in the Cuban missile case? Or in the Dominican Republic? Or in Lebanon?) Similar arguments might be made with regard to the identification of surprise and the assessment of the time available for a policy response. In the end, it may be that crisis, like beauty, is often in the eye of the beholder. Second, is it absolutely clear that completely different processes come into play in times of crisis? It is not inconceivable that both domestic political considerations and bureaucratic infighting influence the perception and formulation of policy even in the most widely acknowledged crisis situations. The decision to cut back the bombing in Vietnam may well be a classic example. We argue that the process alleged to characterize only crisis decisions may operate as well in those decisions considered to be responses to normal stimuli. We may discover, for example, that the process of decision making on the matters of trade expansion, the program of economic reconstruction for Europe, or foreign assistance may differ only in some marginal ways from that in the more clear-cut instances of so-called crisis decision making, such as in Cuba or the Dominican Republic.

Our third criterion for the selection of the case studies in this book derives from our conviction that some historical perspective is essential to a proper understanding of the foreign policy process. We therefore selected cases that span the administrations of Presidents Truman, Eisenhower, Kennedy, and Johnson. In this way, we should be able to compare the roles of individual presidents —that is, the difference that presidential style makes—in policy formulation, and assess the significance of the changing political climate at home and abroad in setting the parameters within which foreign policy is made. Specifically, one could gain insights into such questions as the influence of changing attitudes toward the cold war, toward nonalignment and neutrality, or toward economic assistance on general foreign policy orientations, and thus on foreign policy decisions dealing with similar issues at different points in time.

We do not claim that all these issues can be resolved satisfactorily by examining a relatively small number of cases, but only that through our use of a common analytical framework, one that addresses the five questions raised above, we should be able to gain a clearer understanding of foreign policy than is available either from general theorizing or from single case studies. Moreover, the case studies, taken as a whole, provide the basis for an understanding of the social context of the foreign policy process, a topic that forms the substance of the final two chapters of this book.

In Chapter 13 we present the major prevailing scholarly views about the social context within which the foreign policy process must be placed, and we examine this context in the light of evidence from our case studies. This examination serves three basic objectives: it illuminates a variety of structural aspects of the foreign policy process; it yields insight into the link between interests, ideology, and objectives in foreign policy; and it explains the patterns of continuity and change in the substantive content of that policy. One aspect of this approach is the role of individuals and institutions in the foreign policy process and the principal relationships between them. Here we are drawn to questions of personality, individual influence, and various aspects of institutional and group behavior and how these bear upon foreign policy formulation. At this level one might be inclined to ask, for example, whether a president other than Truman would have acted as he did on the Berlin crisis, or whether institutional arrangements limit the expression of behavioral differences among individuals, as in the case of a secretary of state, whose actions are more influenced by his role than by his personal motivations, preferences, or style. There is by now a considerable literature on the various psychological approaches to decision making (see de Rivera, 1968; Janis, 1972) and on the bureaucratic-politics approach (see Halperin and Kanter, 1973). Although these contributions assist us in clarifying aspects of individual and group behavior in decision-making situations, they tend to underplay the role of power relationships in the shaping of foreign policy.

We seek to compensate for this shortcoming by discussing the issue of locating the center of political power and analyzing the dynamics of the foreign policy process within this center. The addition of this political dimension enriches our analysis and broadens our range of vision of the American foreign policy process. Still, we maintain that in order to fully achieve our objectives, it is necessary to consider a third and final dimension: the broader structure of power—the persistent, underlying structural characteristics—of American society as a whole as this structure relates to the process of foreign policy and its principal outcomes. In our view, the "political center" cannot be divorced from the larger social structure in which it is embedded, or from the temporal and historical dimension that sets the stage for foreign policy decisions. Here, the literature dealing with elitism and pluralism is most relevant, and we have borrowed heavily from the works of Gabriel Almond (1960), Robert Dahl (1971) and C. Wright Mills (1956), among others. As for the relationship among interests, ideology, and the objectives of foreign policy, as well as for the larger issue of continuity and change, whose considerations are natural offshoots of this last factor, we have gained much from the analyses of Hans Morgenthau (1967), Charles Beard (1965), Gabriel Kolko (1969), and Richard Barnet (1969).

As you can see, examining the foreign policy process by analyzing the social context of this process has many advantages. First, it gives us insight into the structure of the policy-making process, identifying the principal actors, their roles, and the patterns of interaction between the actors. It helps us to identify the interests and motivations of these actors, and to probe the ties between these interests and the ideological frameworks through which they are formulated, channeled, and justified. In Chapter 14 we attempt to tackle this issue by tracing the relationship between elites, their interests and ideologies, and foreign policy objectives. Second, this mode of analysis helps us to clarify the "mix" as well as the interplay of foreign and domestic elements within a single decision-making process. Finally, this mode of analysis offers some answers to questions about the persistence or change of broad policy and ideological orientations over time. Unlike other analytical frameworks, it helps us account for the remarkable continuity and consistency of anti-Communism as a foundation for a wide variety of foreign policy initiatives spanning the administrations of such diverse presidents as Harry Truman, Dwight Eisenhower, John Kennedy, Lyndon Johnson, and Richard Nixon.

Ultimately, we agree with Kissinger (1974, p. 16) that a systematic study of the impact of domestic political institutions on foreign policy would involve a thorough comprehension of historical traditions, social values, economic systems, administrative structures, and the formative experiences of leadership groups, as well as the interactions among all of these. Kissinger's is a formidable challenge, one that is much broader than the scope and aims of this book. We hope we have at least taken a short step toward meeting this challenge and thereby advancing our understanding of foreign policy.

REFERENCES AND BIBLIOGRAPHY

ALLISON, GRAHAM T., *Essence of Decision: Explaining the Cuban Missile Crisis.* Boston: Little, Brown, 1971.

ALMOND, GABRIEL, *The American People and Foreign Policy.* New York: Praeger, 1960.

BARNET, RICHARD J., *Roots of War.* Boston: Beacon Press, 1969.

BEARD, CHARLES, "The National Interest," in *American National Security*, ed. Morton Berkowitz and Peter Bock. New York:. Free Press, 1965.

DAHL, ROBERT, "Power in New Haven: The Pluralist Thesis," in *Power in Postwar America*, ed. Richard Gillam. Boston: Little, Brown, 1971.

DE RIVERA, JOSEPH H., *The Psychological Dimension of Foreign Policy.* Columbus, Ohio: Charles E. Merrill, 1968.

HALPER, THOMAS, *Foreign Policy Crises: Appearance and Reality.* Columbus, Ohio: Charles E. Merrill, 1971.

HALPERIN, MORTON H., and ARNOLD KANTER, eds., *Readings in American Foreign Policy: A Bureaucratic Perspective.* Boston: Little, Brown, 1973.

HERMANN, CHARLES F., *Crises in Foreign Policy: A Simulation Analysis.* Indianapolis: Bobbs-Merrill, 1971.

JANIS, IRVING L., *Victims of Groupthink: A Psychological Study of Foreign-Policy Decisions and Fiascoes.* Boston: Houghton Mifflin, 1972.

KISSINGER, HENRY, *American Foreign Policy*, expanded ed. New York: Norton, 1974.

KOLKO, GABRIEL, *The Roots of American Foreign Policy*. Boston: Beacon Press, 1969.

LEPPER, MARY, *Foreign Policy Formulation: A Case Study of the Nuclear Test Ban Treaty of 1963*. Columbus, Ohio: Charles E. Merrill, 1971.

LINDBLOM, CHARLES, *The Policy Making Process*. Englewood Cliffs, N.J.: Prentice-Hall, 1968.

LOWI, THEODORE J., "American Business, Public Policy, Case Studies and Political Theory," *World Politics*, July, 1964, pp. 677–715.

———, "Making Democracy Safe for the World: National Politics and Foreign Policy," in *Domestic Sources of Foreign Policy*, ed. James N. Rosenau. New York: Free Press, 1967.

MILLS, C. WRIGHT, *The Power Elite*. New York: Oxford University Press, 1956.

MORGENTHAU, HANS, *Politics Among Nations* (4th ed.). New York: Knopf, 1967.

PAIGE, GLENN D., *The Korean Decision, June 24–30, 1950*. New York: Free Press, 1968.

ROSENAU, JAMES N., "Foreign Policy as an Issue-Area," in *Domestic Sources of Foreign Policy*, ed. James N. Rosenau. New York: Free Press, 1967.

SNYDER, RICHARD C., H. W. BRUCK, and BURTON SAPIN, eds., *Foreign Policy Decision Making: An Approach to the Study of International Politics*. New York: Free Press, 1962.

SPANIER, JOHN, and ERIC M. USLANER, *How American Foreign Policy Is Made*. New York: Praeger, 1974.

2

The Marshall Plan
1948

After World War II, the cooperative relationship between the two major powers, the Soviet Union and the United States, began to break down. No longer wartime allies, and increasingly distrustful of each other's motives, the newly emerging superpowers entered a new phase of interaction, which we have come to know as the cold war. Through a variety of techniques, the Soviets had succeeded by 1950 in extending their control over 14 countries, 722 million people, and 5 million square miles of land. As a result, Russia's motives became suspect in the United States, and her policies came under severe and critical scrutiny.

During this same immediate postwar period, Communist allies of the Soviet Union succeeded in projecting their influence in a variety of areas. The Chinese Communists defeated the forces of Chiang Kai-shek, compelling him to withdraw from the Chinese mainland and seek refuge on the island of Taiwan. Communist advances in Tibet, North Vietnam, and North Korea had significant results. Communist efforts to advance into South Korea, however, were repulsed, but only after a "United Nations force," which consisted essentially of United States troops, was dispatched to meet this offensive. In Europe, Soviet expansion threatened to engulf Greece and Turkey. The remainder of Europe seemed equally vulnerable to the Soviet threats, especially because of the weakened state of its economy, its notably weak political leadership, and its considerable state of social disorganization, all due in part to the devastation of the war.

The first American response to these perceived dangers came in the form of the Truman Doctrine, which provided economic and military assistance to the beleaguered countries of Greece and Turkey, and served as a precedent for a series of similar measures of aid to friendly and neutral countries in all parts of the world. At the same time, the American government inaugurated the Marshall Plan, a most ambitious program of economic assistance aimed at averting possible economic and political collapse in Western Europe.

Under Truman's direction, discussions within governmental circles regarding the nature and scope of American sponsorship of a generalized program of economic rehabilitation had begun in March, 1947. In high administration circles there was general agreement that a program of economic aid for Europe would be required. Dean Acheson, then undersecretary of state, requested a group of three men from the Departments of State, War, and Navy to coordinate the discussions and activities of an interdepartmental committee whose ultimate purpose would be to prepare the groundwork for the development of such a program. Established in the early months of 1947, this interdepartmental committee, the State, War, and Navy Coordinating Committee (SWNCC), had assisted the president in fashioning the program of aid to Greece and Turkey. It undertook its new assignment diligently, organizing study groups, preparing memoranda, commissioning research on a variety of topics, and engaging in widespread discussion and debate.

At about the same time, William Clayton, then Undersecretary of state for Economic Affairs, drafted a memorandum in which he expressed considerable concern about the prevailing chaos in Europe and pointedly emphasized the serious implications of this situation for the security of the United States. Unless America asserted its leadership immediately, the likelihood of war in the next decade would be increased dangerously. Clayton's grave message accentuated the flurry of activity in Washington policy-making circles and focused increased attention on the need for a program of European reconstruction.

By the time Secretary of State George Marshall returned from the Moscow Conference, in late April, 1947, both SWNCC and a specially organized group within the State Department, the Committee on Extension of Aid to Foreign Governments, had achieved substantial progress. Marshall confirmed Clayton's gloomy observations of conditions in Europe, noting that "the recovery of Europe has been far slower than had been expected. Disintegrating forces are becoming evident. The patient is sinking while the doctors deliberate." (U.S. Department of State, *Bulletin*, May 11, 1947, p. 920) He concluded that "action cannot await compromise through exhaustion" (*Ibid.*, p. 924).

The Policy Planning Staff of the State Department, headed by George Kennan, was requested to begin a study of the problem of aid to Europe and to develop a plan of action. Within less than a week Kennan recruited a staff, organized its activities, and strove to establish contacts with other governmental groups working on related aspects of the problems of European rehabilitation. He soon discovered that much of the basic work had already been done by SWNCC. On May 23, after an exhausting effort, Kennan's group produced a thirteen-page memorandum, which was circulated to top policy makers within the Department of State.

The memorandum addressed itself to the prevailing problems of Western Europe. Although it pointed to Communism as a threat to the stability of democratic regimes in Europe, it perceived the crisis facing Western Europe as primarily the consequence of the disruptive effects of the war. There was no doubt that the Communists intended to exploit this crisis to the ultimate detriment of the United States, but despite this, Kennan's group maintained that "American aid should not be directed to combating Communism, as such, but to the restoration of the economic health and vigor of European society" (quoted in Jones, 1955, p. 244).

On the question of American aid to Western Europe, the Policy Planning Staff called for long-term measures designed to restore economic health to Europe, and a set of short-range steps aimed at creating confidence among Europeans that the overall problems could ultimately be resolved. The memorandum stipulated that the Europeans themselves were to be responsible for developing and initiating such a program of economic assistance. As it noted,

> It would be neither fitting nor efficacious for this government to undertake to draw unilaterally and to promulgate formally on its own initiative a program designed to place Western Europe on its feet economically. This is the business of the Europeans [and] the formal initiative must come from Europe. (Quoted in Jones, 1955, p. 250)

Finally, the Policy Planning Staff hoped that requests for American financial or economic assistance would be made by the Europeans jointly rather than, as in the past, by individual nations.

The first public disclosure of governmental thinking on the problems of European economic rehabilitation was initiated by Acheson in a foreign policy address before the Delta Council in Cleveland, Mississippi on May 8, 1947. Because domestic political problems in Mississippi might have proved politically embarrassing to him, President Truman asked Acheson to substitute for him. Acheson thought that the occasion might be beneficially employed to acquaint the American public with the problems of the European economies and the severity of the economic and social conditions throughout the Continent. He firmly believed in the necessity of shocking the country into facing this growing crisis, and the president concurred wholeheartedly.

In order to ensure widespread public comment and discussion on his address, Acheson lunched with three British newsmen, Leonard Miall of the British Broadcasting Corporation, Malcolm

Muggeridge of the *Daily Telegraph*, and Rene MacColl of the *Daily Express*, before departing for Mississippi. Stressing the importance of his speech to these journalists, and taking care to highlight its significance for European economic rehabilitation, development, and unity, Acheson explained to them the purposes and objectives of a prospective American aid program, identified the principal American interests and major motivations, and reassured the journalists of the presidental resolve to enact such a program.

Acheson's speech marked the first major step in a carefully planned administration strategy to cultivate the support of key sections of American public opinion for a program of European economic assistance. The speech opened with a brief observation on the utter exhaustion and economic dislocation of Europe, cited the increased dependency of the Continent on United States imports, and stressed the necessity for Western Europe to develop new methods by which to finance these sorely needed items. The objective, Acheson noted, was not relief, but the revival of "agriculture, industry, and trade, so that stricken countries might be self-supporting" (Acheson, 1969, p. 306). In order to accomplish these ends, the United States was to undertake two tasks. First, it was to increase its imports from abroad in order to narrow the financial gap between what the world needed and what it could pay for. Second, it was to "undertake further emergency financing of foreign purchases" so that "foreign countries [can] . . . continue to buy in 1948 and 1949 the commodities which they need to sustain life, and at the same time rebuild their economies" (Jones, 1955, p. 24). Such steps, Acheson observed, had to be taken without delay, or the "economic margins" within which human dignity, human freedom, and democratic institutions flourished would prove insufficient to sustain them (see Acheson, 1969, p. 306). Economic well-being, this seemed to imply, was a basic condition for the maintenance of the values and institutions of democracy, and a principal aim of American foreign policy was to ensure a level of economic development that would be conducive to the preservation of democratic regimes. This view—that economic security and stable democratic regimes are linked—continues to be employed, along with a host of other supporting arguments, to justify present programs of foreign aid. (For an analysis of the mounting criticism of recent American foreign aid programs, see Chapter 11.)

Although Acheson delivered this prologue to the Marshall Plan on May 8, it wasn't until early June that Marshall was to deliver his eventful Harvard commencement speech. During that time the reports of SWNCC, the State Department's Foreign Aid group, and the Kennan memorandum provoked considerable controversy and discussion in top policy-making quarters. Of course, by May it was already widely known that the Truman administration would propose a program of aid to Europe. Controversy was centered, however, on the problem of "how to make the transfer of billions of dollars to countries that had not asked for them, and would not ask for them" (Jones, 1955, p. 239). This was by no means a simple problem.

Meanwhile, en route home from Geneva in May, where he had been serving as chief negotiator for trade and tariff negotiations, Clayton penned a second memorandum to the secretary of state in which he urged immediate action in behalf of the program of aid to Europe. He stressed his conviction that American policy makers had underestimated the extent of economic havoc in Europe. Although they appreciated the degree of physical destruction, "the effect of vast economic disruption and political, social and psychological destruction from five years of Hitler's remaking of Europe into a war machine completely escaped [them]" (Acheson, 1969, p. 308). There was, Clayton argued, little need for further study of the problem. Instead, before the situation deteriorated further, immediate steps to alleviate the plight of the Continent should be undertaken. Essentially, this would involve a grant of goods—principally coal, food, cotton, and tobacco—and shipping services by the United States over a three-year period. The three-year grant would be based upon a plan that the European nations would work out.

According to Clayton, the basic problem for the United States was to organize its fiscal policy and consumption patterns so that sufficient surpluses could be extracted from its vast production and "paid for by taxation rather than by adding to [the national] debt" (Acheson, 1969, p. 308). He urged the president and the secretary of state to make a "strong appeal to the American people to sacrifice a little to save Europe from starvation and chaos . . . and at the same time preserve . . . the glorious heritage of a free America" (Jones, 1955, p. 248). His pleas for a direct appeal to the American public to undertake such an enterprise constituted probably the single most important factor that shaped Marshall's decision to make his address at Harvard.

On May 28 Acheson arranged a meeting between Clayton and the secretary of state. Here, Clayton once again urged against delay, and pleaded for the secretary to take the case for aid to Europe to the American people. Although Marshall agreed that immediate action was needed, he expressed some concern about the scope of the program. Should it be confined exclusively to Western Europe, or should it be extended to the entire Continent? The discussions on this issue were inconclusive, although Acheson pointed out that Russian participation in the program might seriously jeopardize its passage in Congress. The conversations concluded with Marshall warning against premature leaks, which he felt might provoke an adverse congressional reaction.

The next day, Marshall informed Acheson of his intention to deliver an address at the Harvard commencement exercises on June 5 on the subject of Europe, despite Acheson's opinion that "commencement speeches were a ritual to be endured without hearing" (Acheson, 1969, p. 310). Charles Bohlen, then special assistant to the secretary of state, was requested to prepare a first draft. Relying principally on the Clayton and Kennan memoranda, Bohlen worked diligently on the speech, concluding it on June 3. It was then screened carefully by Acheson and Clayton before being forwarded to Secretary Marshall. Dissatisfied with those portions of the speech dealing with the necessity for a European initiative in sparking the program, Marshall rewrote it. He revised it further on his plane trip to Massachusetts on June 4.

The speech was preceded by little publicity. Few at that time were aware of the momentous character of the address. Even within the State Department, few were informed about the secretary's intention to launch the European proposal at Harvard. On June 4, however, Acheson disclosed to his three British correspondent friends that Marshall's Harvard speech was of the greatest importance, and he urged them to "telephone the full text of the speech to London as soon as it was released and to make arrangements . . . to deliver the text to Foreign Minister 'Ernest Bevin" as soon as possible (Acheson, 1969, p. 312).

Marshall's speech was brief, clear in the statement of its purpose, and far-reaching in its overall implications. Marshall began with a declaration of the broadest intent, calling for an elaborate, comprehensive program of economic assistance to Western Europe in place of more limited, stopgap measures of economic aid. American economic assistance, Marshall pointed out, "should provide a cure rather than a palliative." Marshall then affirmed the willingness of the United States to cooperate with any country "that is willing to assist in the task of recovery." Most observers could only interpret this as an expression of American willingness to cooperate with the Soviets in the task of economic reconstruction. Although this was undoubtedly a risky strategy, since it could provoke some congressional opposition, the administration believed that whatever losses it suffered would be offset by gains among a bloc of congressmen who were opposed to the Truman Doctrine with its single-minded emphasis on ideological and military resistance to the Soviet Union. Moreover, Marshall made this offer of cooperation in order to weaken any future claims that the United States was responsible for the division of Europe along East-West Lines. At the same time, reasonably confident that the Soviets would rebuff any American pledge, Marshall warned that any "government which maneuvers to block the recovery of other countries . . . will encounter the opposition of the United States." Finally, Marshall set forth the major principles underlying the program for European recovery. Europe was to assume the initiative and responsibility to collectively develop a program of economic assistance; the United States was not to unilaterally proclaim such a program; and America was to limit its role to "friendly aid in the drafting of a European program, and of later support . . . so far as it may be possible [for the United States] to do so." (Marshall's complete address can be found in the U.S. Department of State *Bulletin*, June 15, 1947, pp. 1160-64.)

In July, partly in response to the American initiative, sixteen European nations organized themselves into the Committee on European Economic Cooperation. This group set about to design a blueprint for European economic rehabilitation. Efforts were made to develop a comprehensive economic strategy, to establish an organizational apparatus to flesh out various economic projects and to monitor ongoing activities, and to mobilize needed technical, scientific, and administrative skills. Plans were also inaugurated to map and coordinate the American role in the European recovery program.

In the U.S., Republican Senator Arthur Vandenberg, chairman of the Foreign Relations Committee, proposed the appointment of a "nonpartisan commission at the highest level to advise coordination of our resources with foreign needs" (Acheson, 1969, p. 313). Within the administration, this sparked some concern that such a commission might well oppose any significant change in the American role in Europe. At the same time, since the administration had no wish to offend Vandenberg, whose support for the successful enactment of any major economic aid program was considered crucial, Truman decided to appoint a presidential commission, to be composed principally of prominent citizens from the ranks of agriculture, labor, and industry. This commission would address itself to the problems of the nature, purposes, and scope of the American foreign aid program. In this manner the administration sought to avoid appearing to repudiate Vandenberg's proposal; at the same time it expected that the report of a presidential commission would less likely prove politically embarrassing to administration views.

Commerce Secretary Averill Harriman was recruited to head this group, the administration hoping that his reputation and credentials would deter any serious dissent within the commission. Two other groups were subsequently established by the president, though their tasks were more narrow and technical. The first, headed by Interior Secretary Julius Krug, was mandated to study the available raw materials and potential production of such necessities as coal and steel, both here and abroad. The second, chaired by Edwin Nourse of the Council of Economic Advisers, was assigned to assess the domestic impact of the contemplated foreign assistance program. Undoubtedly, the administration believed that positive recommendations by these two groups would strengthen its case in favor of economic aid.

On July 22 the House passed a resolution offered by Representative Christian Herter of Massachusetts, thereby creating a select House committee to study foreign aid. Comprising nineteen members, who were drawn from a wide range of the standing committees, the Herter Committee departed for Europe on August 28 to investigate the economic and political status of the Continent. Drawing upon the experiences and views gathered during this visit, Herter introduced a bill on November 25 to establish a long-range European recovery program. This bill called for the creation of an independent government corporation to be called the Emergency Foreign Reconstruction Authority, whose appointed chairman and bipartisan board of directors would administer United States foreign aid until 1954. On all questions of policy, it was to be advised by a Foreign Aid Council chaired by the secretary of state. Final decisions on foreign policy would, of course, be left to the president.

Herter's proposal called for Congress to appropriate $500 million for the corporation and to authorize it to issue notes for purchase by the Treasury in an amount to be determined by Congress as the program evolved. The corporation was to distribute food, fuel, and fertilizer, as well as a limited number of consumer goods, to needy countries. These would be available on a noncommercial loan basis. Loans that would permit the European countries to purchase raw materials or capital goods would be handled by the Export-Import Bank, the World Bank, and private industry, and would require security and repayment in accord with current loan standards.

Dissatisfied with the basic philosophy and much of the substance of Herter's proposal, the Truman administration pressed forward with a program of its own. The task of developing the administration's proposals for European recovery was undertaken by the State Department. Three men, Undersecretaries Robert Lovett and Clayton, and Ambassador Lewis Douglas, were chiefly responsible for integrating and coordinating the activities of a vast army of technicians from throughout the government who were working on related aspects of the program. At a later stage in the development of this program, an interdepartmental Advisory Steering Committee, chaired by Lovett and composed of top-level technical representatives from each of the interested departments and agencies of the executive branch, was assembled to "assure that the interests of all appropriate agencies of the government concerned with particular domestic or foreign aspects of the program were taken into account" (U.S. House, 1948, p. 284). The primary responsibility for organizing the presentation of the program to Congress was assumed by the secretary of state.

On December 10, shortly before Congress was scheduled to adjourn for the Christmas recess, the administration's proposal for a European Recovery Program (ERP) was introduced to the House by Representative Charles Eaton, chairman of the House Foreign Affairs Committee. Under the administration plan, the ERP would be authorized for four and a half years—from April 1, 1948 through June 30, 1952. The president's bill called for $17 billion to cover ERP operations during this time.

The measure provided for the establishment of an Economic Cooperation Administration (ECA), to be headed by a single administrator of cabinet rank. The new agency, though responsible to the president, would be directed by the secretary of state and the State Department. The Department of State would be chiefly responsible for initiating ERP agreements and determining the policies under which the new agency would function.

Few limitations were placed on the nature of the supplies or goods to be offered under the program. Whether credit would be extended on a grant or loan basis would be decided by the administrator of the ECA. In the case of grants, however, "commensurable amounts" of local currency were to be set aside and employed for either reconstruction or anti-inflation purposes, whichever was agreed to by the participating nation and the State Department.

The president would be required to submit reports on the operation of ERP to Congress four times a year during the operation of the program and once a year thereafter, until the process of liquidation was completed. Aside from the initial authorization, appropriation, and screening of the quarterly reports, Congress was to play a marginal role in the functioning of the program.

Committee hearings on the Herter proposal opened on December 17 in the House, although support for the measure was limited and far from enthusiastic. The announcement of the administration plan, combined with an endorsement of its basic principles by a number of top congressional figures—including the powerful Vandenberg—forced the leadership in Congress to suspend these hearings and compelled Herter to withdraw his measure from active consideration. After the Herter plan was quietly shelved, hearings on the administration's program resumed before the Foreign Affairs Committee on January 12 and continued for two months. In the Senate, hearings on the administration bill opened on January 8 and concluded by the end of February.

Even before the administration measure had been introduced to Congress, a sustained effort had been made to coax influential congressmen and senators to support the recovery program. Truman went out of his way to give explicit credit to Vandenberg for suggesting the idea of a presidential commission. Moreover, in private conversations with Vandenberg, Marshall sought to impress upon the senator the central importance of the plan and the need for him to exercise his leadership in promoting quick congressional action. "Once his support was forthcoming," Marshall confided to a friend, "success for radical advances in the foreign policy of the United States was assured" (quoted in Jones, 1955, p. 125).

Similar gestures of thanks and overtures to gain support were made by Truman to a wide range of other key congressional figures, including Tom Connally and Tom Lucas from the Senate, and Leslie Arends, Charles Eaton, Charles Halleck, and Sam Rayburn from the House. When the president unveiled the reports of the Krug, Nourse, and Harriman commissions, personal invitations were extended to these congressmen for this occasion, and Truman made a special effort to impress upon them the importance of the recovery program and their central role in its final determination, and to solicit their support for its prompt enactment. This was followed a few days later by letters to the chairmen of the Foreign Affairs Committees in the House and the Senate, in which the president formally requested that they be prepared to act on the measure without significant delay. All of these efforts were undertaken despite the fact that Congress, on the whole, was favorably disposed toward the administration's program for European recovery and shared the administration's desire to assist in the rehabilitation of Western Europe.

In Congress, administration spokesmen, many of whom were provided with testimony by the State Department, which had carefully planned the legislative strategy, defended the proposal on a number of grounds. Some viewed the recovery program as a means of curbing Communist advances in Western Europe. Testifying before the House Foreign Affairs Committee, Secretary Marshall noted that the "situation in Europe has not developed to the point where the grim progression from economic uncertainty to tyranny is probable." But without United States support of European self-help, Marshall warned, "this progression may well become inevitable" (U.S. House, 1948, p. 29). Similarly, in response to a question by Representative John Lodge of Connecticut concerning ERP's utility in deterring the seizure of the governments of Italy and France by Communist-inspired acts of disruption, Army Secretary Kenneth Royall noted, "From the information that I have, . . . I am inclined to think that [such deterrence] is the more probable result [of approving ERP]" (Ibid., p. 403).

Other spokesmen stressed the importance of the ERP in stimulating private investment in Western Europe. Lewis Douglas, the United States ambassador to the United Kingdom, maintained that "if economic and political stability begin to reappear on a solid basis in Western Europe, I think a profitable field for American investment will develop" (Ibid., p. 140). At a later point in his testimony, Douglas was even more direct: "The fundamental purpose of this act is to encourage the restoration of stability in their part of the world, so that private investment may thereafter . . . play its part" (Ibid., p. 182). Similarly, in a speech before the Pittsburgh Chamber of Commerce in January, 1948, Marshall noted that a failure by the United States to provide assistance for the recovery program in Europe would result in the imposition of controls in that area affecting international trade and investment. "It is idle to think," he concluded, "that Europe, left to its own efforts in these serious problems of recovery, would remain open to American business in the same way that we have known it in the past" (Congressional Record, 1947, pp. A283–84).

Some defended the need for the program on the grounds of the new roles and responsibilities inherited by the United States in the postwar era. It was, Senator Vandenberg noted, a repudiation of a wholly inadequate and unwise policy of isolationism." It would be a far happier circumstance if we could close our eyes to reality, comfortably retire within our bastions, and dream of an isolated and prosperous peace. But that which was once our luxury would now become our folly." (*Ibid.*, p. 1915)

Others argued that failure to adopt the ERP might in the long run prove fatal to international peace. As Acheson argued, before the House Foreign Affairs Committee, "With the crumbling of the economy of Western Europe will come . . . quite possibly, the development of situations which will hazard the maintenance of international peace" (U.S. House, 1948, p. 695). Or, as Secretary of Defense James Forrestal observed, [The continued isolation of the United States, brought about by a reluctance to act in this matter, would] "be a threat to the peace of the world" (*Ibid.*, p. 224). Still others looked to the program to stimulate the economic and political integration of Europe, to forestall anticipated budget hikes for the military, and to deter serious alterations in the patterns of international trade. (See, in particular, the testimony of Philip Reed, *Ibid.*, p. 582).

On March 23 the administration measure was brought to the floor of the House. Unlike its Senate counterpart, the House bill contained provisions for economic assistance not only to Western Europe, but to Greece, Turkey, and China as well. The House debate emphasized the anti-Communist features of the bill, considered the problems of trade with Eastern Europe and the loyalty of the personnel to be appointed to administer the act, and explored the wisdom of rehabilitating the German economy. House members seemed intent on considering the recovery program primarily as a cold-war, anti-Communist measure. As Francis Walters of Pennsylvania expressed it, [If ERP is not adopted,] "a vacuum will be created that will be filled by the Communists, and Communism will engulf all of Western Europe within the space of but a few months" (U.S. House, 1948, p. 1830).

Opposition elements in the House criticized the measure as extravagant, untimely, and socialistic in its motivation. One congressman thought that the bill was inspired exclusively by a desire to revive Germany: "A reconstructed, cartel-ridden Germany is the very heart of ERP. Without Germany you would have no

ERP," claimed George Sadowski of Michigan (*Congressional Record*, 1947, p. 3552). Some Republican opponents held the bipartisan foreign policy responsible for such programs as ERP, and accused bipartisanship of failing to offer meaningful foreign policy choices to the American public (see *Ibid.*, pp. 3519, 3718). Some Democrats objected to the omnibus character of the legislation reported by the House Committee on Foreign Affairs, variously criticizing it as bad "legislative procedure" or as "shabby politics" (*Ibid.*, pp. 3620-21). Despite these objections, a substantial majority of both Democrats and Republicans voted for the measure on March 31; the tally was 329 for and 74 against.

Meanwhile, on March 1 the Senate Foreign Relations Committee had placed the bill before the Senate. Echoing the position of the bill's numerous supporters within the upper house, Vandenberg urged the enactment of the bill without unnecessary delay. Between March 1 and March 13, the Senate engaged in a wide-ranging debate on the program. As a result of a number of compromises worked out by Vandenberg within his committee, however, its passage was virtually assured.

The most significant compromise involved the mode in which the program was to be administered. Unlike the proposal offered by the administration, which would have placed the administrator of the recovery program and his agency clearly under the control and direction of the secretary of state, Vandenberg endorsed the principles of a study sponsored by the Brookings Institution, which called for the creation of a separate agency headed by a single administrator of cabinet status. Vandenberg had requested Brookings to undertake such a study in late 1947, in view of the "wide divergence of opinion respecting methods of ERP administration" (see U.S. Senate, 1948, p. 855). A reluctance to antagonize a crucial supporter of the bill, and a lack of harmony of views within governmental circles on this issue, induced the administration to yield on this matter. Along with Robert Patterson, then chairman of a private group supporting the Marshall Plan, the administration agreed that the ERP's "prompt enactment should not be prevented by a protracted debate over the form of administration" (*Ibid.*, p. 760).

On March 13 the Senate concluded its debate and approved

the ERP by a wide margin of 69 to 17. Thirty-one Republicans joined thirty-eight Democrats in supporting the bill; thirteen Republicans and four Democrats voted against the measure. Many amendments had been offered, but only those acceptable to Vandenberg were ultimately approved. A critical test vote occurred when an amendment calling for a substantial reduction in the initial appropriation for the program was proposed by Senator Robert Taft of Ohio. This vote, which defeated the amendment, clearly revealed the extent of disunity within the Republican forces: twenty-three Republicans supported the amendment and twenty-four opposed it.

Persistent opponents of the measure expressed a variety of reasons for their stance. Some, such as Taft, thought the program lacked economic justification and threatened American economic stability (see *Congressional Record*, 1947, p. 2642). George Malone (Nevada) viewed the measure as a step aiming at a "worldwide redistribution of wealth" and parity in living standards between Europe and the United States (*Ibid.*, p. 2208). Senator Joseph Ball (Minnesota) viewed with alarm the increased expenditure of American funds, and another senator claimed that the program would serve largely to prop up faltering socialist regimes.

Private support for the enactment of ERP came from a variety of sources, including the leading associations representing labor, agriculture, and industry, and had been regularly solicited, as we have noted, by means of a long-range and ultimately successful strategy pursued by the administration to sell its program to Congress and the American people. The campaign for broad public support had opened with the floating of a "trial balloon" in Acheson's Mississippi speech in May, continued with Marshall's address at Harvard in June, and culminated in Truman's unveiling of the findings of his commissions in September. The commissions had endorsed the concept of a European recovery program, concluded that the United States could successfully absorb the strain of an additional burden on our resources, and reported that a recovery program would not disrupt the basic health of the American economy. These findings had helped engender widespread acceptance of the ERP within the critical sectors of public opinion. Significant reservations were expressed only by James Patton of the

National Farmers Union, who, in testimony before the Senate Foreign Relations Committee, pointed with trepidation to the "growing tendency of the United States to act independently instead of collaboratively through the United Nations" (U.S. Senate, 1948, p. 928). Even he, however, did not actively oppose the enactment of ERP. The American Farm Bureau Federation, on the other hand, actively supported the program. All the major business associations, including the National Association of Manufacturers, the U.S. Chamber of Commerce, and the Committee for Economic Development, strongly endorsed the plan. The chief labor organization, the AFL–CIO also stood firmly behind the proposal.

Substantial support was also forthcoming from the major elements of the press establishment. According to one observer, the "Marshall Plan remains, among reporters, a classic case where reporters went out of their way to play up the program, in their choice and handling of 'news stories' " (Cohen, 1965, pp. 37–38). Some have even suggested that access to the press was denied opponents of the program. In any event, the major newspapers, including the *New York Times* and the *Washington Post*, enthusiastically favored the plan.

By all indications, the ERP enjoyed substantial support within the population at large. With administration encouragement, an organization called The Citizens' Committee for the Marshall Plan was established in the summer of 1947 in order to mobilize and organize such support. World affairs discussion groups throughout the country helped organize branch committees, which raised money for local education, especially of the press. The central office of The Citizens' Committee supplied pamphlets, speakers, and newsletters and appealed for help in lobbying Congress at critical moments. It bought full-page ads, wrote letters to congressmen, and published a weekly "fact sheet" entitled "Facts About the Marshall Plan." At one point, eight full-time lobbyists were employed by the organization to promote the program in Congress. Their labors were not to be unrewarded, for, as Acheson noted, "All this effort eventually came back to affect the several hundred people in Washington who would write and enact the European Recovery Program into law" (Acheson, 1969, p. 322).

In sum, although the input for the development of the Marshall Plan came from a wide variety of sources within the executive branch, the leadership, as we have seen, was assumed largely by the State Department, and principally by the Policy Planning Staff under George Kennan. Legislative strategy for the presentation of the plan was also developed within the executive establishment, the secretary of state assuming major responsibility for the organization of the administration's case, the order of witnesses, and the preparation of testimony. President Truman himself played an active role in the campaign to ensure congressional support by stressing the bipartisan nature of the program and by actively soliciting, where necessary, the endorsements of key members of Congress. Despite an earnest desire to obtain congressional approval for its proposal, the administration was prepared to compromise in certain areas. Thus, the administration yielded to a congressional preference for an alternate mode of organizing the recovery program.

A broad campaign for widespread public support was carefully constructed and effectively implemented. Systematic efforts were undertaken by the administration to ensure maximum exposure for the proposal and thereby to awaken broad public interest in the program and to encourage community support. With considerable fanfare, three presidential committees were appointed to evaluate the contemplated plan, and their highly laudatory reports of this imaginative new American international effort were given maximum public exposure. The press was openly courted, and their endorsements were also distributed widely. Appeals to the public were often made along patriotic lines that emphasized both the economic strength of America and the need for the United States to fulfill its new international responsibilities in the postwar era. Where necessary, however, the administration was not averse to couching its appeal in more narrow, economic terms. Finally, as we have seen, despite widespread interest-group support, the administration helped establish a citizens' committee that was charged with inducing broad public support of the program.

The Politics of American Foreign Policy: The Social Context of Decisions

REFERENCES AND BIBLIOGRAPHY

ACHESON, DEAN, *Present at the Creation*. New York: Norton, 1969.

COHEN, BERNARD, *The Press and Foreign Policy*. Princeton, N.J.: Princeton University Press, 1965.

JONES, JOSEPH, *Fifteen Weeks*. New York: Viking, 1955.

LOWI, THEODORE, "Making Democracy Safe for the World," in *Domestic Sources of Foreign Policy*, ed. James Rosenau. New York: Free Press, 1967.

TRUMAN, HARRY S., *Years of Trial and Hope*, Vol. II. Garden City, N.Y.: Doubleday, 1956.

U.S. Congress, *Congressional Record*, 1947.

U.S., Congress, House, Committee on Foreign Affairs, *Hearings, United States Foreign Policy for a Post-War Recovery Program*. 80th Cong., 1st and 2nd sess., 1948.

U.S., Congress, Senate, Committee on Foreign Relations. *Hearings, European Recovery Program*. 80th Cong., 2nd sess., 1948.

U.S., Department of State, *Bulletin*, May 11, 1947.

———, *Bulletin*, June 15, 1947.

3

The Berlin Airlift
1948

The decision to undertake an airlift in response to the Soviet blockade of Berlin has been viewed as an extremely successful episode in
United States foreign policy making. It is often cited as a major cold
war coup by which the United States not only withstood a direct
Russian challenge, but also taught Moscow an important lesson in
confrontation politics. At the time, however, the most striking aspects of the decision were the unpreparedness and hesitancy that
characterized the behavior of most of the top decision makers in
Washington. The decision to undertake the airlift was actually
made by the "field commander"—General Lucius Clay, military
governor in Germany—and legitimized by the president, Harry
Truman. In order to understand this discrepancy between the attitudes and actions of the decision makers in Washington and Ber-

lin, we have to examine the background of what came to be known as the first Berlin crisis.

American policy toward Germany in the post–World War II period developed slowly and haltingly. Initially, it was based on the hope that wartime cooperation with the Soviet Union would continue. Consequently some of the crucial aspects of arrangements governing the status of occupied Germany were not formalized in legal documents. In particular, the status of Berlin was left rather vague.

At a series of wartime and immediate postwar conferences, it had been decided that Germany would be divided into American, British, French, and Russian occupation zones. These zones were to be supervised by an Allied Control Council sitting in Berlin and operating under the principle of unanimity (Davison, 1958, p. 3). Although located inside the Russian zone, Berlin was to be divided into four sectors and administered jointly by a Kommandatura consisting of the four sector commandants. The question of Western access to Berlin was treated rather offhandedly. During the war Washington felt that this issue could be settled later by military personnel, and after the war local commanders did reach verbal agreements concerning the use of a highway, a rail line, and two air corridors for the entry of Allied personnel into Berlin (Clay, 1950, pp. 25–26). Even at that early stage, however, the Russians insisted on their right to supervise such traffic (Howley, 1950, p. 25).

During the first months of the occupation, the western powers did not express much concern about either their political or their military position in Berlin, and despite certain points of friction, the first year of the joint administration of the city passed fairly smoothly (Davison, 1958, pp. 30–32). At the end of 1945 the Soviets reluctantly agreed to establish three air corridors linking Berlin to the American and British zones, through which flights could proceed without advance notice. The agreement was formalized early in 1946, and a four-power Berlin Air Safety Center was established to supervise its operation.

Even by American accounts, the access arrangements, the formal air agreement, and the informal procedures for entry by rail, highway, and canal served fairly well until the end of 1947. By then, however, the cold war had set in, and Germany quickly became one of its primary battlefields. The Moscow Conference for a German peace treaty, which lasted from mid March to mid April, 1947, was a complete failure. According to one participant, it "rang down the Iron Curtain" (Murphy, 1964, p. 307). Thereafter, Soviet-American relations deteriorated rapidly. In Berlin, the rising tension was clearly manifested in late 1947 in a three-pronged Soviet challenge to the other three occupying powers. First, an increasingly hostile propaganda campaign was initiated, its statements often concluding with claims that the Western Allies were certain to abandon Berlin (Davison, 1958, p. 64). Second, the joint governing institutions of Germany and Berlin were rendered progressively more impotent by Soviet refusals to cooperate and by the Soviets' repeated use of the veto power (Smith, 1963, p. 98). In particular, the Russians objected to the planned economic integration of the three western zones. The western powers persisted, however, creating the integrated American-British zone (Bizonia), and later the Western zone. When the Allies announced their intention to introduce a common currency in their zone, the Russian delegation to the Allied Control Council walked out, on March 20, 1948, declaring that the council had ceased to exist. Third, early in 1948 the Russians began a "creeping blockade"—that is, interference with traffic between West Germany and Berlin. It was this last tactic that set in motion the sequence of events that led to the blockade and airlift.

In January, 1948 American military trains were boarded by Russian inspectors who asserted their right to check the identification papers of passengers. In response, General Clay placed armed military guards on the trains to confront and bar the Soviets. These cat-and-mouse tactics continued throughout February and March, frequently resulting in train delays of several hours due to clashes between American train commanders and Soviet inspectors (Clay, 1950, p. 354).

The "creeping blockade" was tightened on March 30, 1948, ten days after the Russians had left the Allied Control Council, when the Soviets issued new provisions to be enforced on Berlin traffic, as of April 1, 1948. These provisions stipulated that:

1. American personnel traveling through the Soviet zone by rail highway must present documentary evidence of identity and affiliation with the U.S. Military Administration of Germany.

2. Military freight shipments from Berlin to the Western zones must be cleared through Soviet checkpoints by means of a Soviet permit; civilian freight shipments into Berlin would be cleared by accompanying documents.

3. All baggage must be inspected at Soviet checkpoints, with the exception of personal belongings of American personnel carried in a passenger railway car or a passenger automobile. (U.S. Department of State, 1948, p. 1)

On April 1, the Soviets implemented the new regulations, which amounted to a partial blockade, and decreed, further, that no freight could leave Berlin by rail without permission from the Russian commandant. The result was full control of Berlin trade by Soviet authorities. Rather than submit to Soviet inspection of their military trains, the Americans and British canceled such service and instituted a small airlift carrying 60 to 100 tons of provisions a day to Allied personnel in Berlin (Davison, 1958, p. 64). Ten days later, after some relaxation of the Soviet position, Allied rail service was resumed, but a precedent had been set for the large airlift to come.

Thereafter, the pace of the conflict quickened. New restrictions on the movement of persons and goods, ostensibly for "technical reasons," were reported almost every day. On June 11 the Russians halted all rail traffic between Berlin and West Germany for two days. The next day the highway bridge on the road to Berlin was closed for "repairs." On June 16, at the end of one of many quarrelsome meetings, the Russians walked out of the Berlin Kommandatura. Two days later the western powers announced the introduction of currency reform in the western zones (but not in Berlin). The Soviets reacted by cutting off all traffic into the Soviet zone and insisting on inspection of all freight and personal effects moving into Berlin. Their reason: protection of East Germany from a flood of devalued currency. There followed three days of hurried four-power negotiations on the currency question, in the course of which the Russians announced a currency reform in East Germany. The negotiations did not bear fruit, and on June 24 a complete blockade on traffic was imposed, and, in addition, Berlin was deprived of most of its electric current, which originated in the Soviet sector.

The next day, the British delivered supplies to their garrison by air and were considering the problem of supplying the civilian population of Berlin in that manner. At the same time, General Clay called General Curtis LeMay at Wiesbaden and discussed the possibility of an airlift, and on June 26 the U.S. Air Force delivered the first 80 tons of civilian supplies to Berlin. The airlift grew rapidly, and by the end of the year there was no doubt as to the ability of aircraft to supply the needs of all Berliners. (Admittedly, these were rather modest needs, in view of the extremely low standard of living in postwar Germany.) The "Easter Parade" (April 16, 1949) broke all tonnage records by airlifting 12,940 tons of food and coal in 24 hours, which was more than the total pre-blockade delivery by all means of transportation. On May 12, after three months of negotiations, the blockade was finally lifted.

The decision-making process involved in the Berlin Airlift was dominated not by the authorities in Washington, but by the commander in the field, General Clay. It was he who took command of the situation in the face of nonperceptive intelligence reports, lack of support from the Pentagon, and indecision or lack of a sense of urgency in the State Department. How these factors led to the phenomenon of a local representative making far-reaching foreign policy decisions that were then legitimized by his superiors, including the president, will now be analyzed.

The mounting tensions in Germany early in 1948, in addition to Soviet pressure in eastern and southern Europe, should have alerted U.S. intelligence services to the possibility of a new crisis. Yet the daily reports submitted to Clay contained nothing to arouse suspicion (Clay, 1950, p. 354). On March 5 he reluctantly dispatched the following message to the U.S. Army director of intelligence, warning Washington that beneath the surface all was not calm:

> Within the last few weeks, I have felt a subtle change in Soviet attitude which I cannot define but which now gives me a feeling that it may come with dramatic suddenness. I cannot support this change in my own thinking with any data or outward evidence in relationships other than to describe it

as a feeling of new tenseness in every Soviet individual with whom we have official relations. I am unable to submit any official report in the absence of supporting data but my feeling is real. . . . (Quoted in Millis, 1951, p. 387).

On March 16 the CIA predicted only that war was not probable within sixty days, but later it extended this estimate to cover another sixty-day period (Millis, 1951, p. 395). Two weeks later, the Soviets initiated the partial blockade. Clay's message, which did lead to a speed-up in American defense preparations, "was one of the rare cases in recent American history when the responsible Commander on the spot has not only sensed something that the Intelligence 'experts' had overlooked, but also dared to communicate this feeling to his superiors" (Smith, 1963, p. 102).

The Department of the Army was the government agency involved most directly in the decisions made by Clay and confirmed by President Truman. Its position vis-à-vis Clay's response to the partial blockade foreshadowed its attitude toward the June airlift. On March 30, just prior to the blockade, the Army summoned Clay to a teleconference and requested his views on a proposal to stop the movement of dependents of military government personnel to Germany, and on gradually withdrawing families from Berlin and the American zone. Clay opposed this move, stating that it would be politically disastrous: "Withdrawal of dependents would create hysteria, accompanied by a rush of Germans to Communism for safety" (1950, p. 358).

On March 31, immediately after the Soviet announcement of traffic restrictions, Clay notified Washington. He suggested that Washington respond to the Soviet authorities by declaring that America would refuse to comply with provisions that restricted the right of access to Berlin. He proposed, further, that a test train with several armed guards be sent across the zonal border. The essence of the Clay-Army split, which pervaded the atmosphere throughout June, was foreshadowed by the response of Secretary of the Army Kenneth Royall to Clay's suggestions. During the teleconference Clay detected some apprehension on the part of Secretary Royall and his advisors that a "firm stand on our part might develop incidents involving force which would lead to war" (Clay, 1950, p. 359). Washington reluctantly agreed to Clay's first proposal but vetoed the test train idea. The answer, however, was signed by General of the Army Omar Bradley, who apparently agreed with Clay, and not by Secretary Royall.

The indecision permeating the Department of the Army was demonstrated several times in the following weeks. Clay was told that pressure at home for the return of American families from Berlin was rising, and that "many responsible persons believed it unthinkable that [the families] should stay in Berlin" (*Ibid.*, p. 360). In short, he was being asked if he still wanted to stick his neck out. Predictably, Clay reiterated that "we should stay in Berlin unless driven out by force" (*Ibid.*).

The apprehension in the Pentagon about the consequences of Clay's effort to protect the American position in Berlin was not groundless. The United States was unable to send more than a division (15,000 men) anywhere without partial mobilization (Millis, 1951, p. 411). There were 18,000 Russian soldiers in the Soviet-occupied eastern sector of Berlin and another 300,000 in the East zone, as opposed to about 3,000 American, 2,000 British, and 1,500 French soldiers. Furthermore, many military experts doubted that an airlift of supplies to the American garrison was feasible, even on a limited scale (*New York Times*, April 2, 1948).

The Army's reluctance continued to manifest itself. On the very day the blockade started, and as Clay was arranging for the start of the airlift, the department was urging caution. In a teletype conference, Washington suggested that the introduction of Western currency into Berlin be slowed down. The Pentagon's caution was shared by many of Clay's military advisers in Berlin, who, feeling that withdrawal might be the best course of action, would make no recommendations at the June 24 staff meeting that Clay called to discuss the options open to them (Clay, 1950, p. 366).

Even after the airlift was under way, and had been confirmed by President Truman, the resistance of the military to the policy continued. For almost a month the Air Staff in the Pentagon resisted all efforts to increase the number of transport planes in Europe. Although Clay was assigned many top experts who were capable of organizing such an operation, he did not receive as many planes as he had asked for. This tactic of interference with policy execution was overcome only when Truman specifically overruled Air Force Chief of Staff, General Hoyt S. Vandenberg's objections at a National Security Council meeting in July.

What, from hindsight, were highly significant events in Berlin in early 1948 appeared rather negligible to the State Department at the time. During the latter part of January, Acting Secretary of State Lovett acknowledged to a press conference that there had been a series of incidents in Berlin, but that he saw little indication that they were increasing in severity (Davison, 1958, p. 73). This lack of perception was perhaps predictable in view of the minimal, largely administrative role that the department played in postwar Germany. Numerous attempts made by the Army to reduce its commitments in Germany to purely military duties and to leave the administration of the occupied area to the State Department failed, partly because of the latter's reluctance to take over, and partly because its inexperience was recognized by all the decision makers. Once tensions began to mount, the White House officially decided to maintain the status quo, thereby testifying both to the unpreparedness of the State Department and to the indispensability of Clay. Needless to say, this decision further strengthened Clay's hand in dealing with the problems of the occupation of Germany.

The position of the State Department in late June remained nebulous. In theory, General Clay operated under directives that conformed with the policies of the president and the Department of State. In reality Clay, and not the professional diplomats in Washington, shaped American foreign policy in postwar Germany. Robert Murphy, Clay's chief assistant, was a State Department professional, but he invariably sided with Clay (Murphy, 1964, p. 307). It is significant to note that at this time military influence pervaded the State Department. Secretary of State Marshall, himself a military man, is quoted as saying, "We are playing with fire when we have nothing at all to put it out with." And although he declared, after Truman's rebuff of General Vandenberg in July, that withdrawal would amount to "retreat under pressure," he undoubtedly remained reluctant to urge strong measures.

Others in the State Department expressed like concern. Walter Bedell Smith, American ambassador to Russia at the time, and also a soldier, privately favored the evacuation of Americans from Berlin, asserting that regardless of the outcome of an airlift, Berlin would continue to be a liability to the United States (Clay, 1950, p. 376). To the extent that there was a State Department position, then, it may be summarized as one of cautious pessimism.

We come now to the two individuals who stand at the center of the decision-making process involved in the airlift: General Clay and President Truman. Although Clay was theoretically subordinate not only to the president but also to the Army department and could therefore, again theoretically, only recommend courses of action to Washington, he played a much more active role, as we have seen. Taking a firm stand from the beginning of 1948, Clay first organized the "baby airlift," and then, in response to the full blockade, urged Washington to extend it. In an interview, he pointed out that in initiating "Operation Vittles" (as the full airlift was called) he acted on his own: "I began the airlift with what I had, because I had to prove to Washington that it was possible. Once I'd proved it, it was no longer hard to get help." (Riess, 1952, p. 165)

In view of Clay's central role, it is important to understand the factors that influenced him to undertake the airlift. Despite his military background, his decisions were based primarily on political rather than military considerations. He perceived the situation in Berlin as involving, first and foremost, American prestige. If the Russian squeeze were to succeed, forcing the Allies out of the German capital, images of appeasement, unreliability, and defeat would fill the minds of all Europeans. And although his views were not shared by all his advisors, as we pointed out above, they were strongly confirmed by the German leaders with whom he was in constant touch. Through public demonstrations and publications, these officials long attempted to arouse public opinion at home and abroad and prove to the world that Berlin was a symbol of democracy and deserved every Allied effort to keep it free. On the day of the blockade, Clay called to his office Ernst Reuter, the debarred lord mayor of Berlin, believing that only staunch support from Berliners would assure a successful airlift. Reuter asserted, and public opinion data bear him out, that "the Berliners were prepared to fight for their democratic liberties and would not give in to Soviet demands" (Davison, 1958, p. 105). Clay conveyed this attitude to Truman in June and in subsequent months. In fact, German public opinion was utilized in turn by all three leaders —Reuter, Clay, and Truman—not only as an index of German holdout strength, but also as a justification of the airlift as a "gesture for democracy" to the world once it was undertaken.

Despite the salience of political factors, military considerations were not overlooked. Clay believed that Russia did not want war, since it was not prepared for it. As evidence, he cited the facts that no airlift plane had been shot down and no Western soldier attacked.

The technical aspects of the airlift were also an important consideration. In this light, General Curtis LeMay, the Air Force commander in Germany, influenced Clay by assuring him that a greatly expanded airlift was technically feasible. On June 24, after a conversation with Clay, he mobilized all the aircraft at his disposal, and the first C-47 landed in Berlin with food for the population on June 26. This rapid action convinced Clay of the ultimate success of the undertaking, and helped him to convince Washington.

Perhaps the most interesting aspect of the airlift decision was President Truman's role as legitimizer of the field commander's decisions. A combination of factors brought about this behavior. First, and probably most important, was the aggressive and effective manner in which Clay acted. Since his expertise in German affairs was widely acknowledged, his frequent teleconferences with Truman and his appearances at the White House, before Congress, and at National Security Council meetings carried great weight. Reinforcing Clay's presentations was Truman's tendency to perceive the situation in Berlin, at least in the early months, in rather narrow military terms. In Truman's memoirs, the only reference to the partial blockade is that "our military government authorities rejected these [Soviet] conditions" (Truman, 1956, p. 122). In addition, throughout the first half of 1948 a careful consideration of the Berlin problem ranked fairly low on the list of presidential priorities. The Middle East, the situation in China, the Marshall Plan, and especially the electoral campaign appeared far more pressing. Finally, in contrast with some of his advisers, Truman had displayed a consistently hard-nosed attitude toward the Soviet

Union, which undoubtedly predisposed him to accept Clay's recommendations for tough responses to Russian actions in Berlin. Consequently, it was only after the airlift had begun that serious top-level conferences were held in Washington. On June 25 Truman met with Secretary of Defense James Forrestal, Secretary of the Army Kenneth Royall, and Undersecretary of State Robert Lovett to discuss American legal rights in Berlin. On finding the legal situation somewhat vague—due to the informal Roosevelt-Stalin "understanding"—Truman ordered further study. Nevertheless, the next day he "directed the improvised 'airlift' to be put on a full-scale organized basis, and that every plane available to our European Command be impressed into service" (*Ibid.*, p. 123).

On Sunday, June 27, an emergency meeting of the various secretaries and service chiefs was held in Royall's office to discuss, somewhat belatedly, three possible courses of action: withdrawal from Berlin, defense of the American position there by all possible means, and maintenance of an unprovocative but firm stand. Forrestal points out in his diary that among the few definite conclusions reached at the meeting were that he, Royall, and Lovett should meet with the president on June 28 and present him with the major issues that he might consider in making his decision, and that Clay be consulted once more. The wry comments of Walter Millis, editor of *The Forrestal Diaries*, on this decision-making process are worth quoting:

> Where, one is forced to ask, was all the elaborate machinery which had been set up to deal with such situations—the CIA, which was supposed to foresee and report the approach of a crisis; the National Security Council, which was supposed to establish the governing policy?
> The Berlin crisis was long in the making, but when it finally broke, the response was this ad hoc meeting at 4:00 P.M. on a Sunday afternoon in the Pentagon which . . . incidentally overlooked the potentialities of the airlift. (1951, p. 454)

When Forrestal, Royall, and Lovett met with Truman the next day to present the results of their deliberations, they found that the president's mind was made up. When they presented the withdrawal alternative, Truman "interrupted to say that there was no discussion on that point. We were in Berlin to stay. Period." (*Ibid.*, p. 456) Secretary of the Army Royall countered, rather weakly, by expressing concern about "having to fight our way into Berlin," but Truman stood fast, saying that "we were in Berlin by terms of an agreement and the Russians have no right to get us out by either direct or indirect means" (*Ibid.*, p. 455).

Very little has been written about any other groups or individuals who sought to influence Truman's position on Germany during June, 1948. There are, for example, no discussions of the White House staff's role. This probably reflects Truman's essentially negative attitude toward the staff, and their minimal role in his decision. Truman has expressed his disapproval of the "layer of Presidential aides placed between the President and his appointed officials," who "get in one another's way" and "tend to insulate the President" (Truman, 1953, pp. 228–29).

The direct congressional role in Truman's decision to support Clay's policies was also negligible. Forrestal points out that Truman decided against calling in congressional leaders when informed by Clay, on March 31, of the new Soviet provisions to be implemented. His reasons were that, first, the news would be leaked immediately to the public if the congressional leaders were informed, and, second, this would "add unnecessarily to the creation of war hysteria" (Millis, 1951, p. 408). Interestingly, the advent of the blockade increased congressional support for the administration's draft, rearmament, and universal military training programs.

However, although Truman's decision to legitimize the airlift was executive in origin, the administration attempted to give it a broader base by appealing to the principles of executive-congressional collaboration and bipartisanship. Secretary of State Marshall consulted with Arthur Vandenberg, chairman of the Senate Foreign Relations Committee, and Charles Eaton, chairman of the House Foreign Affairs Committee. In fact, Vandenberg's papers dwell on his close working relationship with Robert Lovett (Vandenberg, 1952). Through John Foster Dulles, the administration also solicited the views of Thomas Dewey, the Republican Party leader. These were, however, essentially ritualistic steps.

The president made his decision, informed the notables of it, and received their public support.

The role of public opinion and interest groups in the Berlin airlift decision can also be quickly dismissed. During his presidential campaign, Truman was justifiably sensitive to public opinion. However, the lack of attention paid by most Americans to Berlin, itself partially a function of the campaign, left Truman the discretion to make policy without fear of encountering negative public opinion. The divergent viewpoints on policy that Truman encountered and grappled with at the top governmental levels were largely absent in the country at large. A general public indifference prior to the Berlin blockade was manifested in a pattern of uncritical acceptance of occupation policy and a declining interest in the German occupation by American newspapers.

Despite the pervasive apathy that facilitated Truman's decision, some groups in the country took definite positions. Among these were the American Association for Democratic Germans, the AFL, and the CIO, all of which urged a strong stand in Berlin. However, their efforts took the form of "foreign policy resolutions" and the sending of CARE packages to German trade-union officials *after* Truman's decision to extend the airlift was made. On the other hand, the new Progressive Party and the American Communist Party opposed the administration's course in Berlin. However, the Progressive Party Convention, with its platform condemning American foreign policy, took place on July 21, after the airlift decision. The American Communist Party was, of course, discounted a priori by the administration. In sum, the fluidity that characterized American public opinion, largely a result of apathy and lack of expertise, gave Truman a carte blanche in dealing with the Russians. As Gabriel Almond has pointed out,

. . . the determination of what constitutes vital American interests to be defended by military means if necessary is a decision which the public tends to leave to its policy-makers. Thus, after official statements were made of our intention to remain in Berlin despite the Soviet blockade, 80 per cent of a national sample were ready to support this policy even if it were to result in war. (1950, p. 105)

Once his decision was made, Truman easily mobilized public opinion on behalf of Berlin, equating Berlin with the cause of democracy and presenting it as a symbol of resistance to Communist aggression. He publicized the struggle of Berliners, his accounts of the "stouthearted Berlin democrats" and their courage under fire evoking admiration among Americans. Thus, although public opinion concerning Berlin had not developed fully when the crisis struck (Davison, 1958, p. 376), Truman, like Reuter and Clay before him, manipulated it to his own advantage.

The United States' two allies in Germany played marginal and conflicting roles in the Berlin decision. The British were prepared to be firm with the Russians and, as we implied above, may even claim priority in starting the airlift. Certainly, they fully supported the effort once it started. The French, on the other hand, were quite dubious. They pressed for negotiations on the evacuation of Berlin, and on June 29, after the start of the airlift, they asked that Clay be restrained from taking independent action or even from making further statements without first consulting the British and French commanders. The record is not clear as to what extent Allied support was considered essential by American decision makers. However, it is fair to say that were the British and French positions reversed, Washington's misgivings about the airlift would have been even greater.

In conclusion, the Berlin airlift decision, which had great consequences for postwar American foreign policy, was made in the field and confirmed almost casually by the president. The decision-making process in this case was a function of two individual initiatives, Clay's and Truman's, both taken in the face of indecisive and divergent advice from the organizations and individuals that are supposed to facilitate rational, effective foreign-policy making.

REFERENCES AND BIBLIOGRAPHY

ALMOND, GABRIEL, *The American People and Foreign Policy*. New York: Praeger, 1950.

CLAY, LUCIUS, *Decision in Germany.* New York: Doubleday, 1950.

DAVISON, W. PHILLIPS, *The Berlin Blockade.* Princeton, N.J.: Princeton University Press, 1958.

HOWLEY, FRANK L., *Berlin Command.* New York: Putnam's, 1950.

MILLIS, WALTER, ed., *The Forrestal Diaries.* New York: Viking, 1951.

MURPHY, ROBERT D., *Diplomat Among Warriors.* New York: Doubleday, 1964.

RIESS, CURT, *The Berlin Story.* New York: Dial Press, 1952.

SMITH, JEAN E., *The Defense of Berlin.* Baltimore: Johns Hopkins, 1963.

TRUMAN, HARRY S., *Mr. Citizen.* New York: Geis Associates, 1953.

————, *Years of Trial and Hope.* Vol. II. Garden City, N.Y.: Doubleday, 1956.

U.S., Department of State, *The Berlin Crisis: A Report on the Moscow Discussions,* Publication 3298. Washington, D.C.: Government Printing Office, September, 1948.

VANDENBERG, ARTHUR H., JR., ed., *The Private Papers of Senator Vandenberg.* Boston: Houghton Mifflin, Riverside Press, 1952.

WINDSOR, PHILIP, *City on Leave.* New York: Praeger, 1963.

4

The Decision
Not To Intervene In Indochina
1954

Most readers are well acquainted with the recent history of American actions in Southeast Asia, especially in the war in Vietnam. The origins of this involvement, however, go back to the end of World War II. In view of later developments (see Chapter 12), it is ironic that the first major policy initiative toward this area consisted of a carefully considered decision *not* to intervene in France's Indochina War in 1954.

Toward the close of 1953, the French position in Indochina was growing increasingly precarious. It was becoming evident in Washington that the French, responding to burgeoning internal discontent in Indochina, were being pushed in the direction of negotiating a settlement of this conflict. Such a settlement, Washington officials contended, could be achieved only by sacrificing Western interests to Communist advances, and would serve merely to reinforce Communist intransigence.

It was in the light of these possibilities, and only with the greatest reluctance, that Secretary of State Dulles agreed to attend a conference on Indochina, to be convened at Geneva in late April, 1954. However, he warned French Foreign Minister Georges Bidault that if Indochina were put on the agenda, "between now and then General Ho Chi Minh [will] make immense efforts to win victories that [will] gain him political advantage. You can expect fanatical attempts to gain a good political position." (Beal, 1957, p. 205)

Dulles's assessment of Communist strategy was not far off the mark. By mid-March, 1954, the French position at Dien Bien Phu, long considered impregnable by most military strategists, was being seriously threatened by a massive assault by Vietminh forces. Most American observers believed that a major French defeat in Dien Bien Phu would not only undermine French morale, but would hasten a French withdrawal from Indochina as well. Although most American officials recognized the unlikelihood of a clear-cut military victory over the Communists in Indochina, they were far from convinced that negotiations would produce meaningful results. Nevertheless, since negotiation appeared to be unavoidable, these officials reasoned that a diligent effort to bolster the French position, both militarily and politically, was an absolutely minimal requirement.

The growing anxiety of American public officials concerning the French fate in Indochina was heightened by the views offered them by General Paul Ely, then president of the French Chiefs of Staff, who visited Washington in late March. He had come to apprise American military advisors and officials of the Eisenhower administration of the situation in Indochina. Although Ely publicly offered an optimistic view of the French position in Dien Bien Phu, and in Indochina in general, his private assessments given to the Joint Chiefs of Staff and to other government officials were apparently less sanguine. It became increasingly evident to American officials that a deeper military commitment to the struggle in Indochina would be required.

On March 21, General Ely met with the Joint Chiefs of Staff to discuss the nature and extent of American military contributions to the French war effort. The Joint Chiefs agreed to send additional troop transports to France, to provide twenty-five more B-26 bombers for deployment in Indochina, and to step up the training of Indochinese pilots in the Philippines. An offer made by the Joint Chiefs to involve the United States in the training of Vietnamese forces was, however, declined by Ely. At this point the Chiefs evidently believed "that a properly trained and equipped Vietnamese army could defend Indochina against the Communists (Randle, 1969, p. 57). To accomplish this purpose, the United States was also prepared to increase its material aid to the French.

Despite this willingness to provide military assistance, Washington officials were for the most part careful to rule out direct military intervention by American ground troops in Indochina. As President Eisenhower had noted in his press conference on February 10, "No one could be more bitterly opposed to ever getting the United States involved in a hot war in that region than I am. Consequently, . . . every move that I authorize is calculated, so far as humans can do it, to make certain that that does not happen." (Congressional Record, 1954, p. 10139) Of course, intervention by the United States under any circumstances was never entirely eliminated. As Eisenhower noted in his memoirs, military intervention would be possible if three basic requirements were fulfilled: "The first requirement was a legal right under international law; second, was a favorable climate of Free World opinion; and third, favorable action by the Congress" (Eisenhower, 1963, p. 340). As it turned out, these conditions did not wholly materialize at any point.

On March 22, Ely, along with the chairman of the Joint Chiefs of Staff, Admiral Arthur Radford, met with Eisenhower. At the conclusion of their discussion, the president directed Radford to provide the French with any material assistance that they requested and, in particular, to take steps to relieve the Vietminh pressure on Dien Bien Phu. After some deliberation, and after his initial proposal to employ tactical nuclear weapons against the Vietminh had been vetoed by other members of the Joint Chiefs, Radford proposed that the Allies—meaning the United

States—"should launch . . . massive air strikes against enemy positions around Dien Bien Phu" (Kalb and Abel, 1971, p. 76). From the decks of two U.S. Navy carriers then on a "training mission" in the South China Seas, and from Clark Air Force Base in the Philippines, some sixty B-29 heavy bombers would carry out several night raids on the beleagured garrison. They would drop, it was contemplated, 450 tons of bombs on each raid. This bombing campaign, Radford assumed, would destroy much of the Vietminh artillery and would severely retard its plans to encircle and destroy the camp. Should the bombing fail to accomplish its purpose, however, Radford was prepared to undertake other military actions, including the possible deployment of American paratroopers and the mining and closing of Haiphong Harbor.

At its meeting on March 25, the National Security Council approved the plan, although with some misgivings. Eisenhower also approved the plan reluctantly, with the stipulation, though, that its provisions would not be carried out without the approval of America's allies and the Congress. Secretary Dulles was even more reticent. He had little confidence in the Radford proposals, not only because he was conscious of Congress's fear that they would lead to a commitment of American ground forces, but because he knew that such a commitment might anger the British and her Commonwealth partners.

General Ely's visit and the ensuing discussions of the Radford plan revealed that the American foreign-policy-making community was far from united in its views on Indochina. Eisenhower appeared convinced that the American people wanted peace and that the military involvement of the United States in Indochina should not be undertaken until all other alternatives had been exhausted. Moreover, he was aware that the decision to intervene might weaken the Republican Party in the upcoming midterm Congressional elections in November. As Timothy Sheehan, the Illinois congressman put it, "If President Eisenhower and the Republican leadership commit our troops into Southeast Asia, . . . the people will show their disgust by returning a Democratic-controlled Congress in November" (*Congressional Record*, 1954, p. 5795; see also p. 5178). Radford, on the other hand, believed firmly that Indochina must not be allowed to fall into Communist hands and that every effort must be made to salvage the French position. He believed that negotiations with the Communists would prove fruitless and would, in the end, lead to a situation seriously detrimental to American interests.

Dulles's views were more difficult to discern. Although he remained skeptical about the utility of negotiating with the Communists, he was not prepared to advocate intervention without a carefully engineered justification of such action and without significant hope for success. This view led him to launch a diligent effort to cultivate and prepare American public opinion for acts of limited intervention and to gain the support of America's allies, principally France and the United Kingdom, for such a venture. It was also imperative, Dulles believed, to mobilize support within key congressional circles before proceeding.

On March 29, Dulles opened his campaign to prepare the American people for the decision to intervene. In a speech before the Overseas Press Club, Dulles touched on a wide variety of topics related to Indochina and Communist China. He defended both the American policy of nonrecognition of Communist China and the administration's decision to oppose seating the Communist Chinese in the United Nations. As for the Indochinese conflict, he detailed the extent of Communist material assistance to the Vietminh and accused the Chinese of interfering with the development of independence in Vietnam. He spoke of the French intention to grant independence to the Associated States of Indochina, and pledged American support for the fulfillment of that objective. Finally, after citing the strategic importance of Southeast Asia to the United States and accusing the Communist Chinese of "indirect aggression," the secretary expressed the major lines of American policy in that region:

> Under the conditions of today, the imposition on Southeast Asia of the political system of Communist Russia and its Chinese Communist ally, by whatever means, would be a grave threat to the whole Free World community [and] should not be passively accepted, but should be met by united action. (*New York Times*, March 30, 1954)

Although the pursuit of this policy would "involve serious risks," the secretary noted, a failure to act at this point could produce an even more serious situation in the future.

The Dulles speech was designed to serve a variety of purposes. First, it sought to alert the American people that the continued broadening of Chinese support for the Vietminh forces might well provoke American intervention. Thus, it attempted to prepare American public opinion for the possibility of United States involvement in Indochina. Second, it sought to assure the French of continued American support for their position in Indochina and to strengthen their morale and their resistance to Communist military advances. Third, it sought to warn the Chinese of the limits beyond which American involvement would be unavoidable. In this regard, James Reston of the *New York Times* observed that "the foreign policy position expressed by the Secretary reflected a basic principle of his behavior, namely, that it is important to state in advance what you will not tolerate, so that your friends know on what they can count and your enemies know what to avoid" (March 30, 1954).

Although the National Security Council at its March 25 meeting had, according to some observers, adopted a provisional decision to fight in Indochina by endorsing Radford's proposals, Dulles's speech marked a significant departure from the plan originally offered by the Joint Chiefs' chairman. The secretary had apparently concluded that the air strikes were a "poor way" of involving the United States in Indochina. Moreover, the secretary seemed convinced that such an action would not seriously alter the military situation at Dien Bien Phu; it would merely deepen American involvement in Indochina without any guarantee of ultimate success.

However, Radford was not prepared to yield his position gracefully. Supported by key figures within the administration, including Vice President Nixon, Assistant Secretary of State Walter Robertson, and a number of State Department officers in charge of Far Eastern affairs, as well as by the right-wing faction of the Republican Party, the Joint Chiefs' chairman pressed his case within the top policy-making strata.

In an attempt to counter this threat to his policy and to forestall immediate unilateral American intervention in Indochina, Dulles convened, with Eisenhower's approval, a meeting with key congressional leaders on April 3. Dulles hoped that a skeptical congressional response at this meeting, which was ostensibly meant to be a forum to notify Congress of the Radford plan, would undermine Radford's position. He was not disappointed.

Attending that meeting, which was held at the State Department, were Radford and Dulles, along with other top administration officials, including Undersecretary of Defense Roger Keyes, Navy Secretary Robert Anderson, and Thruston Morton, then Dulles's assistant for congressional relations. They were joined by a bipartisan group of five senators and three representatives, all of whom occupied key positions in Congress.

In his opening statement to the group, Dulles indicated that the president wanted Congress to approve a joint resolution permitting him to deploy air and naval power in Indochina. The secretary hinted that "perhaps the mere passage of such a resolution would in itself make its use unnecessary" (Roberts, 1962, p. 240). After noting the seriously deteriorating situation in Indochina—in particular, the grievous encirclement of Dien Bien Phu—Radford presented his air-strike plan.

The congressmen, on the whole, appeared unwilling to support Radford's proposal. Would the use of American airpower mean, the congressmen inquired, that the United States would be in the war? Yes, replied the Joint Chiefs' chairman. And, the congressmen continued, should the air strikes fail to achieve their purpose, would the United States engage in further military action? Again Radford responded in the affirmative, although he did not specify the nature of that action. Even Senate Majority Leader William Knowland, who had initially showed great enthusiasm for the venture, eventually lapsed into silence as the discussions proceeded.

Before the meeting broke up, it was evident to Dulles that congressional authorization for unilateral military intervention would not be forthcoming. As he had expected, the meeting with the congressmen had served to scuttle Radford's plan, since these assembled congressional leaders, along with Dulles himself, "doubted the efficacy of an air attack, . . . feared its consequences . . . and . . . regarded unilateral American intervention as undesirable" (Randle, 1969, p. 65). The idea of a congressional resolution, at least at this point, was temporarily shelved. This was satisfactory to Dulles for two reasons. On the one hand, if Congress had approved the resolution, intra-administration pressures might well have compelled the United States to act. On the other hand, had Congress failed to support the resolution, the credibility of the United States "to deter by *threats* of intervention would [have been] appreciably diminished" (*Ibid.*, p. 64).

This group encouraged Dulles to undertake the first step in formulating an American policy by determining which countries would be willing to join the United States in taking "united action" against the Communist threat in Indochina. Reporting to the president on the results of his April 3 meeting, Dulles stated that congressional support for United States intervention in Indochina was contingent upon three conditions:

> (1) United States intervention must be part of a coalition to include the other free nations of Southeast Asia, the Philippines, and the British Commonwealth; (2) the French must agree to accelerate their independence program for the Associated States [of Indochina]; (3) the French must agree not to pull their forces out of the war if we put our forces in (Eisenhower, 1963, p. 347).

At a meeting with the secretary on April 4, Eisenhower indicated his complete agreement with these conditions and urged Dulles to begin fleshing out the program for united action.

Even before Eisenhower had indicated his approval of Dulles's proposal for united action, the secretary of state had met on April 3 with Henri Bonnet, the French ambassador to the United States, to outline his plan. United action, the secretary explained to Bonnet, would involve the formation of a coalition comprising France, Britain, the United States, Australia, New Zealand, Thailand, and the Philippines. This coalition would resist Communist aggression in Southeast Asia. Appearing before the House Foreign Affairs Committee on April 5, the secretary explained that "unity of action" was required to discourage the Communists and to reassure the French and the Indochinese (Bator, 1965, p. 53).

The Dulles policy of united action attempted to serve two purposes. First, it sought to obtain congressional support for a broader involvement of the United States in Indochina by fulfilling a key precondition stipulated by the congressional leadership on

April 3. Second, it aimed to establish "a political and strategic framework where, as in NATO, France and England would no longer be able to take any diplomatic initiatives [such as negotiating peace in Indochina] without Washington's formal agreement" (Devillers and Lacouture, 1969, p. 83).

Dulles's policy, however, was to experience considerable difficulties. Both France and the United Kingdom were hesitant to accept the political implications of the secretary's plan. The French saw Dulles's proposals as curbing their ability to negotiate a settlement of the Indochinese conflict and compelling them to remain militarily tied down in Indochina without any assurance of a broader American military involvement. The British were concerned with the possibility of a more extensive conflict, which they thought could lead to a rupture in their relations with Commonwealth partners and might be regarded as provocation by the Communist Chinese. Although the negative reaction of the French and the British should not have come as a complete surprise to administration officials, these officials do not appear to have been fully prepared for it.

After a brief consultation with the president, Dulles traveled to Europe in early April in an effort to clarify his proposals and to gain Allied support. Although Kalb and Abel assert that Dulles "hoped to persuade [the Allies] that immediate intervention was necessary to save Dien Bien Phu" (1971, p. 80), the evidence suggests that this was not the secretary's principal objective. Instead, Dulles hoped to gain a measure of agreement among the Allies because he believed that a united stand would improve the bargaining position of the West at the forthcoming Geneva Conference. By the time he arrived in London to open discussions with the British, the secretary had abandoned his preference for a joint warning to the Chinese to deter them from further intervention in Indochina in favor of the establishment of a regional security organization in Southeast Asia. He appeared convinced that the existence of such an organization would deter China and make military intervention by the United States unnecessary.

The British, in Dulles's view, "had little enthusiasm for joining [the United States] in taking a firm position" (Eisenhower,

1963, p. 347). Obviously, they did not share the secretary's sense of urgency. Apparently, Britain had decided to rely upon the power of diplomacy to terminate the conflict, and, consequently, to avoid any action that might involve British armed forces in Indochina. Moreover, Britain seemed convinced that the military situation in Indochina could not be settled by military means, and it therefore sought to avoid adopting any policy that might jeopardize the upcoming Geneva talks. Although the chances of success at Geneva appeared slight, Britain believed that all possibilities should be explored thoroughly and patiently.

On April 13, at the conclusion of the talks between Dulles and the British, a joint statement was issued. As the British wanted, the statement did not extend beyond a warning that the Allies "would not allow the work of the Geneva Conference to be prejudiced by Communist military action" (Eden, 1960, pp. 107–8). The British did agree to engage in preliminary discussions on the possibility of forming a collective defense organization for Southeast Asia. Dulles appeared pleased with these results, and he optimistically informed the president that "he had accomplished much toward dispelling the British reluctance to say or do anything before Geneva" (Eisenhower, 1963, p. 348).

Dulles then traveled to Paris to discuss his policy with French officials. On April 14, at the conclusion of their deliberations, a joint statement, which closely resembled the one Dulles drafted with the British, was issued. Conversations with the French political leaders touched most of the topics that Dulles had discussed with the British. The French persistently claimed that no action should be taken that would convey the impression that the "French Government was not sincere in its search for a peaceful settlement, that it was resigned to failure at Geneva, or that it was on the verge of decisions that would enable it to continue the war in a different form" (Devillers and Lacouture, 1969, p. 88).

Despite the hesitations and reservations expressed by the Allied political leaders about the nature and timing of his proposed moves, Dulles returned to Washington convinced that his mission had been moderately successful. He believed that he had Foreign Secretary Anthony Eden's agreement to initiate work immediately on the establishment of a collective security organization in Southeast Asia. Consequently, shortly after his return Dulles invited the French, British, and other "interested powers" to attend preparatory discussions for this purpose on April 20.

On April 18, two days before the first scheduled meeting, Sir Roger Makins, the British ambassador to the United States, telephoned the secretary of state to inform him that the British government had instructed him not to attend. Dulles was visibly angered and shaken by this decision. Apparently he had either misread the British position or Eden had misled him for some reason. Whatever the case it was now evident that Eden and Dulles disagreed on at least two issues. First, the two officials disagreed over whether the defense organization should be formed before the Geneva Conference. Unlike the United States, the British preferred no action prior to the conference. Until the intentions of the Communist states were appraised at Geneva, Britain would not enter into any discussions bearing upon the establishment of a collective defense. Second, Dulles and Eden differed over the question of the organization's membership. Although their discussions in London on this topic were inconclusive, Eden viewed Dulles's action to convene the conference as equivalent to settling "the question of membership in advance on his own terms . . . ." Quite apart "from the timing of such a matter," Eden noted in his memoirs, "it was clear to me that it would . . . be regarded as already constituting the proposed organization" (Eden, 1960, p. 110). Faced with the British refusal to attend, Dulles was compelled to convert the April 20 meeting into a discussion on Korea in order to ensure British attendance.

By the middle of April, therefore, it appeared that the United States had decided, at least temporarily, to take no direct military action in Indochina, particularly since her allies seemed reluctant to support such intervention. Publicly, of course, the administration was pursuing a much less clear-cut course of action. During this period the administration publicly sought to establish the case for possible intervention, in large part to deter the Communist Chinese. On March 29, Dulles stressed the strategic importance of Indochina and hinted darkly that the Chinese might force the administration to take action that could "involve serious risks."

At his press conference on March 31, Eisenhower endorsed the position of his secretary of state. Although it was not possible to lay down a blueprint for action, the president argued, his administration was committed to "united action" against Communist expansion in Southeast Asia (*New York Times*, April 1, 1954). On April 7, Eisenhower presented a more elaborate rationale for possible American military action. Explaining the developments in Southeast Asia, Eisenhower emphasized the multiplying effect of a single falling domino—the "domino theory." "You have a row of dominoes set up," he said, "and you knock over the first one, and what would happen to the last one was the certainty that it would go over very quickly. So you have the beginning of a disintegration that would have the most profound influences." (*New York Times*, April 8, 1954).

In spite of Secretary of Defense George Wilson's remark before the Senate Foreign Relations Committee on April 15 that American military action in Indochina was not imminent, the threat of some form of intervention was not wholly dispelled. Rather, American intentions became even more ambiguous when, on the next day, an "unidentified source" high in the administration (later identified as Vice-President Nixon) announced that if the situation required it, the United States would have to send troops to Indochina, even without substantial contributions from her allies. Nixon had made this statement before a convention of the American Society of Newspaper Editors, then meeting in Washington. Declaring that the situation in Indochina was serious and that the French might stop fighting and withdraw should they suffer a major reversal at Dien Bien Phu, Nixon urged the United States to pursue policies that would deter the communization of Southeast Asia. As Nixon put it, should "the situation in Indochina require that American troops be sent there to prevent that area from disappearing behind the Iron Curtain, the Administration must face the issue and send the troops" (*New York Times*, April 17, 1954).

Nixon's motives in delivering that statement were none too clear. Some viewed his remarks as a "trial balloon" for official administration policy (*New York Times*, April 18, 1954). Others denied this viewpoint. In any event, Nixon was clearly upset by the controversy sparked by his statement. In an effort to reassure Nixon, Eisenhower informed the vice president "that the uproar over his comment had been all to the good because it awakened the country to the seriousness of the situation in Indochina" (Adams, 1961, p. 122). The administration, therefore, apparently welcomed the address as part of its campaign to alert Congress and the American public to the gravity of the situation in Indochina. "The public," as Randle notes, "was put on notice that the warnings Administration officials had been issuing might yet require fulfillment" (1969, p. 94).

Efforts were immediately undertaken, however, to stress the continuity between Nixon's remarks and the basic thrust of American policy. The State Department declared on April 18 that Nixon's statement represented no new policy departure and was in full agreement with the views of the president and the secretary of state. In their view, the deployment of American troops was unlikely, and the withdrawal of French forces from Indochina was highly improbable. On April 19, speaking before a hastily assembled group of journalists, Dulles noted that he "thought it unlikely that American combat troops would be sent to Indochina and the possibility of French withdrawal too hypothetical even to discuss" (*Ibid.*, p. 93). And just in case some doubts still lingered, the secretary claimed that Nixon's remarks had been made off the record and were the vice president's personal views (*New York Times*, April 20, 1954). Nixon himself, in an address on April 20, sought to clarify his position, arguing that a strong and decisive policy was the best guarantee of peace. "If you are weak and indecisive," Nixon warned, "you invite war. You don't keep Communists out of an area by telling them you won't do anything to save it." (*New York Times*, April 21, 1954).

Despite the effort by the State Department and other government officials to gloss over the differences between Nixon's views and those of the administration, the vice president's statement provoked widespread discussion within the Senate. Although the consultation between administration officials and top congressional leaders on April 3 had sparked some debate within the Senate on April 5 and 6, the issue of Indochina had disappeared from the legislative agenda for more than a week. Preoccupied with pressing domestic problems, Congress appeared to show little interest either in the events in Indochina or in Dulles's campaign to mobilize support among the Allies for possible military intervention. The administration, moreover, made little effort to keep Congress informed of the progress in its negotiations with its European partners. Nixon's speech, however, revived congressional interest in Indochina.

Commenting upon Nixon's address, Senator Knowland, then newly appointed majority leader of the Senate, expressed agreement with the vice president's position regarding the use of troops in Indochina. But he added that such a decision should be undertaken in cooperation with the United States' allies, because Congress would not "be satisfied" with the development of another Korean situation in which this country would "assume 90 percent of the burden" (*New York Times*, April 18, 1954).

Opposition to the use of American military forces in Indochina was expressed by Senators Leverett Saltonstall (Massachusetts), Bourke Hickenlooper (Iowa), John Stennis (Mississippi), and Estes Kefauver (Tennessee). (See the *New York Times*, April 18, 1954 and the *Congressional Record*, 1954, pp. 4681, 5291–93.) Senators Hubert Humphrey (Minnesota) and John Kennedy (Massachusetts) stressed the necessity of granting independence to the Associated States of Indochina before contemplating any military action, lest the United States be accused of supporting colonialism. The United States should, Humphrey declared, announce its support for independence, thus dispelling the belief held in some circles that America has, "in the recesses of its official mind, the attitude that Indochina may not be quite ready for independence" (*Congressional Record*, 1954, p. 5117).

A handful of senators criticized the excessive secrecy behind which the administration was developing its policy regarding Indochina. Some urged the administration to make a concerted effort to clarify its position, and in particular to dispel the rumors of imminent military intervention then circulating widely in the Washington policy-making community. "It is imperatively incumbent on the President," Senator Albert Gore (Tennessee) noted, "to make his policies clear with respect to our possible further involvement in Indochina. The country desperately needs clarification. . . ." (*New York Times*, April 19, 1954) Senator Mike Mansfield (Montana) complained about the lack of consultation between the executive and Congress regarding American policy in Southeast Asia. Too often, Mansfield remarked, senators were forced to rely upon the press for information, rather than on their direct contacts with the administration. However, journalist William White observed that such a process of consultation did exist. It tended to focus upon the Democrats, as well as the Republicans, who held powerful party positions and/or powerful positions in the Armed Services Committee (*New York Times*, April 11, 1954). The administration apparently believed that a congressional floor leader would shape legislative opinion more effectively than either a top party figure or a foreign-policy leader. This limited administration contact with Congress, however, served only to widen the gap between the legislature and the executive and, so White informs us, to sadden and in some cases anger many Democratic congressmen who would have responded favorably to Dulles's policy had he chosen to keep them informed of developments while carrying out his plans.

Meanwhile, amidst widespread confusion in Congress concerning American intentions and amidst consternation among America's allies, General Henri Navarre sent a letter to the French cabinet in late April warning its members that French forces in Dien Bien Phu could not maintain their position much longer without immediate and massive air support. During a NATO council meeting on April 23, Bidault informed Dulles of the grievous situation at Dien Bien Phu, and, discounting the value of a British contribution, he asked the secretary of state to reassess the possibility of American intervention. At this point the French were no longer opposed, as they had been in early April, to an internationalization of the war.

The deteriorating French position at Dien Bien Phu reopened the issue of American intervention, although as late as April 20 Dulles had told congressional leaders that American military action in Indochina was neither imminent nor under consideration. Though there was some support within the administration for involvement in Indochina, Dulles continued to be reluctant to enter the conflict. He did not believe, as Bidault had urged, that an air strike would be effective. (For Bidault's position, see Eisenhower, 1963, p. 350.) Moreover, an air strike would be a belligerent act, one that would require prior congressional approval, and this consent depended upon the willingness of America's allies—including, most important, Britain—to join in united action.

On April 24, Bidault informed the secretary of state that the French High Command estimated that a massive air assault by the United States could still save the garrison, and that the attack could well deliver a "decisive blow" to the Vietminh (see Devillers and Lacouture, 1969, pp. 94–95). Although he had attempted unsuccessfully on April 23 to convince Eden of the seriousness of the situation and the need for Britain to support American policy toward Indochina, Dulles continued his discussions on this subject with the British foreign minister throughout most of the next day. Radford was also present at these discussions. Despite the arguments of these two men, Eden refused to yield. He firmly believed that "anything less than intervention on a Korean scale, if that, would have any effect in Indo–China" (Eden, 1960, p. 114), and that, therefore, the contemplated massive air assault would accomplish little.

Later that same day, Dulles and Eden met with Bidault at the Quai d'Orsay. By this time the secretary of state had become convinced that the fall of Dien Bien Phu was inevitable. He was concerned, however, that the capitulation of the fortress would lead to a "collapse of French will," since it had become, he wrote to Eisenhower, "a symbol out of all proportion to its military importance" (Eisenhower, 1963, p. 350). The United States was prepared, Dulles informed the two top policy makers, to set about immediately to organize the defense of the entire region, provided the French would agree to continue the struggle after the fall of the fortress. He was even prepared, Dulles noted, to outline the nature and extent of this assistance more formally in a letter, should the French deem that useful. After some hesitation, Bidault agreed that Dulles should send the letter to him officially (Eden, 1960, p. 116).

Thus, by April 24 it seemed that the United States was prepared to intervene militarily in Indochina if France, and especially the United Kingdom, so desired. If Britain were willing to associate itself, at least symbolically, with American intervention, then a resolution authorizing the president to employ air and naval forces in Indochina—which had already been drafted in anticipation of just such a step—could be approved by Congress as early as April 28, thus clearing the way for military action by the United States before the end of the month. Both Dulles, in his conversations with Bidault and Eden, and Undersecretary of State Walter Bedell Smith, in his discussions with French Ambassador Bonnet in Washington, had spoken of the prepared authorization and had expressed optimism about congressional cooperation in this matter (see Roberts, 1962, p. 246).

Although there appears to be some disagreement about whether the letter outlined by Dulles was ever sent to the French, Eden, concerned about the implications of the secretary's proposals, left immediately for London to consult with his government. He informed Churchill of his disagreement "both with the American belief that such intervention could be effective and with the view that it could be limited to the use of air forces" (Eden, 1960, p. 117). After some discussion, Churchill concluded that Dulles's plan involved an attempt to use Britain in a highly unorthodox manner to mislead Congress into approving a military operation that would certainly prove ineffective and might well bring the world to the verge of a major war (Bator, 1965, p. 69).

Eden and Churchill agreed that Britain should decline giving any military assistance to the French in Indochina. Instead, an effort should be made to strengthen the negotiating position of the French at Geneva, a result, the two statesmen believed, that would not necessarily be achieved by hasty and limited military action. At the meeting on April 25 with the full British cabinet, these views received enthusiastic support. As a result, it seemed evident that the British were not prepared to undertake any action until, as Eisenhower pointed out, "all possibility of settlement by negotiation had been tried and failed" (Eisenhower, 1963, p. 351). Even a second attempt by Dulles failed to bring about any shift in this position. (For the details of this attempt, see Bator, 1965, pp. 70–72.)

News of the British refusal was brought to Washington by Radford on April 26. Dissatisfied with the negative British response, the more "hawkish" elements within the administration made one final effort to obtain a decision in favor of American military intervention. Without consulting Dulles, Undersecretary Smith developed a plan by which the ANZUS Pact powers would provide authorization for American military action, thus bypassing the issue of British participation. Although he was far from enthusiastic about this scheme, Eisenhower appeared willing to go along with it (Eisenhower, 1963 p. 355). Moreover, congressmen who were sounded out on this suggestion on April 26 did not, on the whole, appear to be unfavorably disposed. The entire scheme collapsed, however, when, as Smith reported to Eisenhower, "Australia and New Zealand [withdrew] from their original position favorable to united action" (Ibid., p. 354).

The end of active consideration of the question of American intervention in Indochina occurred on April 29, when Eisenhower noted in the course of his press conference that the United States was prepared "to see what diplomacy could achieve at Geneva before it took any new steps to support France on Indochina" (Randle, 1969, p. 106). As the president pointed out, there seemed at this point no plausible reason for United States intervention, particularly if such action might prejudice the chances of reaching an acceptable modus vivendi at the conference. This new position reflected at least three principal considerations. First, American military experts had informed the president that intervention to salvage Dien Bien Phu at this stage would prove fruitless. Second, congressional opinion appeared firmly opposed to any unilateral American involvement in Indochina, although Congress would probably have acceded to a forceful presidential request. And, third, Eisenhower seemed to share the widespread belief that the American public was strongly opposed to any military action in Southeast Asia (see Devillers and Lacouture, 1969, p. 99).

Let us sum up. On two separate occasions in April, 1954, the administration was confronted with the problem of American military intervention in Indochina. In both cases, the decision not to intervene was made almost wholly within the executive establishment and involved a limited number of actors, including, most prominently, the secretary of state, the president, and agencies such as the National Security Council and the Joint Chiefs of Staff.

The decision rested on a number of considerations: the reluctance of the secretary of state and the president to commit the United States militarily in Indochina without a significant assurance of success; the apparent unwillingness of Congress to support intervention without Allied cooperation; and the conviction within some administration circles that the French failure in Indochina was a result of their refusal to move more rapidly toward granting independence to the Associated States. The development of American policy on Indochina was marked by differences within the administration between those urging intervention and those seeking a nonmilitary response. This debate was carried on both privately and in the press. For the most part, the public presentation was aimed at preparing the American public for possible intervention while alerting the Communists to the American willingness to exercise military force to achieve its objectives. The media, in short, was employed by the administration both to argue its case and to broaden public support.

There was little input by an independent public opinion. The nature of the decision and the major issues were initially posed by the administration, and were presented in such a manner as to prevent the articulation of alternative policies or opinions.

Throughout this period Congress as a whole was consulted only irregularly and only, apparently, on those occasions when Dulles deemed congressional support crucial to his own "moderate" position within the administration (see Randle, 1969, pp. 118–19). At no point, however, did Congress serve as a major obstacle to the secretary's or the president's plans. There appears to be little doubt that even in the absence of Allied support, Congress would have been willing to back any action supported by the president, including intervention, had Eisenhower chosen to request it. As Chalmers Roberts reported, after interviewing a number of congressmen, "Congress would, in the end, have done what Eisenhower asked, provided he had asked for it forcefully and explained the facts. . ." (1962, p. 248).

It would appear in retrospect, therefore, that the decision not to intervene in Indochina cannot be explained satisfactorily by pointing to an aggressive Congress that took a strong and consistent stance and thereby frustrated executive initiatives. Rather, the decision reflected the basic unwillingness of Eisenhower and Dulles to commit American forces to an Asian war.

To Dulles, and perhaps to Eisenhower as well, the Indochina crisis involved a clear case of an American policy of brinkmanship. As Dulles was to argue later,

> You have to take chances for peace, just as you must take chances in war. Some say that we were brought to the verge of war. Of course we were. . . . The ability to get to the verge without getting into the war is the necessary art. If you cannot master it, you inevitably get into war. . . . We've had to look it square in the face—on the question of enlarging the Korean War, on the question of getting into the Indochina War, on the question of Formosa. We walked to the brink and we looked it in the face. (Shepley, 1956, p. 78)

This philosophy was to come under severe attack in the 1960s as being fraught with hazard in an age of nuclear weapons, and as being likely to involve the United States in unwanted military adventures. Yet it was precisely the more "realistic" and "cautious" approach of the 1960s that propelled the United States into a far more extensive military action than was ever contemplated by the allegedly belligerent strategy of Dulles and Eisenhower.

REFERENCES AND BIBLIOGRAPHY

ADAMS, SHERMAN, *Firsthand Report*. New York: Harper & Brothers, 1961.

BATOR, VICTOR, *Vietnam: A Diplomatic Tragedy*. Dobbs Ferry, N.Y.: Oceana Publications, 1965.

BEAL, JOHN ROBINSON, *John Foster Dulles: A Biography*. New York: Harper & Brothers, 1957.

DEVILLERS, PHILIPPE, and JEAN LACOUTURE, *End of a War: Indochina, 1954*. New York: Praeger, 1969.

EDEN, ANTHONY, *Full Circle*. Boston: Houghton Mifflin, 1960.

EISENHOWER, DWIGHT D., *Mandate for Change, 1953–1956: The White House Years*. New York: Doubleday, 1963.

KAHIN, GEORGE MCTURNAN, and JOHN W. LEWIS, *The United States in Vietnam*. New York: Dial Press, 1967.

KALB, MARVIN, and ELIE ABEL, *Roots of Involvement: U.S. in Asia 1784–1971*. New York: Norton, 1971.

The Politics of American Foreign Policy: The Social Context of Decisions

RANDLE, ROBERT F., *Geneva 1954: The Settlement of the Indochinese War.* Princeton, N.J.: Princeton University Press, 1969.

ROBERTS, CHALMERS, "The Day We Didn't Go To War," in *Legislative Politics: U.S.A.*, ed. Theodore J. Lowi. pp. 240–48. Boston: Little, Brown, 1962.

SHEPLEY, JAMES. "How Dulles Averted War," *Life*, January 16, 1956 pp. 70–80.

U.S., Congress, *Congressional Record*, 1954.

5

The Cancellation
of the Aswan Dam Aid Offer
1956

The decisions to offer and later to withdraw a loan to Egypt for the
financing of the High Aswan Dam present an excellent opportunity
to examine both the complexities surrounding U.S. foreign policy
in the Middle East and the problems of the political uses of
economic assistance.

The idea for a dam on the Nile at Aswan was not new. Indeed,
a dam had been there since 1902, and since 1947 plans existed for a
larger structure, to be called the High Dam. After the Egyptian
revolution in 1952, the new government began to implement these
plans. It found ready allies in two high-ranking officials of the U.S.
State Department: Henry A. Byroade, assistant secretary for the
Near East, and Jefferson Caffrey, ambassador in Cairo. On the

basis of the advocacy of these two men, the United States in November, 1954 allocated some funds to Egypt for an engineering survey. The advantages of the project to Egypt and to the United States seemed obvious, although it soon became apparent that the interests of the two countries were by no means complementary.

The proposed dam would be the largest in the world, 250 feet high at the center and 3 miles wide, forming a 300-mile-long lake that would run into the Sudan. The dam would increase the arable land of Egypt by at least 25 percent, permit, by means of extensive new irrigation, one or two new crops to be grown annually, and help control the perennial flood damage. Furthermore, by producing an estimated 10 billion kilowatt hours of electricity—eight times the amount available before then—the dam would dramatically stimulate industrial growth (Finer, 1964, p. 36).

Egyptian leaders were equally impressed by the symbolic and political advantages of the project. In speeches and in the Egyptian press the proposed dam, proudly described as being seventeen times larger than the greatest Pyramid, was seen as a "symbol of reform development, and a higher standard of living for the Egyptian people." Colonel Nasser felt the dam would also have a big payoff for him personally. First, he felt that it would make him the leader of the Arab world; Iraq might have its oil reserves, but Egypt would have the dam and all the advantages that flowed from it. Second, Nasser thought that the construction of the dam would give him world-wide prestige and enhance his chances of becoming a major leader of the neutralist bloc of nations, equal to Marshall Tito of Yugoslavia, and Premier Nehru of India (Dougherty, 1959, p. 22).

The advantages to the United States seemed equally clear. Here was an opportunity to render assistance to a progressive, revolutionary regime in one of the major trouble spots in the world—assistance that would aid the economic development of Egypt, increase the welfare of its citizens, and, hopefully, make Nasser less likely to engage in external aggression and less susceptible to Russian blandishments. And all this at a relatively modest cost to the United States (U.S. Department of State, *Bulletin*, December 26, 1955, pp. 1050–51). It is also possible that the project was viewed, at least in part, as an alternative to Nasser's far more problematic request for military assistance.

The United States did offer arms to Egypt in 1954, but only under some fairly restrictive conditions: (1) dollar payments for the deliveries, (2) an understanding that the arms would be used only for defensive purposes (that is, not for aggression against Israel), and (3) the opening of an American military aid office in Cairo to supervise the use of the arms (Finer, 1964, p. 23). Needless to say, these conditions were unacceptable to Nasser, and although he continued his efforts to obtain U.S. aid until the middle of 1955, he increasingly turned his attention to the other major source of arms, the Soviet Union.

Since it was widely known that the Soviet ambassador in Cairo, Daniel Solod, was actively courting Nasser, and since rumor of an imminent arms deal began to leak out as early as June, 1955, it is hard to believe that Nasser's official confirmation of the deal, on September 27, 1955, "hit [Secretary of State] Dulles and other State Department officials with the force of a thunderbolt" (*Ibid.* p. 28). Nevertheless, it is probably quite true that the full scope and conditions of the agreement were extremely unsettling. Amounting to about $200 million in value, the arms would be supplied by Czechoslovakia, would consist of offensive as well as defensive weapons, and were to be paid for in cotton (*New York Times*, September 24, 1955).

Certain implications of this arms deal immediately became clear to Washington. First, the deal upset the military balance of power between Israel and the Arab nations—which the United States and its allies were supposed to maintain (according to the Tripartite Pact of 1950)—thereby increasing the chances that an intensified arms race in the Middle East would lead to open warfare. Second, Russian penetration of the Middle East was now a *fait accompli*, and this act negated all the efforts that had resulted in the Baghdad Pact, the objective of which was to contain Russia by creating a "Northern Tier" from the Mediterranean to the Himalayas. Arms and technicians from several Communist countries would now flow rapidly into Egypt. Third, Nasser's prestige in the Arab world rose to new heights, *at the expense of the United*

States. Finally, according to American calculations, the fact that Egypt mortgaged its cotton crops to pay for the arms made it extremely unlikely that it could afford both the arms and the High Aswan Dam. Secretary of the Treasury George M. Humphrey, in fact, insisted that the two projects would bankrupt Egypt (Eisenhower, 1965, p. 31).

As if to counteract this last assertion, as well as to add insult to injury, Soviet Ambassador Solod announced on October 10, 1955 in Cairo that Russia would "send economic missions, scientific missions, meteorological missions, and any other kind of mission you can imagine that will help underdeveloped Arab and Asian countries" (*New York Times*, October 11, 1955). Rumors were rampant in Washington that the Soviet Union had also offered Egypt a loan to finance the High Aswan Dam project. It was feared in Washington that Egypt's need for foreign financial help in this project constituted an even more serious opening for Soviet penetration of the Middle East than the arms deal, since the construction of the dam was to take up to fifteen years, thereby allowing Soviet technicians and advisors to have an influential presence in Egypt for a long time. The rumors were lent credibility when, on the same day as Ambassador Solod's announcement, the *New York Times* quoted Dr. Mohammed Ahmed Salim, deputy chairman of the Egyptian National Production board, as saying that "a Soviet offer on the Dam would be difficult for Egypt to refuse even though Western help would be preferred" (*Ibid.*). The offer was finally confirmed on October 13, 1955, when the *New York Times* reported that "Moscow would back the Dam and other major projects in exchange for cotton, rice and other Egyptian commodities on terms running twenty-five years."

These Russian moves strengthened the hand of the pro-Dam forces in Washington and helped overcome whatever economic misgivings there might have been in the administration. State Department advisers, the International Cooperation Administration, and Eric Johnston, the expert who had devised the Jordan River Plan, all recommended that the project be given the go-ahead.

In December, 1955 Dulles attended the annual NATO conference, at which he secured British and French agreement to the project, and on December 16 the official offer was announced: the

United States, Great Britain, and the International Bank for Reconstruction and Development (the World Bank) would jointly help Egypt build the High Aswan Dam. The method of financing the dam that was finally agreed upon was extremely complex, and only the main features need be given here. The total investment over the 15-year construction period would be $1.3 billion. The first stage, coffer dams and diversion canals, would be financed by free grants of $56 million from the United States and $14 million from Britain over a period of about 5 years. The second stage would be financed by long-term, low-interest loans from the World Bank ($200 million), the United States ($130 million), and Britain ($80 million). The balance of approximately $760 million would be provided by Egypt in the form of manpower, materials, and local currency.

Numerous reasons have been given as to why the United States made its offer at this time. It appears that the most probable reason was that the United States "sought to use the High Dam offer as a device for persuading Nasser to cancel the [Soviet] arms deal before the weapons would arrive in large quantities" (Dougherty, 1959, p. 37). The United States hoped that Nasser would direct his resources into social and economic reforms, instead of mortgaging them for arms to be used in confrontations with Israel.

The official explanation was, of course, quite different. Dulles insisted, at a press conference in December, that the offer was merely the culmination of an elaborate negotiation process that had been going on for several years; the arms deal and an alleged Soviet offer of aid for the dam project had no bearing on the decision. He then warned that the United States would not make real offers, involving large sums of money, just to top Soviet "paper offers" (U.S. Department of State, *Bulletin*, January 2, 1956, pp. 11–12).

In early January of 1956, the Soviet Union again entered the picture. Although the details were never confirmed by either Egypt or the Soviet Union, the Department of State learned that Egypt claimed to have received an offer of aid from the Soviet Union for the construction of the High Aswan Dam, an offer that was more generous than the joint offer by the United States, Great Britain, and the International Bank for Reconstruction and Development. The Soviet offer supposedly involved a loan of $300 million over 50 years at very low interest (New York Times, January 3, 1956).

The United States, in the meantime, had received no word from Egypt concerning its offer. Late in January Eugene Black, president of the World Bank, went to Cairo to discuss the implementation of the joint grant-loan, and on February 9, 1956 the New York Times reported Black's announcement from Cairo "that Egypt had accepted terms that required strict guarantees that the Egyptian economy would be able to carry the investment." Mr. Black did not specify the details that had been agreed upon. It should be noted, however, that the loan from the International Bank for Reconstruction and Development would not have come into play until after the first five-year stage of the High Aswan Dam project, which was to be financed by free grants from the United States and Great Britain.

Although Nasser may have been agreeable to the terms of the World Bank loan at this time, he still had not agreed to the conditions of the United States and Great Britain concerning the free grants. Two of the conditions were that the construction contracts would be awarded on a competitive basis, and that Egypt and the Sudan would reach an agreement concerning the division of the Nile River waters (New York Times, July 20, 1956).

However, on April 1, 1956 Colonel Nasser announced that although "negotiations with the United States and Britain for large grants to help get the Nile River project started were progressing" (New York Times, April 2, 1956, p. 1), he was still holding on to a Soviet offer to finance the proposed High Aswan Dam. He stated, further, that "I do not mention the Soviet offer as a threat or bluff. . . . the Soviet offer was very general and, really, we have not studied it." (Ibid.) He added that Egypt was not going to start the project in 1956 "mainly because of many complex difficulties of arranging the details of such a big undertaking" (Ibid.). However, President Eisenhower, Secretary of State Dulles, and Secretary of the Treasury Humphrey began to feel that Nasser was purposely stalling in his negotiations with them, using the Soviet offer in order to obtain a better deal. Others in Washington felt that Nasser had never received a genuine loan offer from the Soviet Union, and that the Soviet Union was merely conspiring with Egypt to obtain as much money as possible from the United States. Nor did Egypt help its cause when, on May 15, it became the first Middle East country to recognize the People's Republic of China.

On July 4, 1956 the Budget of the United States included the first appropriations for the High Aswan Dam project (the initial $56-million free grant). However, in its final report the Senate Appropriations Committee instructed Dulles that it wanted the Eisenhower administration to consult with it before using any of the money appropriated for the project. This restriction was of doubtful constitutionality, but it served to show the Eisenhower administration, and especially Dulles, who had testified before this committee at some length in April, that there was considerable anti–High Aswan Dam sentiment in the Senate.

On July 16, Egypt announced with great fanfare that its ambassador to the United States, Ahmed Hussein, would leave for Washington immediately *in order to accept the American offer.* This sudden Egyptian decision may have been made in reaction to the shift in American sentiment. However, another factor was undoubtedly the meeting between the three major neutralist leaders—Tito, Nehru, and Nasser—that was to take place later that month in Belgrade, Yugoslavia. The High Aswan Dam project would clearly give Nasser added prestige and would lend weight to his claims of equality with Tito and Nehru in leading the "third world."

In Washington the final decision about the loan was not reached until the morning of July 19, the day of Ambassador Hussein's meeting with Dulles. In this one-hour meeting Dulles informed Hussein that the United States had rescinded its offer.

The sequel to this decision can be summarized quickly. On July 20 Britain also withdrew its offer, and since the World Bank's participation clearly depended on the Anglo-American grants, the withdrawal of that aid killed the entire package. On July 26, in retaliation for these unfriendly acts, Nasser nationalized the Suez Canal, precipitating the invasion of Egypt by Israel, France, and Britain.

With this background in mind, we can now examine the process by which the Aswan Dam decisions were made. As we shall see, the Eisenhower administration had great freedom of action, since there was little active interest or participation, either pro or con, by the public, interest groups, or even Congress. The issue simply had low salience until after the cancellation of the offer and Nasser's strong reaction.

Public opinion was quite general. It opposed Soviet penetration of the Middle East, supported Israel—the bastion of democracy in that area—and resented Nasser's intemperate attacks on "Western imperialists." Most of this opinion was channeled through permanent interest groups and transmitted to Congress. The major interest groups involved in this channeling of opinion were, of course, the Jewish organizations, and even they could not make a very strong case against a policy that would help raise the standard of living in an underdeveloped country. They had to fall back on indirect arguments: the United States should not support a regime advocating aggression and expansion, and the United States should finance projects that would benefit the whole region instead of just one country.

Some of the major United States cotton growers may also have lobbied Congress to oppose the aid; at least some Congressmen stated as much. However, the argument that the dam would enable Egypt to enlarge its cotton crop and compete with American cotton does not sound very convincing, since one of the dam's major purposes was to allow Egypt to raise *other* crops, thereby decreasing its dependence on cotton—a commodity that was already saturating the world market.

Finally, there is some evidence (Beal, 1957, p. 257) that foreign nations tried to pressure Washington to cancel the offer. In addition to Israel—obviously an interested party—some of the United States' economically developing friends informed the State Department that they objected to neutrals receiving so much more aid than allies.

The mass media—perhaps the best indicator of public concern over a foreign policy issue—did not show great interest. The *New York Times* reported the developments in considerable detail but did not editorialize about them. Two *Newsweek* articles critical of the project were read into the *Congressional Record* (1956, p. 5392).

Of necessity, Congress played a larger role, but by no means a major one. When the loan was first announced, in December, 1955, only a few congressmen commented on it, and they did so in rather neutral tones. In January, 1956 the Senate Committee on Appropriations held hearings concerning the "Financing of the Aswan High Dam in Egypt." Undersecretary of State Herbert Hoover Jr. used the occasion to defend the more basic question of long-term foreign aid as a means of counteracting the new Soviet policy of giving economic aid to uncommitted nations. He concluded by simply pointing out that the dam was exactly the kind of project that would achieve this goal.

Criticism of the proposed loan took two major forms. First, there was the complaint that no provision had been made regarding the ownership of the additional arable land (some two million new acres) that the High Aswan Dam project would make available. Carl Hayden, chairman of the Senate Committee on Appropriations felt that the United States should have a firm commitment from Egypt that the new land would be distributed to the needy and would not fall into the hands of a few wealthy landowners. Comments were made to the effect that in other instances of foreign aid from the United States, only a few wealthy families in the recipient countries had benefited from the program. The second group of critics consisted of Southern senators, led by Spessard Holland of Florida, who feared that Egypt's new arable land might be used for the growing of cotton, so that the United States would in effect be paying Egypt to compete with it on the world's cotton market. Undersecretary Hoover responded, first, that although there were no formal commitments from Egypt on these points, a land distribution program to benefit only the needy peasants was currently being worked out, and, second, that Egypt had promised the United States that the new arable land would not be used for the growing of cotton. The hearings closed with the committee's senators instructing the undersecretary of state to supply them with more detailed information concerning Egypt's promises on land reform and crop diversification.

The second time that aid for the High Aswan Dam project was subjected to questioning was in a closed session of the Senate Committee on Foreign Relations in April and May of 1956. This time Dulles presented the administration's views. The same points were raised again, and Dulles replied that he still had no firm commitments from Egypt (*New York Times*, July 15, 1956 and July 17, 1956). Also, by late May Nasser had recognized Red China and had made increasingly pointed anti-West statements in Cairo, thereby causing a number of senators to wonder if Egypt was not already lost to the Communist bloc. Senator Walter F. George of Georgia, chairman of the committee, who apparently was not consulted by the Eisenhower administration about the High Aswan Dam, was very critical of our proposed involvement in the project. First, he felt that it was "wholly inconsistent" for the United States, in the climate then existing between the Arab states and Israel, to enter the Middle East in this way. Second, he felt that if Egypt grew cotton on the new land, United States cotton growers would be hurt. In addition, George stated that it was wrong in principle "to tie strings to any aid we give." Senator William F. Knowland (California) added that a number of congressmen were against giving aid to any neutral nation, and also that no country that recognized Red China should be given foreign aid (*New York Times*, April 23, 1956).

Dulles had two catchall answers, which he repeated with minor variations. First, despite its arm deal with Czechoslovakia and its many instances of friendship with the Soviet Union, "Egypt was far from becoming a tool of the Soviets"; however, it "could drift that way if we did nothing to prevent it" (Adams, 1961, p. 248). Second, although many congressmen thought that the United States should cut off aid to all countries who tried to deal with both the East and the West, Dulles still considered Egypt to be neutral, and stated that the United States would continue to honor aid requests from neutrals. He noted, however, that America would continue to give the lion's share of the balance to its friends, since the interests of the United States must take priority.

According to Eisenhower (1965, p. 32), Dulles warned Egypt on July 13, 1956 that the United States was not then "in a position to deal with this matter [the aid offer] because we could not predict what action our Congress might take, and our views on the merits of the matter had somewhat altered." Then, on July 15 the Senate Appropriations Committee in its final report ordered the Eisenhower administration not to use any funds appropriated for the High Aswan Dam project "without prior approval of the Committee on Appropriations." Eisenhower mentions that the committee's report "did reflect the existence of an anti-Dam coalition in Congress. It included Senators with pro-Israeli sympathies, Southerners concerned over the cotton market, and those who were opposed to any assistance to foreign nations other than our own allies." (Ibid.)

A number of things appear clear at this point. First, in no way was Congress the initiator of the offer of aid. Second, the administration made little effort to woo Senator George, chairman of the Foreign Relations Committee. (This seems strange, considering that George was very much against long-term foreign aid, of which the Aswan Dam loan was a classic example.) Third, Dulles met with a number of leaders of both parties in Congress shortly after the final hearings in Congress (about June 2, 1956), but he did not succeed in changing anyone's mind. Indeed, it appeared to some that Dulles, too, was beginning to look less favorably upon the loan.

We may conclude that Eisenhower and Dulles initially felt that the loan offer would probably sail through Congress. However, when Nasser became increasingly more belligerent toward Israel and the West, not only did some members of Congress become increasingly critical of the aid offer, but Eisenhower and Dulles also began to have second thoughts.

When President Nasser nationalized the Suez Canal, one week after the administration rescinded its offer of aid to Egypt, many in Washington accused Dulles of being shortsighted in not foreseeing this reaction. Those in the administration generally responded that "it was extremely doubtful if the President could have obtained Congressional approval of the grants and loans to the Egyptians at that point, had he asked for them" (Adams, 1961, p. 249). However, Senator J. William Fulbright, who was on the Foreign Relations Committee at that time, said that the opposition in Congress was not very strong, that few senators were involved, and that the secretary of state "could either have persuaded the opposition to abstain, or could have overridden them by the votes of other Senators" (Finer, 1964, p. 49). Furthermore, Eisenhower firmly rejected the stipulation that the money appropriated for the dam project was not to be used without prior approval by the

Committee on Appropriations: "I would not admit that the Committee's announcement could have any real effect on negotiations, because if such a report could have the standing of law it would render the Executive powerless in his conduct of foreign relations" (1965, p. 32). The inescapable conclusion is that Congress did not have the significant role that the Eisenhower administration tried later to attribute to it, but instead served primarily as a partial legitimator of the decision to deny the aid to Egypt.

The two official State Department statements regarding the financial aid offer by the United States to Egypt for the construction of the High Aswan Dam read as follows:

I. HIGH ASWAN DAM PROJECT: Statement by the Department of State, December 17, 1955.

Mr. Abdel Moneim El Kaissouni, Egyptian Minister of Finance, met yesterday with Acting Secretary of State Herbert Hoover, Jr., British Ambassador Sir Roger Makins, and World Bank President Eugene Black, for final talks before his departure for Cairo.

During their stay in Washington, Mr. Kaissouni and his colleagues have been carrying on discussions with the management of the World Bank and representatives of the United States and United Kingdom Governments concerning possible assistance in the execution of the High Aswan Dam project.

The United States and British Governments assured the Egyptian Government through Mr. Kaissouni of their support in this project, which would be of inestimable importance in the development of the Egyptian economy and in the improvement of the welfare of the Egyptian people. Such assistance would take the form of grants from the United States and the United Kingdom toward defraying foreign exchange costs of the first stages of the work. This phase, involving the Coffer Dam, foundations for the main dam, and auxiliary work, will take from four to five years. Further, assurance has been given to Mr. Kaissouni that the Governments of the United States and the United Kingdom would, subject to legislative authority, be prepared to consider sympathetically in the light of then existing circumstances further support toward financing the later stages to supplement World Bank financing.

Mr. Kaissouni plans to leave Washington for Egypt today, and it is understood that he will report to his Government on his talks here. Final understandings with the British and American Governments and the World Bank will await Mr. Kaissouni's consultation with the Egyptian Government. (U.S. Department of State, *Bulletin*, December 26, 1955, pp. 1050–51)

II. UNITED STATES WITHDRAWAL FROM THE HIGH ASWAN DAM PROJECT: Announcement by the Department of State, July 19, 1956.

At the request of the Government of Egypt, the United States joined in December 1955 with the United Kingdom and with the World Bank in an offer to assist Egypt in the construction of a high dam on the Nile at Aswan. This project is one of great magnitude. It would require an estimated 12 to 16 years to complete at a total cost estimated at some $1,300,000,000, of which over $900,000,000 represents local currency requirements. It involves not merely the rights and interests of Egypt but of other states whose waters are contributory, including Sudan, Ethiopia, and Uganda.

The December offer contemplated an extension by the United States and United Kingdom of grant aid to help finance certain early phases of the work, the effects of which would be confined solely to Egypt, with the understanding that accomplishment of the project as a whole would require a satisfactory resolution of the question of Nile water rights. Another important consideration bearing upon the feasibility of the undertaking and thus the practicability of American aid was Egyptian readiness and ability to concentrate its economic resources upon this vast construction program.

Developments within the succeeding 7 months have not been favorable to the success of the project, and the U.S. Government has concluded that it is not feasible in present circumstances to participate in the project. Agreement by the riparian states has not been achieved, and the ability of Egypt to devote adequate resources to assure the project's success has become more uncertain than at the time the offer was made.

This decision in no way reflects or involves any alteration in the friendly relations of the Government and people of the United States toward the Government and people of Egypt.

The United States remains deeply interested in the welfare of the Egyptian people and in the development of the Nile. It is prepared to consider at an appropriate time and at the request of the riparian states what steps might be taken toward a more effective utilization of the water resources of the Nile for the benefit of the peoples of the region. Furthermore, the United States remains ready to assist Egypt in its effort to improve the economic condition of its people and is prepared, through its appropriate agencies, to discuss these matters within the context of funds appropriated by the Congress. (U.S. Department of State, *Bulletin*, July 24, 1956, p. 188)

If one were to rely just on these documents and on a few of Dulles's press conferences, one would conclude that the decision to rescind the aid offer was strictly economic in character, and that it was reached after careful and thorough analysis and discussion within the appropriate executive agencies. However, from what we have seen thus far we know that this was not the case.

There is no doubt that economics did have some weight in the decision to rescind the offer, but it is far more likely that the Eisenhower administration was using the economics of the situation as an ex post facto rationale. This conclusion has been reached for the following two reasons. First, Eugene Black, president of the International Bank for Reconstruction and Development, was highly respected by President Eisenhower and his advisers both as a very astute diplomat and as a knowledgeable economist. One of the conditions of receiving a loan from the World Bank was that the bank had the right to investigate a receiving nation's accounts to insure that the Bank's member nations would receive the interest and capital due them on the loan. Colonel Nasser frequently complained in public that the West, through this loan, was trying to colonize Egypt economically. However, as we mentioned earlier, Mr. Black announced in Cairo on February 9, 1956 that Nasser had agreed to the Bank's requirements, and it appears that Black never wavered from his belief that the *loan was economically sound*. Second, after the loan was withdrawn, the State Department argued that Egypt's purchase of Communist arms, which were to be paid for with Egypt's cotton reserves, put Egypt's economy in a precarious position, one that would not allow Egypt to undertake the High Aswan Dam Project. However, the loan offered by the United States was made almost three months after the details of the arms deal were announced.

Two other reasons advanced by the Department of State were that an agreement had not been reached between Egypt and Sudan on the division of the Nile waters, and that Nasser had not agreed to competitive bidding on the contracts for the construction work. However, considering the whole political environment at the time the loan was offered—and considering especially the hope of the Department of State and of President Eisenhower that the project would put the United States and all of the West in a favorable light in the Arab nation's eyes—it is very hard to believe that these two reasons held much weight in the final decision to rescind the loan.

If the economic reasons were only a façade, what, then, were the actual reasons for the denial of the loan? To answer this question, we must briefly go back in time. In so doing we will also gain some insight into the role played by the State Department. Colonel Nasser first entered the Egyptian political scene when he, along with General Naguib, led a successful coup against King Farouk's corrupt regime in 1952. Nasser then deposed Naguib and declared himself premier in 1953. Jefferson Caffrey, United States ambassador to Egypt during Nasser's rise to the top, impressed upon the Department of State his belief that Colonel Nasser was a sincere reformer committed to raising the standard of living in Egypt, and that the Egyptian leader was a worthy model for other Arab countries to follow. Therefore, when Nasser mentioned to him his desire for a high dam at Aswan, Caffrey pushed very hard in the Department of State for the project. Caffrey felt that this was a chance for the United States to make a lasting friendship with an Arab nation, increase its influence in the Middle East, and help the impoverished people of Egypt.

This line of reasoning was not unique to Caffrey. Apparently, it was shared by all the Middle East specialists in the State Department. These "Arabists" felt that American interests in the area could best be served by a pro-Nasser policy that would overcome the image of America as the imperialist successor to Britain and France (Kraft, 1971). Even when Dulles and Eisenhower began to display disenchantment with Nasser, there is no indication that these experts urged the cancellation of the dam project.

Only one major figure in the administration was opposed to the project almost from its beginnings: Secretary of the Treasury George Humphrey. His opposition seems to have been based on purely financial grounds, and was undoubtedly related to his general fiscal conservatism and his opposition to most large, long-term foreign-aid projects. Yet although Humphrey was close to Eisenhower and Dulles, there is no evidence that he played a major role in the decision-making process. However, it is possible that his views made it easier for Dulles to reach the decision to cancel the aid offer; they were certainly used in the official justification quoted above which was issued after the fact by the State Department.

Even the secretary of state did not begin to express serious doubts until after Nasser's announcement that he would consider accepting Soviet aid for the High Aswan Dam. Evidently, in Dulles's eyes the major sin a neutralist could commit was to try to bargain for the best deal with both East and West. In succeeding weeks, both Eisenhower and Dulles made several statements about the immorality and shortsightedness of neutralism. At the same time, Nasser was rapidly losing his popularity in the United States as a result of the widely reported displays of Russian weapons in Egypt, Russian and Chinese trade contracts with Egypt, continued border incidents between Egypt and Israel, and what seemed to be deliberately hostile and provocative anti-Western, anti-American speeches and editorials by the Egyptians. Perhaps in response to the rising public pressures, Dulles told a July 10 press conference that it was "improbable" that Egypt would receive the loan (Finer, 1964, p. 44).

And yet as late as July 15, the day Egypt suddenly announced that its ambassador was coming to Washington to accept the American offer, the final decision had not been made. Dulles instructed his staff to prepare a press communiqué explaining the rescinding of the offer, but on July 18, *the day before* his appointment with Ambassador Hussein, he told British Ambassador Sir Roger Makins only that he was dubious about the loan, not that he was committed to refusing it.

From this meeting between Dulles and Makins we also gain some insight into the role played by Britain in the decision. Because the British also had misgivings about granting the loan, they advised Dulles to proceed very carefully. A few days earlier, the French had also warned of the dangers of refusing the loan, suggesting that the likeliest consequence would be the nationalization of the Suez Canal. We may conclude, then, that Washington consulted its allies only in a rather perfunctory manner, even though one of them, Britain, was supposedly an equal partner in the venture. Moreover, there is no evidence that the World Bank was consulted.

The decision seems to have been made at the meeting between Dulles and Hussein on July 19. After presenting some of the arguments against the loan, Hussein supposedly referred to the Soviet offer, whereupon Dulles retorted that Egypt should accept the Russian bid. Robert Murphy typified State Department reaction when he confessed to Herman Finer that he did not understand why Dulles made the decision in that way at that time, unless he simply did not like the ultimatumlike tone in Hussein's message.[1]

Little information is available about the role President Eisenhower and his staff played in the decision to rescind the aid offer. Although most of the sources we consulted tend to imply that President Eisenhower was an innocent bystander, wishing to be consulted by Dulles only when Dulles had made up his mind, a closer examination of the facts reveals a more complex, and to us more credible, interpretation of their relationship.

From the information we have, it seems fairly certain that the president was originally in favor of granting aid for the Aswan project, that he did not want to contribute to the Middle East arms race, but that he felt deeply committed to Israel's continued existence.[2] Eisenhower had hoped that such aid would deter Egypt from buying more arms; he was very disturbed about Egypt's recognition of Red China; he, like Dulles, had become exasperated by Nasser's anti-imperialist, polemical attacks against the West; and, overriding all his other concerns, he genuinely desired world peace. Thus, it appears that although Dulles had much room in which to maneuver, he was aware of, and stayed within, the bounds of Eisenhower's sentiments. For example, although Dulles was a great exponent of the cold war diplomatic strategy of brinkmanship, not once during the whole course of the High Aswan Dam decision-making process did Dulles rattle America's sabers at either the Soviet Union or Egypt. As Richard E. Neustadt maintains,

> It appears that Dulles kept Eisenhower's confidence in the same way he had won it. During the entire Suez crisis, for example, he apparently cleared every move with Eisenhower in advance, emphatically including cancella-

---

[1] This account of the July 15–July 19 period is based on Herman Finer's report of his personal interviews with participants and his perusal of restricted documents (1964, pp. 46–48).
[2] He is alleged to have said, in private, at the 1954 American Jewish Convention in Washington, "I don't know what I would have done had I been President when the question of Israel's independence came up, but Israel is now a sovereign nation to which we do have obligations. We shall keep them." (Finer, 1964, p. 13)

tion of the Aswan Dam. . . . As I read the record, Eisenhower was no "patsy" in this process. Far from it, he was laying down the law: *He* wanted "peace." Dulles strained to keep it. (1970, p. 105)

According to Herman Finer, Eisenhower and Dulles met on July 17, 1956, the day after Egypt announced her acceptance of the offer, and "discussed the issue cursorily" (1964, p. 46). Although Eisenhower did not order Dulles to rescind the loan, he told him of his disappointment in not dissuading Nasser from an arms build-up in the Middle East, and said that if the secretary should decide to rescind the loan, he would concur. However, Robert Murphy reports that "Dulles summoned no staff meeting . . . and Eisenhower was not consulted until the morning of Hussein's visit" (1964, p. 377). Nor do the memoirs of Sherman Adams, Eisenhower's most trusted assistant, contain anything about the president's specific role in this decision.

In conclusion, it seems that President Eisenhower did not play an active role in this decision, that the input from other participants in the foreign-policy-making process was minimal, and that Secretary of State Dulles made the decision by himself, albeit on the basis of Eisenhower's broad guidelines and with his concurrence. Yet we doubt whether the decision would have been any different had Eisenhower been less passive, for all the evidence indicates that Eisenhower and Dulles viewed the situation in the Middle East through the same ideological spectacles.

REFERENCES AND BIBLIOGRAPHY

ADAMS, SHERMAN, *Firsthand Report.* New York: Harper & Brothers, 1961.

American Foreign Policy: Current Documents, 1955, 1956.

BEAL, JOHN ROBINSON, *John Foster Dulles: A Biography.* New York: Harper & Brothers, 1957.

COOKE, M. L., *Nasser's High Aswan Dam.* Washington, D.C.: Public Affairs Institute, 1956.

DOUGHERTY, JAMES E., "The Aswan Decision in Perspective," *Political Science Quarterly,* 74, No. 1 (1959), 21–45.

EISENHOWER, DWIGHT D., *Waging Peace, 1956–1961: The White House Years.* New York: Doubleday, 1965.

FINER, HERMAN, *Dulles Over Suez*. London: William Heinemann, 1964.

KRAFT, JOSEPH, "Those Arabists in the State Department," *New York Times Magazine*, November 7, 1971, pp. 38–96.

MURPHY, ROBERT, *Diplomat Among Warriors*. Garden City, N.Y.: Doubleday, 1964.

NEUSTADT, RICHARD E., *Alliance Politics*. New York: Columbia University Press, 1970.

U.S., Congress, *Congressional Record*, 1955, 1956, 1957.

U.S., Department of State, *Bulletin*, Volumes 33, 34, and 35 (1955 and 1956).

U.S., Senate, Committee on Appropriations, Hearings, *Financing of Aswan High Dam in Egypt*. 84th Cong., 2nd sess., January 26, 1956.

The Intervention
in Lebanon
1958

The landing of the United States Marines on the shores of Lebanon in July, 1958 and their withdrawal some three months later do not constitute a major chapter in the military history of either the Marine Corps or the United States. Not only was the number of troops low—14,000 at the height of the operation—but their stay was completely peaceful. From a political point of view, however, the action was far more significant. It represents the unequivocal entry of the United States into the Middle East as the successor to Britain and France. The United States, of course, had been deeply involved in the Middle East since World War II, but it generally saw itself—and was perceived by others—as Britain's ally and as having only secondary interests of its own in the area. The decision to intervene in Lebanon made it quite clear that the United States had acquired a major stake in the region and had become a principal player.

The origins of the Lebanese intervention must be traced back to American efforts to recoup some of the political losses suffered by the West in the Suez War. That war, as we suggested in Chapter 5, was caused in no small part by the withdrawal of the American offer to support the construction of the High Aswan Dam. When Nasser retaliated by nationalizing the Suez Canal, Britain, France, and Israel invaded Egypt. The United States reluctantly joined the Soviet Union in working to end that war, but as a consequence it lost the good will of its allies without gaining any particular favor with the Egyptians, the rest of the Middle East, or the Soviet Union. In fact, Nasser was seen as the leader who "stood up to the imperialists" (thus strengthening his position as a neutralist world leader); the Russians were praised for helping in this noble enterprise; and the United States was still viewed as one of the imperialists, a country that for strictly tactical reasons had temporarily abandoned its allies.

Hoping to stop what it considered a dangerous drift toward neutralism and the growth of pro-Russian orientations in the Arab world, the United States devised the Eisenhower Doctrine. In January, 1957 President Eisenhower informed Congress that the power vacuum in the Middle East must be filled by the United States before it was filled by Russia, which appeared to be doing its utmost to increase instability in the region so that it could dominate it. In view of this threat—and because the independence of the nations involved was vital to the interests of the United States, Eisenhower argued—the United States should increase economic and particularly military aid to the region, and the president should, at his discretion, be empowered to use the armed forces to protect countries that request aid "against overt armed aggression from any nation controlled by international Communism." After three months of discussion, in the course of which several congressional leaders expressed doubts and reservations, Congress passed the Joint Resolution to Promote Peace and Stability in the Middle East (71 Stat. 5, 1958), in the form proposed by the administration.

Unfortunately, the formalized Eisenhower Doctrine was

greeted with almost universal hostility abroad. Even the British—whom Dulles hoped to please, since the doctrine implied that they acted in the Suez War only in reaction to Soviet provocations—denounced the measure, claiming that it was an attempt to curtail their role in the Middle East (Meo, 1965, p. 115). The Arab world, of course, had to object to the tone and substance of the doctrine as constituting a clear effort to maintain a Western imperialist presence in the area. Two of the most pro-Western Arab leaders, King Hussein of Jordan and King Ibn Saud of Saudi Arabia, joined President Nasser of Egypt and Premier Chukri al-Quatli of Syria in a communiqué denouncing attempts by foreign powers to turn their countries into spheres of influence.

Trying to salvage something from this deplorable situation, the president appointed Representative James P. Richards, chairman of the House Foreign Affairs Committee, as his special envoy to the Middle East in the spring of 1957. The only support Richards found for the doctrine was in Lebanon, where President Camille Chamoun and he issued a joint statement affirming that Lebanon would request, and the United States would deliver, aid to combat attacks by international Communism. In Washington, the Eisenhower administration was delighted by this "victory" for its doctrine; in Lebanon, however, the act helped precipitate the civil war that in turn led to the American intervention.

Lebanon in 1957 was experiencing severe domestic problems. Since gaining its independence from France in 1943, this small country had managed to maintain a measure of internal stability and external security unique in the region and unusual elsewhere. Lebanon's domestic stability was built on an explicit political compromise between its Christian and Moslem populations. The political parties, which were formed along religious lines, agreed to share the top offices: Christians occupied the presidency and foreign ministry, Moslems the offices of prime minister and speaker of the house. In foreign affairs, Lebanon was careful to behave as neutrally as possible. Thus, it took no side in inter-Arab disputes, was pro-Western in sentiment but did not join the Baghdad Pact, and was even regarded as the one Arab country that might be able to make peace with Israel. Even the Communist Party, outlawed in most Arab countries, was allowed to operate in

Lebanon for most of the postwar period. As a result of this happy state of affairs, Lebanon became a haven for foreign business investment, gaining some right to the title of "Switzerland of the Middle East."

In the 1950s, however, this situation began to change. The basic domestic political arrangement began to crumble. The higher birth rate of the Moslem population meant that the Christians would soon lose their slim majority. The influx of Palestinian refugees further increased the Moslem population and, more important, introduced a volatile new element into Lebanese political life. With the rise of Arab nationalism, Lebanon found it much harder to maintain a neutral posture in foreign affairs, especially when that nationalism became increasingly anti-Western.

Thus, when Chamoun attempted to obtain parliamentary approval for the Eisenhower Doctrine, the stage was set for a major political crisis. Opposition to Chamoun increased, and even some Christian leaders joined in it, feeling that the doctrine would do nothing for Lebanon except antagonize Cairo and Moscow. Chamoun used the issue fairly successfully in the parliamentary elections of June, 1957, helping to defeat his party's opponents by tagging them "Nasser's candidates." However, the debates merely increased in vehemence, and as it became widely known that Chamoun wanted to seek a second term (for which a constitutional amendment was needed), even some of his leading Christian supporters left him, in part, no doubt, from personal ambition. Bombings and riots—blamed by the government on foreign agents from Egypt and Syria—occurred early in 1958, and these continued and were augmented by violent demonstrations in the spring of that year. In February, when Egypt and Syria formed the United Arab Republic, many in Lebanon wanted their country to join. The United Arab Republic did nothing to discourage such intentions; in fact, its arms and ammunition found their way into Lebanese hands (Barnet, 1968, p. 143).

On May 7 the crusading editor of an anti-Chamoun newspaper was assassinated. Demonstrations and riots, during which the U.S. Information Agency library was destroyed, followed the assassination. On May 13 the Eisenhower administration received a communique from President Chamoun inquiring about the possibility of American assistance. Eisenhower responded that aid, especially the use of troops, would have certain conditions attached to it. On May 27, at the request of Lebanon, the United Nations Security Council convened. The Lebanese charged before the council that the United Arab Republic was intervening in the internal affairs of Lebanon. On June 10 the Security Council voted to send an observation team to Lebanon in order to investigate the charges. The same month, Secretary General Dag Hammarskjöld also paid a visit to Lebanon. The observation team reported, with Hammarskjöld concurring, that there was insufficient evidence to sustain Lebanon's charges against the United Arab Republic.

On July 14 a military coup in Iraq shocked the Western powers, whose intelligence services apparently had given no advance warning that this was a possibility. President Chamoun's fears now appeared more credible, and his new, formal request for United States troops was taken more seriously. High-level meetings between President Eisenhower, Secretary of State John F. Dulles and CIA Director Allen Dulles were held, and the president called in congressional leaders to brief them on the Middle East crisis. On July 15, a day after troops had been officially requested, 1,700 Marines walked ashore in Lebanon, where they met no resistance either then or at any time during their presence. (This lack of resistance, however, did not prevent an ultimate increase to 14,000 troops—a force twice the size of the entire Lebanese army, and considerably better equipped and supported.) The same day, Eisenhower sent a message to Congress explaining his actions, and in the evening he addressed the American public on radio and television. At the United Nations, on July 15 and 16, Ambassador Lodge explained to the Security Council that the United States sent troops into Lebanon at the request of its official government. He argued that the instability in Lebanon had been produced by outside influences that threatened the country, and he called upon the United Nations to field an emergency force in Lebanon to replace American troops. On July 16, President Eisenhower appointed Robert Murphy as his special representative and sent him to Lebanon to coordinate the American military presence there.

Other nations were also active during this period. On July 16

Great Britain moved troops into Jordan at the request of King Hussein. On July 19 Nikita Khrushchev, who for several months had been making special efforts to increase Soviet influence in Egypt and Syria, proposed a summit conference to resolve the crisis. He argued that the Big Four Powers plus India should work out a solution to be presented to the Security Council. Eisenhower rejected Khrushchev's proposal, replying that the United Nations was the appropriate forum to handle such problems. In a letter to Khrushchev, Eisenhower suggested that the heads of state or foreign ministers could have a summit meeting within the confines of the Security Council. Surprisingly, Khrushchev accepted the American proposal and even suggested July 28 as the date for the first meeting, but he insisted that India and the Arab states involved in the crisis should take part in the meeting. On July 25 Eisenhower replied to Khrushchev that July 28 was too early a date for the United States; he also insisted that the Security Council itself must determine which nations, other than its own members, should partake in its proceedings.

On July 21 the Lebanese Parliament elected General Fuad Chehab, Chief of the Army, to replace Chamoun as president. Since Chehab was acceptable, at least initially, to the major factions in Lebanon as well as to Nasser and the United States, the crisis was over.

On August 5 Khrushchev announced that he was no longer interested in a summit meeting, but both the United States and the Soviet Union asked for a special session of the General Assembly. The assembly convened on August 8, and when Eisenhower addressed it on August 13 he called for the formation of a permanent United Nations peace force in the Middle East and presented an economic development plan for the region. On August 21 a resolution submitted by ten Arab states was adopted. It pledged noninterference by the Arab states in one another's affairs, and instructed Secretary General Hammarskjöld to arrange the withdrawal of the West's troops from Lebanon and Jordan. President Eisenhower commented that with the adoption of this resolution the crisis had ended.

Even though the rather mild civil war in Lebanon had clearly ended with the election of Chehab, American troops stayed in Lebanon. Only on October 8 did the State Department announce that they would be withdrawn, and by October 25 all had left.

The reaction of the American press prior to the American intervention was one of deep but cautious concern. The United Nations was identified by most leading papers as the proper agency for resolving any threat to Lebanon's government. The *Memphis Press-Scimitar*, for example, observed on May 22, "We cannot police the world alone. When Britain and France intervened in Suez, our Government insisted on the U.N.'s jurisdiction. By failing to apply that rule now, Washington risks injuring the already weak U.N., jeopardizes the frail Anglo-American position in the Middle East, and is unwittingly aiding the enemy." The *New York Times* editorialized on July 10 that "the U.N. should be able to prevent a Lebanese Anschluss by Nasser's U.A.R." That newspaper, as well as the *New York Herald Tribune* and the *Washington Post*, urged that the United Nation's peace-keeping machinery be fully utilized to resolve the crisis. Joseph Alsop criticized the secretary of state for indicating that the United States might bail Lebanon out of its crisis. He also charged that Dulles failed to consult with the secretary of defense in formulating foreign policy.

The reaction of the press to the landing of the troops was mixed. Those newspapers supporting the administration's response saw the action within the context of the cold war. The administration's argument that the Lebanese crisis was an extension of Communist aggression was accepted by these newspapers. Some newspapers rationalized that the United States was following the same principles that justified aid to Greece and Turkey and involved us in the Korean conflict; some reminded their readers of the importance of Western oil interests in the Middle East; and several argued that the United States had to exercise force in order to maintain itself as a credible major world power.

Newspapers that criticized the administration's actions in Lebanon did not view the American-Soviet struggle in world politics as the basis of the recurring Middle East crisis. Some of these newspapers accepted Nasser as a neutralist seeking to advance his position by playing East against West. They rejected the notion that

Nasser was a tool of world Communism, pointing to the outlawing of the Communist Party in Egypt. The critical press thought that the intervention was a mistake based on a misunderstanding of Arab nationalism, and/or the result of an absence of policy planning toward the Arab nations. These newspapers argued that the American approach to the area was, at best, inconsistent, and that our intervention worked against the interests it claimed to be protecting. If oil were important, we were putting its critical supply to the West in jeopardy. If our prestige were important, we were lowering it. A short-term solution was seen as centering in a resolution of the crisis by the United Nations. A long-term solution would be possible only in the context of a general improvement in American relations with the Arab Middle East, which would require a major reappraisal of existing American policies regarding that area.

A similar division of opinion also characterized the leading columnists and the numerous letters to the editors written by former government officials and academics.

The available indicators of public opinion show that the majority of Americans supported the American military intervention in Lebanon. The *Wall Street Journal* found that 80 percent of 300 people surveyed supported the intervention (July 16, 1958). Most of those interviewed stated that although they didn't know much about the crisis, they felt confident that the president knew what he was doing. It is also interesting to note that most people, critics and backers alike, expressed dissatisfaction with the way American interests were treated in the Middle East. A substantial number of those interviewed believed that the United States intervened in order to save face: "When Lebanon asks for help and we have previously promised to give, we've got to go in" (*Ibid.*). *Newsweek*'s correspondents on July 28, 1958 reported that most of the people they interviewed believed that the president had to act, and deserved their support. In fact, 58 percent of the people surveyed in a Gallup poll approved of the way Eisenhower was performing as president, an increase of 6 percent in his popularity since the previous Gallup poll (*U.S. News and World Report*, July 25, 1958).

Beirut, Lebanon's capital, is one of the major commercial centers in the Middle East. Located there are many American businesses, including offices of American oil companies and oil-equipment supply companies. The oil companies employ economists and other social scientists as consultants, whose job is in effect to provide the companies with a foreign policy for each nation within which they operate. The American businesses in Lebanon appreciated that country's relatively stable political atmosphere. Therefore, when the crisis began one company encouraged negotiations between Chamoun and Nasser, and actually sent a representative to talk to both presidents. The American business community also seemed to have a significant degree of influence in Washington. Raymond Hare, the American ambassador to Egypt, said that there was a "New Look in Washington—thanks largely to the new influence of unofficial reports of businessmen in Beirut which, by the time they got to the State Department, had strong endorsements from parent companies" (Copeland, 1969, p. 238).

The American business community in Lebanon supported President Chamoun. While the United Nations was receiving reports from its observers that there had been no evidence of interference by the United Arab Republic in Lebanon, the oil companies were sending reports to their home offices that the crisis pitted Nasser forces against loyalist Chamoun forces. These reports, which were passed on to Washington, substantially reinforced similar CIA reports from Lebanon.

The oil companies continued to play a role after American troops landed in Lebanon. Secretary of the Interior Fred Seaton, fearing that the Arab countries would cut off their supply of oil to Western Europe, convened a meeting of the Foreign Petroleum Supply Committee (FPSC). Composed of sixteen major American oil companies, the FPSC performs two principal functions:

(a) When requested by the department, it provides advice on how the government may obtain needed information relating to foreign petroleum operations and to requirements and supplies of petroleum. (b) It may consider and make recommendations designed to prevent, eliminate or alleviate shortages of petroleum supplies in friendly foreign nations threatening to, or adversely affecting, the defense mobilization interests or programs of the United States." (U.S. Department of the Interior, 1959, p. 212)

The oil companies, in a plan outlined to FPSC by Seaton, were to pool their foreign facilities, free from antitrust considerations. If an oil emergency was declared, the companies were to use this plan in formulating their own policies.

Three other organized interest groups took a public position on the American intervention in Lebanon, although there is no evidence that any of them had an impact on American policy. The New York Committee for a Sane Nuclear Policy denounced the intervention. Negotiation to settle differences, this committee maintained, is the only rational approach to conflict in an era in which nations are capable of bringing about the destruction of the world (*New York Times*, July 18, 1958). The other two groups supported the intervention. The Czechoslovak National Council of America believed that "the Communist threat to Lebanon must be stopped whatever be the consequences" (*Ibid.*). And the AFL–CIO stated in its *News* that the intervention "was a necessary move to preserve peace and freedom in the Middle East and to uphold the principles of the U.N." (*New York Times*, July 24, 1958).

The lack of opposition by any major interest group or major segment of the public freed the administration from the need to convince the public of the correctness of its decision. This obviously contrasts with the Vietnam War, during which a sustained governmental campaign was necessary to counter well-organized interest groups and vocal segments of the population. Moreover, the eroding of the power of cold war rhetoric has obliged two recent administrations to find different lines of reasoning for their action. The Eisenhower administration was under no similar constraint during the Lebanese intervention.

Congress, as a body, offered no opposition to the intervention. And although a few senators criticized the action harshly, there is no evidence that their dissent had any substantial impact. The critics were for the most part those senators who did not perceive the situation in Lebanon in the context of the cold war, and who believed that disruption in the world order could come from sources other than the Soviet Union.

Early comment on the Lebanese crisis came from three members of the Senate Foreign Relations Committee who later became the leading critics of the intervention. Senator Mike Mansfield (D-Montana), the Democratic Senate whip, told the Senate on May 22 that the United Nations should have an emergency force that could be dispatched to the border of any nation that believed itself subject to foreign aggression (*Congressional Record*, 1958, pp. 9284–89). He stated on June 17 that the introduction of American forces could not solve the problems of the Middle East. Mansfield believed that the United Nations could handle the problem best, and suggested an embargo by the United Nations of any aggressor nation in the Middle East (*Ibid.*, p. 11452). On June 26 Hubert Humphrey (D-Minnesota) echoed Mansfield's statements about the United Nations. He also criticized the administration for its lack of a policy in the Middle East. In addition, Humphrey felt that the Eisenhower Doctrine was not applicable in the Lebanese situation; he did not believe that Lebanon was subject to any external Communist aggression (*Ibid.*, p. 13942). On June 17 Senator Wayne Morse (D-Oregon) stated that if the administration believed that there was a possibility of introducing American forces into Lebanon, then it should receive authorization from Congress for such an action (*Ibid.*, p. 11453).

During the pre-intervention crisis the administration apparently did not keep either the Senate Foreign Relations Committee or its chairman informed of the developments in the Middle East. However, on the eve of the American intervention President Eisenhower invited twenty-two congressmen to be briefed on the crisis. Both Secretary of State John Dulles and CIA Director Allen Dulles were present at the briefing. Eisenhower recalled that when the role of the United States was discussed, John Dulles "had to explain Article 51 of the United Nations Charter, which permitted a country to act on an emergency basis pending the first opportunity to turn the problem over as soon as the United Nations was able to act" (1965, p. 272). Even by Eisenhower's account, none of the congressional leaders were enthusiastic about American intervention in the Middle East. Speaker Rayburn wondered whether the United States was not involving itself in a civil war. Eisenhower stated that the "most skeptical of all was Senator Fulbright, who seemed to doubt seriously that the crisis was Communist inspired"

(*Ibid.*). In reality, congressional opinion had no impact on the president, who had already decided how to handle the Lebanese situation. The briefing session was held in order to present the appearance of concern for congressional advice.

For the most part, congressmen followed a bipartisan approach to foreign policy after the landing of Marines in Lebanon on July 15. The congressional leadership, except for Senator Mansfield, supported the administration's actions. Speaker Rayburn swallowed his doubts and used his congressional role to quell criticism within the House. He actually cut off a critical speech being delivered by Representative Henry Reuss (D-Wisconsin). The speeches given in favor of the intervention were for the most part framed in cold war rhetoric, the blame being assigned to Nasser, to Soviet Communism, or to an unholy alliance of the two. Senator Alexander Wiley (R-Wisconsin) delivered a constitutional argument in favor of the intervention. He said that the Eisenhower Doctrine was approved by Congress and became a public law, and that since the U.S. Constitution charges the president to take care that the laws be faithfully executed, Eisenhower, by sending troops to Lebanon, merely did what he had to do.

The congressional critics denounced the action until Congress adjourned on August 24. In a show of loyalty, all said that they would support the troops while they were in Lebanon, but that they considered the intervention a mistake. Lebanon was viewed as a nation in the midst of a civil war involving Arab nationalism, not international Communism. Senators Humphrey, Fulbright, and Morse, the leading critics, also became the most vocal advocates of the summit meeting proposed by Khrushchev, which they urged the reluctant Eisenhower to attend.

While discussion was taking place on the floors of the two legislative chambers, the House Foreign Affairs Committee and the Senate Foreign Relations Committee were holding closed hearings. Various members of the administration briefed the committees almost daily on the developments in the Middle East. Among the officials who appeared were Undersecretary of State Christian Herter; William B. Macomber, Assistant Secretary of State for Congressional Affairs; David Newson, the State Department officer in charge of Arabian Peninsular Affairs; CIA Director Allen

Dulles, and Gerald C. Sanders, Assistant Secretary of State for Planning.

The only official action that Congress took was to pass a resolution supporting the administration's stand at the United Nations in favor of establishing a permanent United Nations emergency force. The most active opponent of the administration's course of action, Senator Morse, introduced two Congressional resolutions. The first, Senate Resolution 391, denounced the president for taking an action that should have required congressional authorization. The other, Senate Joint Resolution 203, called for the withdrawal of American troops from Lebanon within thirty days of its passage. In justification, Morse declared, "I do not propose to sacrifice the lives of American boys for oil for Europe" (*Congressional Record,* 1958, p. 14934). The resolutions were futile gestures. Introduced on August 23, they were immediately referred to the Foreign Relations Committee, but on the very next day Congress adjourned until January of the following year, by which time the troops had long been recalled from Lebanon.

For the Eisenhower administration, where the Lebanese decisions were made, the world of 1958 was dotted with trouble spots. The deteriorating conditions in these areas were attributable to the activities of the Soviet Union. Eisenhower wrote that

> although temporarily pursuing a "soft" propaganda line, the Soviets were pushing everywhere, stirring up trouble in Venezuela, Indonesia and Burma, not to mention the Middle East. . . . against similar provoca, ons in the past the United States had for one reason or another been ur .ble to lend a hand. But here was one case where, it appeared, if the Lebanese Government should call upon us for help, we might move firmly and in full accord with the local government and the principles of the United Nations. (1965, p. 266)

After receiving Chamoun's May 13 letter inquiring about American aid, Eisenhower held a meeting with the Dulles brothers. Eisenhower recalls, "We met in a climate of impatience because of our belief that Chamoun's uneasiness was the result of one more Communist provocation" (*Ibid.*). Eisenhower and Allen Dulles listened to John Dulles outline the probable reactions of different nations if the United States sent troops into Lebanon. The secretary of state favored such an action despite his assessment that the pipelines across Syria would probably be blown, the Suez Canal might be blocked, and widespread Arab resentment could be expected. Eisenhower apparently was not ready to order a dispatch of troops. Instead, he instructed Dulles to reply to Chamoun that "troops would not be sent to Lebanon for the purpose of achieving an additional term for the President; that the request should have the concurrence of some other Arab nation; and that the mission of the United States troops in Lebanon would be twofold: protection of the life and property of Americans, and assistance to the legal Lebanese government" (*Ibid.*, p. 267). No other action was taken at this point, except that of placing American troops in Europe on alert.

If the period between May and July was characterized by major soul searching in the administration, no record of such a process is available. The various governmental agencies involved in the Lebanese decision apparently agreed with Dulles's definition of the situation, although there seems to have been some debate about the specific measures to be taken.

According to Emmet Hughes (1962, p. 263), for example, the American military did not favor sending troops into Lebanon. The navy worried about possible supply problems. The army, having seen the French tie up over half a million men in Algeria without being able to control the situation, feared that this would also happen in Lebanon. The air force believed that its bombers would be too vulnerable in a region in which the Soviet Union could deploy its troops quickly. In sum, the military was in favor of showing some sign of strength—ship movements or plane overflights—but not of committing land forces.

The CIA, on the other hand, shaped the information it supplied in such a way that military intervention seemed the only solution. Several factors combined to lend extra weight to the CIA's reports from Lebanon. First, the CIA had a long record of involvement in the country, and some of its agents were extremely close to the Lebanese president and foreign minister, who supposedly consulted them before they consulted their own colleagues (Halpern, 1964, p. 257). Some observers even claim that the CIA helped elect Chamoun in 1952. Second, in addition to its resident chief, the CIA had a section chief in Lebanon who had the trust of the Dulles brothers, so that CIA dispatches received at least the same attention as the Ambassador's reports. And, third, the CIA reports reinforced prevailing Washington beliefs. It was the CIA that reported in very certain terms that the Iraqi coup was part of a massive plot that supposedly included the elimination of both King Hussein of Jordan and President Chamoun (Barnet, 1968, pp. 147–48).

The State Department was apparently less certain of the nature of the threat and of the appropriate response. Although we have found no explicit evidence for this observation, it is likely that the Arabists (the Middle East specialists) in the department were not too enthusiastic about military intervention, being perfectly capable of distinguishing between Arab nationalism and international Communism. It is even possible that some members of the department urged greater reliance on the United Nations, for as late as the eve of the Iraqi coup, Robert McClintock, U.S. ambassador to Lebanon, informed Chamoun that since the United Nations observation team had found no substantial evidence of outside intervention, it would be impossible to have United States troops sent to Lebanon.

It is therefore barely conceivable that scattered misgivings in the administration, the Pentagon, Congress, and the press, when added to the United Nations reports and Chamoun's decision not to seek reelection, might have deterred Eisenhower and the Dulles brothers from deciding to intervene militarily (Eisenhower, 1965, p. 268). The Iraqi coup, however, dispelled all such doubts.

When Eisenhower received news of the Iraqi coup, he decided to send troops to Lebanon. He made this decision *before* his discussion with his principal advisors: "Because of my long study of the problem, this was one meeting in which my mind was practically made up regarding the general line of action we should take, even before we met" (*Ibid.*, p. 270). Here was Eisenhower's opportunity to save a pro-Western nation, to stand up to Communism, and to demonstrate to America's allies that the United States was capable of taking action, and all of this would be accomplished by responding to the official invitation of the Lebanese government to intervene in its affairs.

Eisenhower met with the Dulles brothers on July 14 in order

to hear their analysis of the situation. Allen Dulles believed that the Iraqi coup was pro-Nasser but that there was no evidence to prove that Nasser was behind it. John Dulles then analyzed the Arab reaction to American troop intervention in the same way that he had done two months earlier. The secretary thought that the United States could count on Western European and Latin American support and Asian and African disapproval. Dulles doubted that the Russians would do anything. Eisenhower shared this view: "Personally I had always discounted the probability of the Soviets doing anything as a 'reaction.' Communists do little on impulse; rather, their aggressive moves are invariably the result of deliberate decisions" (*Ibid.*, p. 282).

After his meeting with the Dulles brothers, Eisenhower met with twenty-two congressmen. The congressmen did not seem to desire American intervention in Lebanon, and some questioned whether the administration was perceiving the situation correctly. According to Eisenhower,

> at the end of the meeting I felt sure that Congress, while not attempting to impede our intervention in Lebanon would not, in the absence of some greater emergency, support anything more extensive than had been discussed at the meeting. Except for a very few . . . none of the leaders was outspoken in his support of intervention in Lebanon; but authority for such an operation lay so clearly within the responsibility of the Executive that no direct objection was voiced. In any event, the issue was clear to me—we had to go in. (*Ibid.*, p. 272)

There is a discrepancy in the accounts of this meeting: some congressmen reported that Eisenhower never mentioned the possibility of intervention at the meeting. Be that as it may, neither the lack of strong congressional support for intervention nor the lack of substantial evidence of United Arab Republic or Communist aggression in Lebanon had any effect on Eisenhower's chosen course. The orders were given to intervene in Lebanon.

The first two public actions the president took after making his decision were aimed at rallying support for it. First, on July 15 he sent a message to Congress explaining his action and reminding Congress of the support it had given the Eisenhower Doctrine. Second, he addressed the American public via radio and television that evening. The gist of the message was that the United States was helping Lebanon, which was suffering from the same type of aggression that Greece, China, Czechoslovakia, and Korea had experienced. The Soviet Union and the United Arab Republic were clearly to blame for fomenting the crisis. Eisenhower also explained that Article 51 of the United Nations Charter permitted nations to join together in actions for their collective defense, and that the area was of vital interest to the United States (*Congressional Quarterly*, 1958, pp. 936–37).

We have already seen that these largely ritualistic gestures had the desired effect of mobilizing public and congressional support and stilling domestic criticism. They had little to do with the actual decision-making process. Likewise, much of the administration's subsequent public maneuvering in the United Nations, its correspondence with Khrushchev, and its testimony in Congress had very little to do with the decision to recall the troops. That decision, too, was made in the White House, when Eisenhower and his principal advisers concluded that the situation in Lebanon had stabilized—a conclusion that was reached after the election of a new Lebanese president—and, more important, that the United States had achieved its primary objective of regaining sufficient prestige in the Middle East, thereby countering the feared Soviet designs.

REFERENCES AND BIBLIOGRAPHY

BARNET, RICHARD, *Intervention and Revolution*. New York: World Publishing, 1968.

Congressional Quarterly, 1958.

COPELAND, MILES, *The Game of Nations*. New York: Simon & Schuster, 1969.

EISENHOWER, DWIGHT D., *Waging Peace, 1956–1961: The White House Years*. New York: Doubleday, 1965.

HALPERN, MANFRED, "The Morality and Politics of Intervention," in *International Aspects of Civil Strife*, ed. James N. Rosenau. Princeton, N.J.: Princeton University Press, 1964.

HUGHES, EMMET JOHN, *The Ordeal of Power*. New York: Atheneum, 1961.

MEO, LEILA, *Lebanon: Improbable Nation*. Bloomington, Ind.: University of Indiana Press, 1965.

MURPHY, ROBERT, *Diplomat Among Warriors*. New York: Doubleday, 1964.

U.S., Congress, *Congressional Record*, 1958.

U.S., Department of the Interior, *Annual Report of the Secretary of the Interior*. Washington, D.C.: Government Printing Office, 1959.

7

The Trade Expansion Act
1962

On October 11, 1962, almost nine months after he had introduced it in Congress, President Kennedy signed the newly enacted Trade Expansion Bill, calling it the "most important international piece of legislation . . . affecting economics since the passage of the Marshall Plan in 1948" (*Congressional Record*, 1962, p. 23174). Basically, this measure gave the president greater flexibility in negotiating tariff changes with foreign nations. On the surface, this would appear to be merely an extension of a well-established pattern of international economic relations between the United States and other countries. Was the president, then, simply exaggerating the significance of this action for symbolic reasons, or as a means to some domestic political end?

Tariff or other international trade decisions often do have

worldwide repercussions. After all, a hike in the United States tariff rate on such commodities as cotton or wheat, or on simple manufactured goods such as textiles, could adversely affect the economies of all those states throughout the world whose economic well-being depends upon the existence of a relatively unrestricted American market. Thus, tariff policy has been employed as an important weapon in the arsenal of American foreign policy. At the same time, tariff changes can exert a significant impact on the domestic economic front, since changes in the tariff structure bear directly upon certain domestic economic interests. Therefore, we should find that the policy-making process involved in the Trade Expansion Act displays a more intimate and direct interplay of domestic and foreign elements than in any of the cases we have examined so far.

In the first months of 1961 a careful evaluation of American trade and tariff policy was conducted within high administration circles. The existing trade legislation, the Reciprocal Trade Act, was due to expire in mid-1962. Various versions of a new trade act were prepared under the leadership of George W. Ball, Undersecretary of State for Economic Affairs, who was assisted by Robert Schaetzel of the State Department and Howard Petersen, a Philadelphia banker. These proposals were based in part on the recommendations of a task force report on foreign economic policy prepared by Ball for the president-elect prior to Kennedy's inauguration. In that document, Ball had advocated the development of a new trade policy for the United States, one that would provide for increased presidential authority to negotiate tariff reductions, open up trade with the Soviet Union and the Eastern bloc, and facilitate the economic integration of the Atlantic community. As Ball observed, unless the United States pursued a trade policy aimed at reducing tariff barriers in the early stages of Western European economic integration, not only would it suffer the damaging economic loss of access to the European market, but its failure to act would contribute to the "disintegration of the Free World Economy into separate trading systems" (New York Times, January 8, 1962).

Despite Ball's urgent plea, Kennedy was at first far from convinced of the political wisdom of pushing for a new trade program in 1962. Other key political advisers also questioned the advisability of advocating a new trade program before the midterm elections of 1962 (see Schlesinger, 1965, pp. 846–47). By late 1961 Kennedy's relationships with Congress were beginning to show signs of strain and tension. Some evidence for a growing disenchantment with Kennedy's proposed trade program was emerging within the Democratic Party, and the Republican opposition, particularly its more conservative wing, was clearly hardening. The absence of any major legislative victory for Kennedy, the increasing bitterness of presidential-legislative relationships, and Kennedy's misadventures in Berlin and Cuba only served to reinforce the reticence within the administration to seek the enactment of a trade bill before the end of 1962.

By November, 1961, however, Kennedy had decided to support the enactment of a new trade expansion measure and to commit the resources of his administration to its passage. Ball, along with Petersen and Schaetzel, had been actively urging the president to pursue such a course of action, for economic as well as political reasons. Economically, Ball argued, the new trade measure would strengthen the economic relationship between Western Europe and the United States, serve to alleviate the growing American balance-of-payments problem, and assist Britain in her efforts to gain entrance into the Common Market. Ball was also quick to point to the domestic implications of presidential support for trade expansion by claiming that a major legislative triumph on this measure would benefit the Democrats as well as the president. Should Kennedy suffer a defeat, Ball argued, he could always exploit this issue during the forthcoming congressional campaign and attempt to reverse the defeat in 1963.

The bill itself was drafted by Ball, Schaetzel, and Petersen, who were joined later by Meyer Rashish, an economist who had served as a staff member on the House Ways and Means Committee and the liberal-trade Committee for a National Trade Policy (CNTP), an organization representing businessmen whose interests lay primarily in exports. Schaetzel had served as Ball's assistant in the State Department, and Petersen, the Philadelphia banker, was an expert in international economics who had been recruited by the president in August, 1961 to serve as special assistant for trade policy. Basically, the bill contained broadened tariff negotiating powers for the president, provided for a multilateral negotiation of tariff rates by categories of goods rather than on an item-by-item basis, as previously established, permitted negotiations for the total elimination of tariffs in some circumstances, and authorized government compensation for injury to domestic interests.

The opening round in the struggle to enact the newly drafted trade measure began with Ball's address before the National Foreign Trade Council on November 1, 1961. In his speech Ball attacked the prevailing pattern of American trade policy, pointing to the weaknesses of the Reciprocal Trade Program and emphasizing the necessity of developing fresh approaches and perspectives to the problems of international trade. The advent of the Common Market, the development of new international trading patterns, and the growing imbalance in American balance-of-payments transactions demanded, Ball asserted, a change in prevailing trade practices and programs (*New York Times*, November 2, 1961). Within the month, leading figures in Kennedy's administration had endorsed Ball's pleas for a fundamental overhaul of American trade policy.

In speeches delivered on two successive days in December before business and labor audiences, Kennedy echoed Ball's position. Before the National Association of Manufacturers, the president revealed his intention to replace the prevailing trade legislation with a wholly new program for expanding trade. Such action, Kennedy assured the assembled businessmen, was crucial if America was to increase her exports, promote the economic integration of the Common Market countries, and maintain the economic and political leadership of the Western world. Calling it a "new and bold instrument of American trade policy," Kennedy endorsed the proposed trade program in order to ensure Western "initiative in the economic arena," encourage adaptation to the "revolutionary changes which are taking place throughout the world," and guarantee the preservation of American exports "in the world market" (*New York Times*, December 7, 1961). Then, in his State of the Union message on January 11, 1962, Kennedy spelled out further details of his anticipated program. We need, he repeated, "a bold new instrument of American trade policy" (*Congressional Quarterly*, 1962, p. 264). Finally, on January 25 the president sent a draft bill to Congress with a supporting special message.

Urging Congress to act swiftly on his trade measure, Kennedy's message stressed the growing irrelevancy of the existing trade policy for the needs of the 1960s. Pointing to a host of new developments in international trade, such as the growth of the European Common Market, growing pressures on our balance-of-payments position, the need to accelerate our economic growth, the Communist aid and trade offensive, and the need for new markets for Japan and the developing nations, the president urged that novel approaches and procedures in the foreign trade area be established in order for the United States to cope more effectively with these new conditions. (See the *Congressional Quarterly*, 1962 pp. 122–26.)

In testimony on the Kennedy tariff program before congressional committees, key administration officials elaborated the president's rationale, developed and refined his arguments, and sought diligently to bolster his case. Speaking before the Ways and Means Committee, a leading State Department figure pointed to the proposed act as a means of "strengthening those forces in Europe that are seeking to liberalize the Common Market's trading policies" (U.S. House, 1962, p. 638). Secretary of the Treasury Douglas Dillon noted the anticipated contribution of the bill to improving the American balance-of-payments position: "If broad and substantial mutual tariff reductions by the Common Market and the United States are effected . . . , we can then expect the resulting expansion of two-way trade to bring with it a significant increase in the commercial trade surplus of the United States —with corresponding benefit to our balance of payments position" (*Congressional Quarterly*, 1962, p. 478). Secretary of Commerce Luther Hodges and Roswell Gilpatrick of the Defense Department emphasized the value of the measure in the cold war struggle against the Soviets. Hodges, for example, described the act as "an essential weapon in the cold war" (U.S. House, 1962, p. 3775) and pleaded strongly for favorable congressional action.

An intensive lobbying effort was undertaken by the White House to mobilize public and congressional support behind the trade measure. Centered in the executive office so that the president could be kept continually informed of the latest developments in the legislative campaign, the lobbying activities were under the overall supervision of Petersen. The White House trade staff was enlarged so that they could help gather technical information and data, draft speeches, and prepare congressional testimony. Tom Finney was "temporarily detached" from the staff of Senator Mike Monroney (D-Oklahoma) and assigned to coordinate the legislative activities of all governmental departments and agencies on behalf of the trade bill. Collaborating closely with Larry O'Brien, Kennedy's special assistant for congressional relations, Finney served as O'Brien's special assistant on trade matters.

The distribution of information to Congress regarding trade matters was centered in Finney's office. Some positions within this office were filled by recruits from private industry and interest groups that were favorably disposed toward the president's program. One congressman, angered by the presence of these men within the White House, denounced this practice as the "informal integration of pressure groups into the machinery of government at the highest policy levels" (Congressional Record, 1962, p. 6368).

Kennedy himself was an active participant in this lobbying campaign. He invited groups of congressmen to the White House to discuss his program, spoke privately with a smaller number of particularly recalcitrant legislators, and on occasion made phone calls to those who appeared to waiver in their support, in order to strengthen their resolve. He employed the mass media frequently in order to promote widespread public support for his trade bill. In virtually every press conference between January and June, the president emphasized the significance of his trade measure in furthering the foreign policy objectives of his administration. (See, for example, the report of a Kennedy press conference in the March 7, 1962 issue of the New York Times.) Members of his administration were dispatched on speaking tours throughout the country in order to drum up support for the bill. (See, for example, the address by Petersen in the Congressional Record, 1962, p. A2736.) On May 24 Kennedy, appearing on a special CBS news broadcast devoted to an analysis of the Trade Expansion Act, called the measure "the most important piece of legislation before the country this year" (*Congressional Quarterly*, 1962, p. 273) and urged Republicans as well as Democrats to support it. Two stalwarts of the Republican Party, former Secretary of State Christian Herter and former President Eisenhower (both of whom joined Kennedy in his broadcast), announced afterwards their endorsement of his trade program (*Congressional Record*, 1962, pp. 12065–69).

In an effort to strengthen the persuasiveness of its case, the White House sought allies among a wide variety of groups and associations, including the AFL—CIO, the American Farm Bureau Federation, and the United States Chamber of Commerce. In particular, the administration established close contact with and revivified the virtually moribund CNTP. Established in 1953 largely through the efforts of Ball and Ralph Straus, an executive of Macy's Department Store, the CNTP gradually became the chief "spokesman" for reciprocal trade and tariff liberalization. Although it largely failed during the 1950s in "its original objective to wage a cold-facts campaign based on self-interest, bolstered and defined by research," the committee did "establish itself as a place to go to for information and help" (Bauer et al., 1962, p. 386).

As a key liberal-trade lobby, CNTP led and coordinated the activities of the other major groups that were favorably disposed toward Kennedy's trade proposal. In the 1962 trade struggle, the CNTP doubled its full-time professional staff in Washington from four to eight and took on additional clerical workers. Information about congressmen's voting records and current leanings, the districts of "swing" congressmen, and the status of the administration's trade measure was exchanged frequently between CNTP's Washington office and the White House, the AFL–CIO, the Chamber of Commerce, and other groups. The CNTP staff concerned themselves with a broad range of tasks: preparing bulletins, organizing studies of trade issues, explaining critical problems of foreign trade, and countering the arguments of protectionist forces. In conjunction with other allied groups, or independently, the CNTP conducted or sponsored studies designed to produce information useful to the advocates of trade liberalization.

Meanwhile, support from a variety of sources, including economists, trade officials, and private citizens, was forthcoming for the president's proposal. Claude Wickard, speaking for the Public Advisors to the General Agreement on Tariffs and Trade (GATT), agreed with the president that "the item-by-item bargaining under the present law is extremely cumbersome and inadequate to meet our needs" (*Congressional Quarterly*, 1962, p. 478). Henry Cabot Lodge, Director General of the Atlantic Institute and the 1960 Republican vice-presidential candidate, also testified in support of the bill. Congress's failure to approve the president's trade act, Lodge asserted, would "cut us off from our major allies, worsen our balance of payments position, and injure the interest of millions of Americans whose jobs depend on exports and imports" (*Ibid.*). Representatives of such diverse organizations as the American Association of University Women, the League of Women Voters, the Board of Christian Social Concerns of the Methodist Church, and the U.S. Council of the International Chamber of Commerce also testified in support of the measure.

Labor, agriculture, and business generally favored the bill. George Meany, AFL–CIO president, testified in favor of the measure but hoped that "certain modifications" would be made. In particular, he pleaded for the expansion of adjustment benefits to those industries injured by import competition. By no means, however, was labor wholly united behind the trade program. Describing Meany as a "trained seal," a president of a local steelworkers' union roundly denounced the trade measure. Moreover, at the AFL–CIO's December, 1961 convention, there were notable dissents from the leadership's stand by the United Brotherhood of Carpenters and Joiners, the International Brotherhood of Carpenters and Joiners, the International Brotherhood of Operative Potters, the United Textile Workers, and the United Shoe Workers (*Congressional Record*, 1962, p. A4196).

Although it opposed the administration's Farm Bill, the American Farm Bureau Federation (AFBF) endorsed the major provisions of the president's trade measure, but it called for amendments designed to protect American agricultural interests against discriminatory practices that limited competition. "We have never been stronger in our support [for a liberal trade policy] than this year," claimed the AFBF spokesman (*Congressional Quarterly*, 1962, p. 405).

The Chamber of Commerce, meanwhile, announced its support of the president's bill on February 24. As the *Congressional Quarterly* noted, although the "Chamber [had] consistently supported liberal trade, . . . its 1962 announcement was greeted with relief by the Administration . . . who had feared that dissent among some members might force a change in position" (1962, p. 404). The Chamber did indicate, however, that a concern with other issues of interest, such as taxes and medical care, would prevent it from fully employing its resources in the legislative campaign in behalf of the bill. Internal disunity, on the other hand, neutralized the National Association of Manufacturers and prevented it from playing any role in the legislative struggle over the tariff issues. It prepared no testimony and filed no formal statement on the bill. It was forced to content itself with a candid admission that the "Association does not attempt to speak for its members on tariff matters." "The Association's lack of a position on the subject of tariffs," the NAM sheepishly admitted, "is a consequence of the size and diversity of its membership." (U.S. House, 1962 pp. 3924–25)

Kennedy's legislative strategy to shepherd the trade measure through Congress involved three basic maneuvers. First, the president and key administration officials and supporters in Congress persistently emphasized the bipartisan character of Kennedy's trade legislation. On the CBS broadcast of May 24, Kennedy took particular note of the "non-partisan character of [this] legislation. It belongs to the Republicans as much as the Democrats." (*Congressional Record*, 1962, p. 12069) As evidence, he alluded to Herter's and Eisenhower's endorsement of his program. Presenting the trade act before Congress after his committee had concluded deliberations on it, Chairman Wilbur Mills noted, "We have before us a bill today that is as nonpolitical and as bipartisan as any bill that has been reported from the Committee on Ways and Means . . . for this bill is not the handiwork of just the Democratic members of the Committee" (*Congressional Record*, 1962, p. 11991). In addition, Mills offered a picture of widespread support for the measure among the top leadership of both the Democratic and Republican Parties.

Second, from the outset the president sought to place the

trade bill within the overall context of American foreign policy. Hence, its role in preparing the United States for negotiations with the Common Market, Japan, and the underdeveloped world was pointedly stressed, and a diligent effort was made to underplay its domestic economic ramifications. By treating the measure within the perspective of foreign relations, moreover, Kennedy hoped to undermine the opposition in Congress by capitalizing upon the presumption of executive predominance in international affairs. As *The New Republic* noted,

> Because the new legislation does break with the past, the way the Administration puts the case for it can go far toward deciding what the Congress will do. If the case is put in bread and butter terms alone, it will arouse the jealousies of the Congress, which traditionally regards itself as the main arbiter of the nation's economic interests. But if the Administration puts the case in terms of how the legislation fits into the grand design for a new Atlantic partnership—and it has begun to do this in recent days—it will bring to the support of the measure the inherent strength the President has whenever he invokes his own special authority as the chief architect of foreign policy. (1962, p. 5)

Despite this effort, some congressmen were quick to object that the president's program was an infringement on congressional authority. "The President," declared Congressman Noah Mason (R-Illinois), a staunch opponent of the trade program, "proposed to take over the whole trade agreements program, practically speaking, which the Constitution says rests on the shoulders of . . . Congress" (*Congressional Record*, 1962, p. 11913). A few others who were skeptical of the president's measure criticized the manner in which Kennedy had chosen to ignore the domestic economic implications of the program and the extent to which, they believed, the president was prepared to sacrifice domestic interest to foreign policy needs and concerns. These congressmen agreed with O. R. Strackbein, a leading critic of the act, that the "bill call[ed] for the subordination of domestic economic interests to the considerations of foreign relations as judged and evaluated by the State Department" (U.S. House, 1962, p. 1317). Finally, one congressman denied that the proposal was motivated by a desire to liberalize trade, viewing it instead as a critical development in the effort by the federal government to establish control over the private market.

Individuals in the Kennedy administration who claim they are for free trade, Congressman Thomas Curtis explained, want "to control trade through the political machinery of the Executive Branch of the Federal Government. [They] have been trying to get control of the domestic market . . . and put it under the control of the . . . Federal Government. [Now they] are engaged in the same thing and using the international market." (*Ibid.*, p. 3256)

Such extreme opinions as those held by Curtis, were not widely shared among members of Congress. The administration forces countered the opposition arguments by emphasizing the marginal role that Congress had played in the tariff-setting process, at least since 1934. As Charles Gilbert, the CNTP chairman, noted, "Every Congress since 1934 has . . . agreed that in tariff setting the standard of the national interest can best be applied by the President, acting under authority delegated to him by the Congress" (*Ibid.*, p. 1876). Therefore, efforts to restore Congress's role in the negotiation of individual tariff rates or to unduly hamper the president in the performance of this activity were, the administration argued, misdirected and uninformed. "Tariffs are perhaps," as Fred Greenstein noted, "the best example of the kind of policy which is not made effectively by Congress" (1963, p. 90). The supporters of the trade expansion act concurred wholeheartedly.

Perhaps the most significant component of the president's legislative strategy was a diligent effort to prevent the formation and, most important, the consolidation of a powerful protectionist bloc within Congress. The presence of this bipartisan, protectionist coalition had been principally responsible, almost since 1934, for preventing innovations in American trade policy. Kennedy sought, therefore, to satisfy "in advance the demands of enough injured industries [that is, protectionist interests] to neutralize them or even give them a stake in the passage of the bill" (Bauer et al., 1963, p. 78). The successful enactment of the trade expansion act therefore rested primarily on the president's ability to attract normally protectionist interests away from their conventional alliance with other protection-minded elements within Congress. This was to be accomplished by offering concessions to these interests, which, without sacrificing the commitment of the administration to liberalized trade, would induce the more protectionist-minded firms and industries to sever their allegiance to the anti–free trade group in Congress.

The bargaining with these special interests was inaugurated by White House political aides, especially Meyer Feldman. Feldman's strategy of special concessions, although motivated by a desire to neutralize opposition to the trade program, provoked concern within Congress and the State Department and among the foreign-trade staff of the White House. Every week Feldman was beseiged by calls and letters from many of those who had worked on the drafting of the bill, pleading that he not sell out their principles. Feldman sought to oblige by pursuing a strategy aimed at preserving the basic features of the bill intact but making concessions outside of it. When the bill was subsequently enacted, few formal changes had in fact been made: the "concessions that were made and the obligations that were incurred concerned Administrative action or special bills" (Ibid.).

Bargains that Feldman made with protection-minded interests in order to obtain their support for the president's measure were to prove crucial in the legislative deliberation of the bill. A few "textile senators," for example, provided the necessary votes for the defeat of an amendment offered by Senator Prescott Bush that would have reintroduced the "peril-point" provisions of earlier trade legislation. Moreover, the critical assistance of Senator Robert Kerr, who assumed the management of the bill in the Senate, was based in part on an informal understanding that the administration had reached with domestic oil interests. But despite the fears expressed by some administration officials, these concessions would not fundamentally weaken the major principles and objectives of the program. As the *New York Times* wrote, shortly before the bill's enactment,

> Some free traders believe that the grand design of a "bold new instrument" has been impaired by the many administrative and legislative devices for dividing and conquering the opposition. The Administration's view, however, is that all the concessions and compromises fade into insignificance when viewed in the light of the legislation's potential effectiveness in expanding world trade. . . . The apparent consensus of impartial commentators is that . . . it is a substantive as well as political triumph, despite all concessions and compromises. (September 23, 1962)

The outstanding case of presidential bargaining with protectionist-minded forces was that of textiles. Here, the president sought to "isolate the textile problem from the trade bill and prevent representatives of districts with textile interests from opposing [his] bill" (*Congressional Quarterly*, 1962, p. 288). On February 15, 1962, much to the dismay of protectionist forces, Kennedy announced the successful negotiation of a nineteen-nation textile import quota agreement by which imports of foreign textiles were to be limited. Shortly thereafter, the textile industry was provided with a liberalized tax depreciation schedule. These concessions apparently had their intended effect. On March 31 the American Cotton Manufacturers Institute, which represented 80 percent of the textile industry, announced its support for the major provisions of the Kennedy trade program. The leaders of the textile bloc endorsed the trade expansion act, and a substantial number of congressmen representing textile interests ultimately voted for the bill.

Opponents of the act denounced these developments and accused the Kennedy administration of duplicity and unprincipled bargaining. Representative Curtis, for one, criticized the announcement of the textile endorsement as a political deal in which textile interests had been "bought off" by administrative action. "Let the Textile Institute," he charged, "state what kind of political deal . . . has been made. . . . I think President Kennedy or his Cabinet officers who have been part of this obvious political deal need to tell the American people what it is." (U.S. House, 1962, p. 3255) On April 10, testifying for a second time before the Ways and Means Committee, Secretary of Commerce Hodges denied that any deal had been made with the textile interests. There appears little doubt, however, that the response of the textile industry to a presidential trade program that included no concessions to them would not have been entirely favorable.

Despite the defection of the textile interest from the protectionist forces, it was by no means evident that Congress would act favorably on the trade act. In order to obtain wider support within Congress and further weaken the protectionist coalition, Kennedy approved tariff increases on carpets and glass products. Moreover, on July 26 he announced a program of import limitations designed to assist the hard-pressed lumber interests of the Northwest.

On the whole, Kennedy's strategy of undermining the cohesion of the protectionist coalition was eminently successful. The union of various protectionist interests such as textiles, coal, and lumber—which, acting together, could have severely hampered the bill's success—failed to materialize. And as Raymond Bauer and his associates observed, "the Administration's calculated and massive individualized approach to such industries as chemicals and textiles" played a significant role in "cutting the protectionist coalition to shreds" (1963, p. 79).

Despite the administration's predictions of a major legislative struggle, Kennedy's measure moved through Congress with relative ease. Hearings opened in the House on March 12 and continued for twenty days, during which 245 witnesses appeared. On May 23 the Committee on Ways and Means tentatively approved an amended bill, which contained, however, all the basic authorities requested by the administration. Then on June 4, over some opposition within his Ways and Means Committee, Chairman Wilbur Mills introduced the bill on the House floor. It was brought to a vote on June 28, after two days of debate, and it was approved by the substantial majority of 298 to 125.

There were two objections, clearly related to each other, to Kennedy's program in the House, and these were expressed most often by Republicans, despite a recent observation that "trade [by the time of the trade expansion measure] evolved from a highly partisan issue to a mixed issue" (Manley, 1970, p. 210). At the broadest level the opposition was concerned about the possible results of what they perceived as a change in the traditional philosophy of American tariff policy. Specifically, they maintained that this measure abandoned the view "that our negotiators refrain from agreeing to a reduction in duties which will bring about serious injury to the domestic industry" (*Congressional Quarterly*, 1962, p. 1028). To counter this threat, the opposition demanded assurance that domestic interests would be adequately protected under the new trade program. A second expression of displeasure was directed against the dominant role assumed by the president in the tariff-making process. Since the president, in negotiating tariff rates, was no longer strictly bound by their possible detrimental impact on the economic health of domestic economic interests, he could determine in effect that "certain United States industries —entire whole industries—are expendable" (*Congressional Record*, 1962, p. 12062). There was thus a serious built-in potential for the abuse of executive power. Not only would this dominant role reinforce the power of the presidency but it would contribute to the tendency to see tariff policy almost exclusively as an instrument of American foreign policy, thus discounting even further its economic impact on American industry.

To these charges, the Kennedy administration responded in two ways. First, it pointed to the wide range of procedures in the measure that were designed to identify and articulate threatened domestic economic interests so that tariff changes would not unwittingly burden American industry. "We have tried," argued Chairman Mills in behalf of the Administration case, "to establish *machinery* to prevent the making of mistakes, [to provide] full opportunities for hearing for all interested parties, [and to ensure] that people are heard with respect to the pre-negotiation phases of this program" (*Ibid.*, p. 11991). The administration countered the second charge by claiming that although trade policy was indeed a critical instrument in the fulfillment of foreign policy, an effective tariff policy was not incompatible with the interests of American industry and could be designed without sacrificing these interests.

On the same day the bill was enacted in the House, a last-ditch but unsuccessful effort was made by staunch trade-expansion opponents to obstruct final legislative approval of the measure. The bill was scheduled for debate under a closed rule, which according to the traditional procedure for debate on trade bills, excludes all but committee amendments from the floor. Under a closed rule, a pending bill may be changed only by the approval of a recommittal motion. As ranking Republican member of the Ways and Means Committee, Representative Noah Mason of Illinois proposed a motion to recommit the pending trade bill with instructions that a substitute that would extend the existing trade legislation for a year be reported back to the House. Since the negotiating authority of the president under the existing trade act had been virtually exhausted, passage of the Mason motion would have spelled defeat for Kennedy's trade program. On June 26, the day before debate opened in the House on the trade bill, the Republican Policy Committee discussed, but did not adopt any party position regarding, a recommittal motion. Then, in the final moments of the two-day debate the House Republican leadership announced their support of the Mason motion.

Administration supporters in the House counterattacked immediately. Speaker of the House John McCormack urged his colleagues to reject the recommittal motion. Viewing its approval by the House as a repudiation of the Ways and Means Committee, McCormack sought to capitalize upon the willingness of congressmen to defer to the congressional committee leadership structure. Passage of the Mason motion, McCormack charged, "would be a vote of 'no confidence' in the Ways and Means Committee leadership . . . , as well as a vote of 'no confidence' in the other members of that great Committee" (*Ibid.*, p. 12063). The Democratic Steering Committee was promptly convened in order to drum up support for the trade bill. At his news conference on June 27, the president emphasized the urgent need to enact his trade measure and warned that "to recommit this bill back to the Committee is to defeat it" (*New York Times*, June 28, 1962). Kennedy also convinced Eisenhower to urge House Republican leader Charles Halleck not to endorse the recommittal motion. Halleck ultimately supported the Mason motion, although he hesitated in doing so. Finally, the administration let it be known that it was prepared to accept—within limits, to be sure—modifications in the trade adjustment provisions of the act if this "appeared necessary in order to gain additional votes to beat the Mason motion" (*Congressional Quarterly*, 1962, p. 279).

The Mason motion was defeated on June 28 by a wide margin of 253-171. This defeat vastly improved the chances for the adoption of Kennedy's trade program by the House. Left with the choice of either approving the pending trade bill or killing trade legislation entirely, most House members opted for the more moderate of the two alternatives. Apparently, few congressmen were prepared to support such drastic action as the scuttling of the entire United States trade program. Even Congressman Byrnes,

one of the more outspoken critics of Kennedy's measure, ultimately supported the trade bill in order, he argued, to keep the
trade issue alive so that congressmen would have an opportunity to
"protest against sections of the bill they disliked and the denial of
an opportunity to change them" (Ibid., p. 1084).

Despite the generally more protectionist sympathies in the
Senate, the trade measure fared equally well in this chamber. After
four weeks of hearings, a bill emerged from the Finance Committee containing most of the major provisions requested by the administration. Praising the work of the Finance Committee, Kennedy urged the Senate to enact the bill in "substantially this form."

Debate within the Senate differed little from the discussions
in the House. There was almost none of the traditional debate on a
liberal as opposed to a protectionist trade philosophy. No significant changes were made in the bill on the Senate floor, and
amendments proposed by the Finance Committee were endorsed
without opposition. Measures designed to strengthen the retaliatory powers of the president were approved over the mild objection
of administration supporters. A series of protectionist amendments
proposed in the Finance Committee were successfully opposed,
however.

The most important victory for the administration in the Senate, though, occurred over the struggle to beat back the Bush
amendment. The approval of this amendment, sponsored by
Senator Prescott Bush (R-Connecticut) would have restored the
"peril-point" provisions of the existing Trade Agreement Act
under which specific industries who felt that their interests were
jeopardized could appeal adverse tariff decisions directly to the
Tariff Commission. Had this amendment been approved, it would
have critically limited the negotiating flexibility of the president in
tariff matters. Accusing Bush of pursuing a no-decrease trade policy, Senator Paul Douglas (D-Illinois) charged that the Connecticut
senator was seeking to "replace the President as a negotiating authority" with "the Tariff Commission" (Congressional Record,
1962, pp. 1878–79). The administration concurred wtih Douglas's
view, claiming that the adoption of the Bush amendment would
"nullify the [pending] trade bill and render it useless except as a
vehicle for curtailing Foreign trade" (Ibid., p. 1887). Despite the
seriousness of these charges, the amendment came perilously close

to being adopted. Forty Democrats provided a slim margin of victory for the administration against twenty-five Republicans joined by thirteen defectors from the Democratic camp. The day after, the Senate enacted the Trade Expansion Act by a substantial margin.

The proceedings of the Conference Committee that were convened to reconcile the outstanding differences between the Senate and House versions of the trade bill were on the whole uneventful. The administration was forced to accept the retention of many of the escape-clause provisions of earlier trade legislation. Also, the administration was unable to obtain congressional approval for extending the principle of most-favored-nation treatment to trade with Poland and Yugoslavia. Despite these setbacks, the Trade Expansion Act, as approved by Congress, contained most of the provisions advocated by the administration. It provided the president with substantial negotiating authority, redefined the role of Congress in the tariff-setting process, and legitimized foreign trade as a major instrument of American foreign policy. Of no less importance, it marked a distinct triumph for the Kennedy administration, whose rhetoric in the past had too often barely concealed its slender success in the legislative arena.

Our examination of the passage of the Trade Expansion Act of 1962 reveals a novel configuration of forces, roles, and institutions within an overall policy matrix not present at any previous time in the history of trade legislation. As we have seen, the details of this proposal were developed within the White House under the direction of a key presidential adviser (Ball). Although initially reluctant, the president, once he was convinced of the necessity of a new policy, assigned it top priority in his legislative program. He played a leading role in the elaboration of legislative strategy, in the mobilization of public support, and in the orchestration of compromises.

The initiative clearly lay with the executive. Kennedy carefully engineered a strategy designed to induce congressional support. This plan centered chiefly in an effort to weaken the power of the protectionist coalition in Congress to deter new departures in trade policy. By inducing normally protectionist elements in Congress to break with their erstwhile allies, Kennedy took a major step toward ensuring the successful enactment of his legislation.

The president clearly dominated the legislative process, but his relationships with economic groups that had a stake in the passage of this act were no less manifest. The administration openly encouraged these groups to endorse the new trade program, and in at least one case it sought to restore the declining status of a virtually moribund group. In return, these groups provided critical assistance to the administration in the form of widespread publicity and educational campaigns. There was little independent expression of public opinion, although the interested public expressed its positions through the regularly constituted interest groups. The major role of public opinion was in an administration-directed effort to arouse support for the trade act, an effort that was especially notable in the campaign undertaken by the Committee for a National Trade Policy.

The successful passage of the Trade Expansion Act reflected the conjunction of international economic developments, domestic ideological changes, and a carefully planned and executed presidential strategy that capitalized on these. The growing awareness of international economic interdependence and the widespread concern over export trade in the face of Common Market competition, combined with a general decline of protectionist ideology in the United States, provided a favorable climate for Kennedy's trade program. (Tables 1 and 2 show the growth of U.S. foreign trade and the increasing importance of U.S.-European economic relations which motivated the passage of this Act.)

However, there is little doubt that the success of the bill depended primarily upon the administration's careful handling of the issue in Congress and among the American public. President Kennedy utilized to maximum advantage two conventional arguments of American chief executives regarding trade policy. First, he referred to the widespread belief that "tariff-making is and should be primarily the business of the executive" (Manley, 1970, p. 331). Second, he maintained that a "liberal, low-tariff international trade policy was in the best interest of this nation's national security" (Bailey, 1966, p. 22). These views, which had characterized presidental attitudes on foreign trade policy at least since the adoption of the Reciprocal Trade Program in 1934, enabled Kennedy to claim an intimate connection between tariffs and foreign policy objectives, and to use the mantle of national security to offset opposition based on domestic economic considerations.

TABLE 1[1] U.S. Merchandise Exports to Western
Europe and Western Hemisphere,
1948–1971 (in millions of U.S. dollars)

Year	Western Europe	Western Hemisphere
1948	4,279[2]	5,307
1949	4,118[2]	4,861
1950	3,280	4,902
1951	5,118	6,607
1952	5,088	6,682
1953	5,709	6,514
1954	5,112	6,520
1955	5,119	6,903
1956	6,423	8,243
1957	6,751	9,001
1958	5,452	7,999
1959	5,464	7,692
1960	7,204	7,684
1961	7,237	7,673
1962	7,633	7,724
1963	8,171	7,944
1964	9,096	9,207
1965	9,224	9,917
1966	9,805	11,429
1967	10,187	11,890
1968	11,132	13,411
1969	12,392	14,713
1970	14,465	15,618
1971	14,190	16,850

[1]Data from: 1948–49; U.S. Department of Commerce,
Business Statistics, 1969 (Washington, 1969), p. 111;
1950–66: U.S. Bureau of the Census, *Highlights of the
U.S. Export and Import Trade*, Report FT 990, August
1967 (released October 1967), pp. 96–97; 1967–70: U.S.
Department of Commerce, *Overseas Business Reports*,
February 1971, Report OBR 71–009, p. 18; 1971:
Economic Report of the President 1972 (Washington,
1972), p. 299.

[2]All Europe, including USSR.

Source: David P. Calleo and Benjamin Rowland,
*America and the World Political Economy: Atlantic
Dreams and National Realities* (Bloomington: Indiana
University Press, 1973), p. 156.

TABLE 2[1]   Trade between the U.S. and the EEC
—Agricultural and Non-agricultural
Goods (in millions of U.S. dollars)

	EEC→US	Total Trade US→EEC	Balance
1958	1,664	2,808	1,144
1959	2,371	2,651	280
1960	2,242	3,830	1,588
1961	2,232	4,054	1,822
1962	2,447	4,458	2,011
1963	2,563	5,051	2,488
1964	2,849	5,438	2,589
1965	3,425	5,693	2,268
1966	4,098	6,022	1,924
1967	4,424	5,898	1,474
1968	5,769	6,393	624
1969	5,958	7,335	1,377
1970	6,633	9,038	2,405

[1]Data from: Statistical Office of the European Communities: *Foreign Trade—Monthly Statistics*, 1972–No. 1; 1971–No. 8–9 & No. 12; 1970–No. 6; 1969–No. 5; 1968–No. 3 & No. 8–9; 1967–No. 10; 1966–No. 8–9; 1964–No. 5.
Source: David P. Calleo and Benjamin Rowland, *America and the World Economy: Atlantic Dreams and National Realities* (Bloomington: Indiana University Press, 1973), p. 160.

REFERENCES AND BIBLIOGRAPHY

BAILEY, STEPHEN, *The New Congress*. New York: St. Martin's, 1966.

BAUER, RAYMOND A., ITHIEL DE SOLA POOL, and LEWIS ANTHONY DEXTER, *American Business and Public Policy: The Politics of Foreign Trade*. New York: Atherton, 1963.

Congressional Quarterly, 1962.

GREENSTEIN, FRED I., *The American Party System and the American People*. Englewood Cliffs, N.J.: Prentice-Hall, 1963.

LOWI, THEODORE, "American Business and Public Policy: Case Studies and Political Theory," *World Politics*, 16, no. 4 (July 1964).

MANLEY, JOHN, F., *The Politics of Finance: The House Committee on Ways and Means.* Boston: Little, Brown, 1970.

SCHLESINGER, ARTHUR M., JR., *A Thousand Days.* Boston: Houghton Mifflin, 1965.

SORENSEN, THEODORE. *Kennedy.* New York: Harper & Row, 1965.

"Trade Bill Salesmanship," *New Republic,* February 5, 1962. pp. 4—5.

U.S., Congress, *Congressional Record,* 1962.

U.S., Congress, House of Representatives, Committee on Ways and Means, *Hearings, Trade Expansion Act of 1962.* 87th Cong., 2nd sess, 1962.

U.S., Congress, Senate, Committee on Finance, *Hearings, Trade Expansion Act of 1962.* 87th Cong., 2nd sess, 1962.

The Cuban Missile Crisis
1962

In late 1962 the world watched in horror as the most frightening post–World War II nightmare seemed about to come true: the two superpowers, the United States and the Soviet Union, engaged in nuclear confrontation. Marked by tension, uncertainty, and the threat of nuclear holocaust, the Cuban missile crisis affords us a unique view of what has come to be known as "crisis diplomacy." (See, for example, Bell, 1971.) But it is equally significant as a vehicle for analyzing the American foreign policy process in crisis situations.

Although the reasons for the Soviet actions that precipitated the missile crisis will probably never be completely known, two events appear to have been particularly relevant. The first was the dismal failure of the Bay of Pigs invasion of 1961. Here, American support for an armed effort to overthrow the Castro regime had proved insufficient. The Russians apparently concluded from this incident that the Americans were not prepared to exist peacefully with the Communist regime in Cuba and that they seemed prepared to resort to military means in order to dislodge Castro. Second, as a result of the 1961 Vienna summit meeting, Chairman Khrushchev became convinced that President Kennedy would prove unable to counter Russian ambitions effectively, whether in Berlin or in the Western Hemisphere (Abel, 1966, pp. 35–36; see also Allison, 1971). Whatever the precise reasons, the Soviet decision to deploy long-range nuclear missiles in Cuba was apparently reached sometime in the spring of 1962. By the end of July military shipments began to arrive. Thirty-seven Soviet dry-cargo ships docked at Cuban ports during August, and some twenty of these carried arms shipments. Finally, sometime in September the first Soviet strategic offensive missiles arrived in Cuba, accompanied by missile trailers, fueling trucks, and special radar vans. During that month these shipments increased, and surface-to-air missiles (SAMs) and jet bombers capable of carrying nuclear weapons were added to the lethal cargoes. In addition, Soviet military personnel ultimately comprising some 22,000 soldiers and technicians, were dispatched to Cuba to assemble, operate, and defend these weapons.

The shipment of Soviet military equipment to Cuba was undertaken with the utmost secrecy. Few ports were used, and Cubans residing near the docks that were used were evacuated. Military shipments were landed at night and transported by trucks over specially designated routes to isolated sites for unloading. Only in late September, after the story of the military build-up had been acknowledged widely in official policy-making circles in Washington, did the Soviets choose to announce the fact.

The American intelligence community had been aware of the shipments for at least a month—that is, since the end of August. In a note to the president, the CIA reported that "something new and different" was occurring in Soviet aid operations to Cuba (Schlesinger, 1965, p. 797). On the whole, however, the intelligence community seemed convinced that the Soviets would confine their military assistance to defensive weaponry. To support their position, they pointed out that the Russians had never stationed offensive missiles outside the Soviet Union, not even in Eastern Europe, and argued that the Soviets had to recognize that the development of an offensive missile base in Cuba might induce an American military response. Moreover, on a number of occasions the Russians sought to assure Kennedy that they would take no action that might "embarrass" him before the upcoming congressional elections (Kennedy, 1971, p. 4).

On the basis of this evaluation, key administration officials found it easy to deny that the military build-up in Cuba was offensive in character. On August 24 the head of intelligence in the State Department, Roger Hilsman, in a briefing on the militarization of Cuba, assured his audience that the equipment appeared to be largely defensive. On September 4 the president asserted that there "is no evidence of the presence of offensive ground-to-ground missiles" in Cuba, although he pointed out that were "it to be otherwise, the gravest issues would arise" (Halper, 1971, p. 135). The September 19 report of the United States Intelligence Board again concluded that the Soviet Union would not introduce offensive missiles into Cuba, although it urged that the intelligence agencies "maintain a continuous alert" (Hilsman, 1967, p. 135). And as late as October 14, a day before photographic evidence was to reveal conclusively the existence of offensive missiles in Cuba, presidential advisor McGeorge Bundy claimed in a television interview that "there is no present likelihood that the . . . Cuban Government and the Soviet Government would in combination attempt to install a major offensive capability" (Abel, 1966, p. 13).

Meanwhile, a number of Republicans attempted to exploit this foreign-policy issue for electoral purposes. As Theodore Sorensen noted, "Ever since the Bay of Pigs, Cuba had been the Kennedy Administration's heaviest political cross; and the approach of the 1962 Congressional elections . . . encouraged further exacerbation of the issue" (1966, p. 754). Relying upon the reports of some Cuban refugees, as well as upon information supplied by disgruntled elements within the military and intelligence apparatus, Senators Kenneth Keating and Barry Goldwater launched a campaign in late August to force the administration to act in some manner. Criticism of the administration's policy of "inaction" continued through September. Finally, on October 10 Keating charged that six intermediate-range ballistic missiles (IRBM) bases were being constructed in Cuba (Hilsman, 1967, p. 177). Not to be outdone, other Republicans were quick to join in the attack. William Miller, chairman of the Republican National Committee, called Cuba the "symbol of the tragic irresolution of the Administration" (Halper, 1971, p. 132). The Republican Senatorial and Congressional Campaign Committees proclaimed that Cuba would be the dominant issue in the forthcoming congressional elections. And Senator Homer Capehart (Indiana) demanded that the president stop "examining the situation and start protecting the interests of the United States" (Ibid.). Condemning the inaction of the administration, these critics called for a variety of measures, such as a blockade, an invasion, or simply "action."

The administration launched a campaign of denial designed to discredit the critics' claims. On August 29 the president stated that "we cannot base the issue of war and peace on a rumor or report which is not substantiated" (Sorensen, 1966, p. 755), and he labeled as "irresponsible" calls for an invasion of Cuba. On September 4, as we have seen, Kennedy denied the provocative nature of Soviet actions in Cuba. He followed this by arguing in his September 13 press conference that the new shipments of military equipment to Cuba did not, at that point, constitute a serious threat. But he indicated, as he had previously done, that should Cuba become an offensive military base for the Soviet Union, the United States was prepared to do "whatever must be done to protect its own security and that of its allies" (Schlesinger, 1965, p. 799). And on October 13, while campaigning in Indiana, he lashed out against those "self-appointed generals and admirals who want to send someone else's sons to war" (Koenig, 1964, p. 372).

Despite persistent denials by the administration of the offensive nature of the Soviet military build-up in Cuba, Republican criticism, coupled with a growing concern in certain governmental quarters, forced the president to undertake some preventive measures. Attorney General Robert Kennedy was dispatched to meet with Soviet Ambassador Anatoly Dobrynin in order to convey the president's deep concern about the events in Cuba. Naval ships and planes photographed every Soviet vessel bound for Cuba. A series of special daily intelligence reports on the Cuban situation were initiated in late August. Moreover, as a result of the discovery on August 29 of SAM sites under construction in Cuba, the frequency of aerial reconnaissance flights over that country was doubled. Finally, in late September Congress passed a joint resolution indicating their determination to "prevent in Cuba the creation or use of an externally supported military capability endangering the security of the United States" (Halper, 1971, p. 133). Although the president had initially recommended such a resolution, he made every effort to ensure that its language was as nonprovocative as possible (see Sorensen, 1966, p. 757).

Photographic evidence from U-2 flights over Cuba provided conclusive evidence of the continuing militarization of the island. U-2 overflights on September 5, 17, 26, and 29 and October 5 and 7 gathered substantial information on SAM sites, coastal defense missile sites, MIGS, missile patrol boats, and IL-28 light bombers. Not until October 14, however, after a bureaucratic dispute between the CIA and the Defense Department had been resolved, did a U-2 flight provide conclusive photographic evidence of the existence of Soviet offensive missiles in Cuba. (For a discussion of this bureaucratic dispute, see Allison, 1971, pp. 122–23.)

On the evening of October 15, photographic and intelligence analysts from the CIA informed Bundy of their discovery. Due to the lateness of the hour, and in an effort to avoid arousing the Washington community, Bundy decided to postpone informing the president until the next day. As he explained later, "At that point the President could only have fretted; and it seemed best to give the staff a chance to get rolling and get the intelligence materials in order, for the central requirement at that time was not haste, but the development of an effective plan of action" (Hilsman, 1967, p. 194; see also Sorensen, 1966, pp. 758–59).

On the morning of October 16 the president was informed. He reacted with anger to the announcement. Viewing Soviet actions in Cuba as a betrayal, Kennedy reasoned that if "Khrushchev could pull this, after all . . . his denials, how could he ever be trusted on anything?" (Schlesinger, 1965, p. 802). He resented the fact that in spite of all his efforts to develop a mood of mutual confidence between himself and the Soviet leader, Khrushchev had evidently lied to him, and, worse, appeared to be challenging him personally.

As the president perceived the situation, Soviet missiles in Cuba represented less a military threat than a political one. Although strategic considerations could not be ignored entirely, the Soviet missiles, the president felt, posed a serious threat because they "would have politically changed the balance of power" (Halper, 1971, p. 140). A president responsive to public opinion, Kennedy was concerned that inaction by his administration in the face of this latest Soviet move might crack the "brittle surface of [his] public image and self-esteem" (*Ibid.*, p. 141). Finally, decisive action seemed called for in order to preserve the image of the United States as a great power. Failure to act forcibly, Kennedy seemed convinced, would undermine his confidence among members of his administration, weaken his reputation with Congress, stimulate public distrust, encourage dissident elements in his administration to attack all of his policies, and perhaps induce another Bay of Pigs (Allison, 1971, p. 194). From the outset, therefore, the president was determined to stand fast and act forcefully.

Kennedy instructed Bundy to arrange a meeting in which the president and a number of top officials would discuss the case, examine the evidence more closely, and explore alternatives. Included among this group were cabinet members, personal advisers, and former top governmental officials, including Dean Acheson, a former secretary of state, and John McCloy, a former high commissioner to Germany.

The group that assembled in the Cabinet Room at 11:45 A.M. on October 16 was eventually christened the Executive Committee of the National Security Council. It was composed of (1) individuals in whom the President had the utmost personal confidence and (2) government officials who occupied positions of authority in the State Department, the Defense Department, the CIA, and other agencies that had a crucial role to play in this crisis situation. No member of Congress was invited to join this group, nor was a single expert in the area of congressional relations pressed into service. Kennedy apparently felt that since Congress could neither significantly limit or aid him at this juncture, it was unnecessary to include Congress during this early phase of the crisis. Moreover, to "include some Congressmen [would have been] to exclude others," and the president perhaps believed that it was "politically less risky, at least at this stage of policy formation, to bypass this decision by excluding them all" (Halper, 1971, p. 149).

Throughout the crisis the major organ of deliberation was this Executive Committee, an ad hoc group, rather than more formally constituted executive agencies, such as the cabinet, the Joint Chiefs of Staff, or the National Security Council. The cabinet as an organ of consultation was bypassed because the president distrusted the abilities of some of its members and considered it substantially unqualified as a collective entity to offer crisis advice. Moreover, its cumbersomeness made it particularly unsuited for crisis decision making. Neglect of the Joint Chiefs stemmed largely from Kennedy's apparent distrust of the military, and more particularly from his disappointment with their role in the ill-fated Bay of Pigs episode. Finally, the National Security Council was not convened because Kennedy, along with some other members of his administration, may have been convinced that it too had become too large and cumbersome. Whatever the reason—and Halper suggests (1971, p. 148) that the president's reliance on the Executive Committee was related to his "distrust of formalism and his pervasive concern for pragmatism"—the essential elements of American strategy during the missile crisis were not developed in the constitutionally prescribed organs of government.

Ex-Com, as the Executive Committee came to be called, was to meet two and sometimes three times a day during its first week of life. The president demanded that its existence and the nature of its deliberations be carefully shielded from public view. "Any premature disclosure," he warned, "could precipitate a Soviet move, or panic the American public, before we were ready to act" (Sorensen, 1966, p. 762). Moreover, Kennedy believed that if the United States wished to prevent the initiative from slipping into the hands of the Soviets, it was essential that there be "no public disclosure of the fact that we knew of the Soviet missiles in Cuba until a course of action had been decided upon and readied" (Hilsman, 1967, p. 198). In order to avoid suspicion, Kennedy indicated his intention to carry on routine business as much as possible, and he urged his advisers to do the same.

Extraordinary steps were undertaken to ensure maximum secrecy for the meetings of Ex-Com. Secretary of State Dean Rusk recalls meeting in a variety of places in order to avoid discovery. Ex-Com members were cautioned to tell their wives and secretaries nothing. Senior officials often did their own typing and operated with virtually no staff. "Some of my own basic papers were done in my own handwriting," Rusk remembers, "in order to limit the possibility of further spread" (Abel, 1966, p. 49). The assistant secretary of state for Latin American affairs, Edwin Martin, refused to travel to the White House with other advisers for secret meetings because he feared that his presence might reveal that Cuba had once again become a principal source of concern. Martin has written, "if I had been seen entering the White House with the others, it would have clearly pointed to Cuba" as the latest subject of the Washington rumor factory (Halper, 1971, p. 150). An effort was also made to "manipulate" White House news in order to provide additional security. Throughout the entire crisis, in fact, a systematic campaign to control and manage information that emanated from the White House was carefully carried out.

Although the president attended many meetings of Ex-Com, a number of preliminary sessions were held without him. This was done in order to prevent what Arthur Schlesinger has termed (1965, p. 802) the "constraining effect" on deliberations, which the presence of the president frequently induces. Discussing this point, Robert Kennedy noted that "personalities change when the President is present, and frequently even strong men make recommendations on the basis of what they believe the President wishes to hear" (1971, p. 11).

Every effort was made to ensure free and open discussion of issues and alternatives. Everyone, according to Robert Kennedy, "had an equal opportunity to express himself and to be heard directly" (Ibid., p. 24). Distinctions of rank and status within the group were downgraded, if not eliminated: "Rank mattered little when . . . the nation's life was at stake . . . and when secrecy prevented staff support" (Sorensen, 1966, p. 765). Insofar as possible, interpersonal conflict was kept to a minimum and discussion was focused on the topic at hand. The president made every effort to ensure the widest possible airing of views, and as a means to this end he had frequent personal contact with lower-ranking advisers. Thus, "despite the pressure of time and the temptations to resolve issues simply by asserting authority, the President's eventual decision on the missiles followed a process of relatively open debate" (Halper, 1971, p. 167).

At the very first meeting of Ex-Com, a variety of alternatives were outlined and explored. Some advisers argued for an air strike, which would eliminate the missile complex before it became operational. Others claimed that an air strike, to be successful, would have to extend beyond the missile sites and would not necessarily preclude an invasion. A third group called for a naval blockade, combined with a warning and increased aerial surveillance. A fourth group favored a diplomatic approach.

On the first Tuesday morning when Ex-Com convened, October 16, it appeared that the choice was between an air strike and acquiescence. Secretary of Defense McNamara was initially a strong advocate of the "do-nothing" approach, as it later came to be called. Attempting to avoid the threat of nuclear conflict, McNamara posed the issue as a straightforward strategic problem. The Soviet missiles, in his view, made no real difference, since, as he put it, "A missile is a missile, [and] it makes no great difference whether you are killed by a missile fired from the Soviet Union or from Cuba" (Hilsman, 1967, p. 195). This position was apparently shared by McGeorge Bundy, who also initially supported some form of diplomatic approach. McNamara's argument received little support within Ex-Com, however, and in two or three days it was quietly shelved. The president himself was definitely opposed to a policy of acquiescence. From the first meeting of the committee he rejected a policy that simply assented to the Soviet actions, arguing instead that the "United States could not accept what the Russians had done" (Kennedy, 1971, p. 11).

The group supporting an air strike to remove the missile bases initially included General Maxwell Taylor, chairman of the Joint Chiefs of Staff, Paul Nitze, an assistant secretary of defense, and Secretary of the Treasury Douglas Dillon. These men, who tended to view the crisis primarily in military terms, naturally found a military solution quite attractive. By Wednesday, the views of this group were endorsed by Bundy and by former Secretary of State Dean Acheson, who ultimately became the "leader of the air-strike advocates" (Allison, 1971, p. 207).

At least initially, the idea of an air strike—a "surgical strike"—enjoyed widespread support within Ex-Com. Even Kennedy was apparently drawn to this solution at this stage (see his comments to Adlai Stevenson in Abel, 1966, p. 49). It had the virtues of speed, apparent effectiveness, and forceful action. The Joint Chiefs enthusiastically supported military action, convinced that the president lacked any other viable alternative. For the military chieftains, the missiles were a convenient pretext to pursue their real objective, the elimination of Castro's Cuba from the Western Hemisphere (Allison, 1971, p. 198).

By Wednesday, however, elements within the committee began to question the advantages of the air-strike option. Undersecretary of State George Ball was the first to argue vigorously against the air-strike idea. Then Secretary McNamara and Undersecretary of Defense Roswell Gilpatric announced their opposition to an air strike and their support for a blockade of Cuba. Finally, Robert Kennedy, who had sought from the outset of the crisis an alternative to an air attack, labeled the option a "Pearl Harbor in reverse" and claimed that "America's traditions and history would not permit such a course of action" (1971, p. 16).

The idea of a blockade had originally been proposed on Tuesday, but McNamara's announced preference on Wednesday for this form of indirect military action converted it into a formidable alternative to the air strike. McNamara became the blockade's strongest advocate, marshaling strong arguments in its behalf and fending off the objections of its leading critics. In the defense secretary's view, the blockade deserved support because it was an action of "limited pressure, which could be increased as the circumstances warranted," and because it would "still leave us in control of events" (Ibid., p. 12).

The air-strike option, the secretary argued, would prove unsuccessful for a number of reasons. First, such a step was inconsistent with either American traditions or history, and in the end it might prove harmful to American prestige throughout the world. Second, air action would foreclose many options, and obviously any nonmilitary initiatives. Third, McNamara stressed the "military impracticality" of a "surgical" air strike, a view, he noted, that was corroborated by the Joint Chiefs themselves. Finally, he warned of the likelihood of escalation should the air-strike alternative be chosen. Any such "surgical" air strike, he pointed out, "would have to include all military installations in Cuba, eventually leading to an invasion" (*Ibid.*).

By Thursday evening, according to Hilsman, a consensus within Ex-Com began to develop around the idea of a blockade. Robert Kennedy, who, according to most observers, played a leading role in the development of this consensus, aligned himself firmly with the blockade proponents, because this course of action "had more flexibility and fewer liabilities" (Kennedy, 1971, p. 15).

By this time the president was evidently becoming attracted to the blockade proposal. First, it was consistent with the basic strategic concepts of American military policy. Second, it appeared to limit the threat of escalation into a nuclear war. According to Sorensen, Kennedy felt that the blockade had "the advantage of giving Mr. Khrushchev a choice, an option [other than direct military contact]. [He] did not have to have his ships . . . stopped and searched. He could turn them around. . . . In this age of nuclear weapons, [an option] . . . is very important." (Sorensen, quoted in Halper, 1971, p. 156) Moreover, it permitted "a more controlled escalation . . . , gradual or rapid, as the situation required" (Sorensen, 1966, p. 776). The blockade, in addition, would increase the president's freedom of action, since it could be formulated and executed with the greatest precision and speed.

By Thursday evening, when the Ex-Com was convened by the president, a majority of the group expressed themselves in favor of a blockade. Initially, the blockade was to be directed against offensive weapons only, so as to insure its clear connection with the problem of the missiles. By now, the president had also shifted from the air-strike to the blockade camp, and he indicated this preference to the group.

Kennedy's abandonment of the air-strike option resulted from a number of considerations. For one thing, Robert Kennedy's persuasive case against the air strike on moral grounds struck a responsive chord in the president. The "Pearl Harbor in reverse" analogy, the president felt, was not wholly inaccurate. Second, the limited aim of the blockade—namely, the removal of the offensive missiles —and the fact that it exploited United States superiority in conventional power appealed to Kennedy (see Schlesinger, 1965, pp. 804–5). A third factor was the emergence of a powerful coalition of advisers within Ex-Com, including his brother, McNamara, and Sorensen, in "whom the President had the greatest confidence, and with whom he was personally most compatible" (Allison, 1971, pp. 203–4; see also Kennedy, 1971, p. 129). Finally, the coalition that supported the air-strike option provided President Kennedy with reason to hesitate. Composed of the Joint Chiefs, John McCone of the CIA, Nitze, and Acheson, this group did not consist of the "President's natural allies" (Allison, 1971, p. 204). Though he was to return to the question of the air strike, on Thursday evening Kennedy apparently was convinced that this was no longer a live option.

According to Hilsman, the president was waiting to make his decision final mainly because of the continued opposition of the Joint Chiefs to a blockade, and because of their preference for more direct and militant action (1967, p. 205). Nevertheless, Kennedy instructed Sorensen to begin work on a speech announcing the imposition of a blockade, or quarantine, as he preferred to call it. The State, Defense, and Justice Departments were ordered to assign their legal experts to develop the juridical grounds for a blockade proclamation.

Before leaving Washington Friday morning for previously announced campaign appearances, commitments the president met to avoid arousing suspicion, Kennedy saw the Joint Chiefs in order to hear their case once again. Although their arguments failed to convince him, Kennedy was concerned lest "more delays and dissension . . . plague whatever decision he took" (Sorensen, 1966, p. 780). He urgently requested that the attorney general and Sorensen work diligently to "pull the group together" (Allison, 1971, p. 207). Kennedy wanted to announce the quarantine to the nation on Sunday, so as to implement it by Monday. Time was obviously a significant factor.

Although the proponents of a blockade argued that a decision had been reached the night before, the air-strike advocates chose to reopen the issue at the Friday morning meeting of Ex-Com. Acheson remained adamantly opposed to the blockade, despite his personal conversation with the president on Thursday morning. Concerned about the security threat posed by the presence of missiles in Cuba, the former secretary of state urged military action before the weapons became operational. After all, he pointed out, the "nuclear weapons already there . . . were capable of killing eighty million Americans" (Allison, 1971, p. 198). He emphatically rejected the view that an air strike would compel the Soviets to respond. "That would be possible . . . , but analysis," he wrote later, "seemed to show it unlikely" (1969, p. 77). Finally, he observed, the blockade would not necessarily ensure the removal of the missiles from Cuba. Even as strong an advocate as Sorensen was forced to agree with this point (see Sorensen, 1966, pp. 775, 781).

Despite the heated debate in this Friday meeting, by the afternoon it was apparent that the air-strike advocates had lost. Acheson left Washington the next day, and attended few committee sessions during the remainder of the crisis. Robert Kennedy had apparently had the strongest impact on the group's decision to reject the air strike in favor of a blockade. His speech in which he flatly asserted that the president could not possibly support an air strike proved decisive, according to most accounts (Hilsman, 1967, p. 206). Dillon, originally a supporter of the air-strike option, has written, "What changed my mind was Bobby Kennedy's argument that we ought to be true to ourselves as Americans, that surprise attack was not in our tradition" (quoted in Abel, 1966, pp. 80–81). Other advocates of the air strike eventually transferred their support to the blockade, particularly when the "military representatives conceded that a quarantine . . . would not exclude an [air] strike later" should the blockade prove unsuccessful (Schlesinger, 1965, p. 807).

Sorensen's draft of a blockade speech to be delivered by the president was approved by Ex-Com on Saturday morning. It reflected a policy that Sorensen was to describe as "an amalgam of the blockade-air-strike routes" (1966, p. 781). Its major provisions had been discussed within the committee, and the blockade concept had been strengthened by linking it to the concept of further armed action. A blockade would first be imposed, but, as Nitze recalled, "if, after a reasonable period, we saw that the Russians were going ahead with their missile bases . . ., then we would go to an air-strike" (quoted in Abel, 1966, pp. 89–90).

A formal meeting of the National Security Council—the first of this body during the crisis—was scheduled for Saturday afternoon. By this time Kennedy had committed himself firmly to the blockade option. The arguments in behalf of the two dominant options blockade versus air strike—were presented by McNamara and Bundy, respectively. Undersecretary of Defense Gilpatric summarized the presentations by noting, "Essentially . . . this is a choice between limited action and unlimited action," and he concluded that "most of us think that it's better to start with limited action" (Allison, 1971, p. 208). According to Sorensen (1966, p. 782), the president nodded his agreement with the formula of limited action.

Before making a final decision, however, Kennedy agreed to meet once more with the Air Force Tactical Bombing Command in order to satisfy himself once again that a truly surgical air strike was not possible. The inability of the Tactical Command to guarantee that an air strike would eliminate all the missile sites and nuclear weapons in Cuba convinced the president that even though a blockade might not remove the missiles, an air attack "could not accomplish that task completely, either" (Kennedy, 1971, p. 27).

Diplomatic moves to accompany the announcement of the blockade were also discussed at the National Security Council meeting. United Nations Ambassador Stevenson urged the president to offer to withdraw American forces from the Guantanamo base in Cuba and to dismantle the Turkish and Italian missile sites, in exchange for the removal of the offensive missiles by the Russians. The president rejected both of these suggestions. At this stage, he argued, the United States could not possibly consider giving up Guantanamo. And although the Jupiter missile sites were clearly obsolete, they could not be dismantled during this crisis period, lest such an action be interpreted as a "concession under pressure." (Well before the crisis, the president had ordered the removal of these missile sites, but for a variety of reasons these orders had not been carried out. For a brief review of this decision, see Allison, 1971, pp. 141–43.) Other members of the council, including Dillon and McCone, denounced Stevenson's proposals more harshly. The thought of negotiations at this point, they believed, "would be taken as an admission of the moral weakness of our case and military weakness of our posture" (Schlesinger, 1965, pp. 810–11).

Because of these views, Stevenson was to be considered by some contemporary analysts as "wanting a Munich." In all fairness to Stevenson, however, given his position as United Nations ambassador, he was merely reflecting his preference for negotiation rather than a policy of confrontation (see Abel, 1966, pp. 95-96). In an effort to explain Kennedy's rebuff of Stevenson, it has been suggested that Kennedy sacrificed Stevenson to the "hawks" in order to allow himself to choose a more doveish alternative. Be that as it may, the "bitter aftertaste of that Saturday afternoon," notes Abel, "stayed with [Stevenson] until his death" (*Ibid.*, p. 96).

Although the president disagreed with some of Stevenson's proposals, preferring instead to concentrate on a single issue —namely, the Soviet emplacement of the missiles in Cuba and the necessity for their removal—he did support the ambassador's desire to go before the United Nations before the Russians did in order to "seize the initiative." To ensure that the American position in the United Nations would not be weakened because of Stevenson's obvious preference for a negotiated settlement, John McCloy was sent by Kennedy to assist the ambassador. Schlesinger, who was recruited to help draft the speech to be given before the United Nations, was informed by Robert Kennedy to "stand absolutely firm now." "Concessions must come at the end of negotiations," the attorney general emphasized, "not at the beginning." (Schlesinger, 1965, p. 811)

Meanwhile, Sorensen continued working on the "quarantine" speech. It was to be revised several times, in some cases by the president. Representatives of the Defense Department set about to draft a quarantine proclamation which sought to provide legal sanction for the planned naval action, and State Department officials began to organize their approach to the Organization of

American States (OAS). Despite his disagreement with the decision to implement a blockade, Acheson was pressed into service to inform De Gaulle and NATO of the intended action. The United States Information Agency prepared a special hookup with private radio stations in order to transmit the president's message in Spanish to Cuba and Latin America. Finally, a wide variety of precautionary military steps were undertaken, including the establishment and coordination of a sea and air blockade by Admiral George Anderson, Chief of Naval Operations.

The speech was scheduled for 7 P.M., Monday, October 22. That day, the president attended a series of conferences. He met with Ex-Com in the morning, and then with the National Security Council. Later, he met with his cabinet for the first time since the advent of the crisis to inform them of the events of the past week. This meeting was notably brief and included no questions or discussion. Finally, at 5 P.M. Kennedy met with a group of congressional leaders.

Up to this point, Congress had been informed neither of the events in Cuba nor of the discussions by Ex-Com. To the twenty congressional leaders of both parties, Kennedy simply described the crisis and stated his intention to impose a blockade. Although he anticipated opposition from Republicans, he evidently did not expect any disagreement by congressional Democrats. Surprisingly, Senator Richard Russell argued that a quarantine was too slow and too risky and advocated an invasion. The president was even more astonished when Senator William Fulbright, a persistent critic of Kennedy's Cuban policy since 1961, sided with Russell, contending that "since blockade could lead to a forcible confrontation with Russian ships, it was more likely to provoke a nuclear war than an invasion pitting Americans only against Cubans" (Halper, 1971, p. 171). Republican Congressman Charles Halleck indicated that although he would support the president's policy, he wanted the record to show that he had been informed, but not consulted, on its development.

Emerging from this meeting in a "smoldering rage," according to Abel, Kennedy muttered to Sorensen that "if they want this job they can have it—it's no great joy to me" (Sorensen, 1966, p. 792). Later, while discussing the meeting with Schlesinger, Kennedy was to remark, "[The] trouble is that when you get a group of Senators together they are always dominated by the man who takes the strongest . . . line. After Russell spoke, no one wanted to take issue with him." (Schlesinger, 1965, p. 812) But despite this congressional opposition to his policy, Kennedy expressed no intention of altering his decision.

From his White House study the president addressed the nation and the world to explain the situation in Cuba and the reasons for the quarantine. He began by describing American surveillance and what it had discovered. Reviewing the evidence of a Soviet build-up of offensive weapons in Cuba, and emphasizing Russian duplicity, the president carefully sought to place the blame for the crisis squarely on Russian shoulders. He accused the Soviets of deliberately upsetting a precarious strategic status quo by installing missiles in Cuba, and he asserted that such action "cannot be accepted by this country if our courage and our commitments are ever to be trusted again by either friend or foe" (quoted in Hilsman, 1967, p. 210). The United States' "unswerving objective," the president proclaimed, was to eliminate this nuclear threat. Then he proceeded to indicate what the United States planned to do.

Among other things, Kennedy talked about a quarantine on all offensive military weapons under shipment to Cuba, an intensification of air surveillance, the convening of the OAS and the United Nations Security Council to consider this threat to world peace, and a full retaliatory response upon the Soviet Union should any missile be launched from Cuba against any nation in the Western Hemisphere. Finally, he called upon Chairman Khrushchev to halt and eliminate this "clandestine, reckless and provocative threat to world peace." Throughout his address Kennedy emphasized that the quarantine was an "initial" step, which, if it failed to achieve his goals, would be followed by other, more forceful actions. (See Abel, 1966, pp. 121–23, for a brief analysis of the speech.)

The next day witnessed widespread foreign and domestic support for the President's policy from a variety of quarters. Both NATO and the OAS approved resolutions calling for the withdrawal of the missiles. The support of the OAS was very important, since in its absence the Soviets might have been encouraged to press their challenge to the legality of the quarantine. The American case in the United Nations was strengthened immeasurably when in the course of a verbal debate with Soviet Representative Valerian Zorin, Stevenson presented photographic evidence of the Soviet missiles. One African delegate, for example, buttonholed an American to announce that his government fully approved the Kennedy decision, even though it did not dare say so in public (*Ibid.*, p. 133). Congress, on the whole, flocked to the president's side. One congressman who had attended the earlier briefing session telephoned Kennedy shortly after the speech to indicate that he "now understood and supported the policy more fully" (Sorensen, 1966, p. 794).

A concerted effort was made by the administration, and especially the president, throughout the remainder of the crisis to "pace and manage events so as to give the Soviet leaders time to think out the consequences of each move" (Hilsman, 1967, p. 213). In particular, Kennedy wanted to avoid any action that "—for reasons of 'security' . . . or 'face'—would require a response by the other side, which, in turn, would . . . bring about a counterresponse and eventually an escalation into armed conflict" (Kennedy, 1971, p. 40).

Although the announcement of the quarantine had been made on Monday, it was not put into effect until Wednesday morning. The timing was intentional: it gave the Soviets forty-eight hours —the time it would take the nearest Soviet freighter to reach the quarantine line—to decide on an appropriate response. Furthermore, on Wednesday evening, over violent Navy objections, the blockade was drawn in closer to Cuba in order to give the Russians even more time. (There appears to be some disagreement over whether this order was really carried out. See Allison, 1971, p. 130.)

The president, meanwhile, made every effort to manage the critical details of the crisis himself. He was to decide what ships were to be stopped and when, how the announcements of such haltings were to be made, and what was to be said publicly and privately. Soviet ships were to be kept in view, but none was to be boarded without specific presidential orders. Thus, on Thursday the Soviet tanker *Bucharest* was permitted by presidential command to pass through the quarantine without being boarded. One high-ranking naval official undoubtedly expressed the sentiments of many when he wrote that this was a "hell of a way to run a blockade" (Allison, 1971, p. 129). It was not until Friday that a specific presidential directive was used to enforce the blockade: on that day a Lebanese freighter under Soviet charter was stopped, boarded, and, since no arms were found, allowed to proceed.

The president made every attempt to establish a clear line of communication with Khrushchev during the crisis. Private as well as public letters between the two heads of government were exchanged regularly. These were supplemented by a wide variety of other communications. (See Allison, 1971, p. 217 for a brief list.) In fact, an unofficial communication line was to figure most prominently in the development of the major elements of the subsequent settlement.

By Friday, October 26, although Kennedy now believed that Khrushchev was not exhibiting the behavior of a man who wanted war, he still considered the removal of the missiles a matter of great urgency. Although the Russians had not chosen to breach the blockade, work at the Cuban missile sites continued unabated. The missiles, Kennedy knew, would shortly be operational. At the White House it began to appear that a "choice between expansion of the blockade and some form of air action" would soon be unavoidable (*New York Times*, November 3, 1962). At the regular State Department noon briefing, the department spokesman Lincoln White underlined Kennedy's threat, initially asserted in the Monday quarantine speech, of further military action should the blockade fail to dislodge the missiles. Privately, Robert Kennedy informed Ambassador Dobrynin that the president could not postpone military action beyond the next two days.

That afternoon the first significant break in the crisis occurred. Alexander Fomin, a Soviet Embassy official who was known to be the KGB station chief in Washington, contacted John Scali, the State Department correspondent for the American Broadcasting Company, and transmitted a proposal from Khrushchev that he would withdraw the missiles from Cuba under United Nations supervision if President Kennedy would declare publicly that the United States would not invade Cuba. Scali carried the message to

Hilsman, who in turn delivered it to Rusk. After some discussion by Ex-Com, it was decided that Scali would inform Fomin that the administration saw real possibilities in the proposal but that the time needed for a negotiated settlement was rapidly running out. Scali conveyed this message, and a short time later a letter from Khrushchev arrived. (For a review of these events, see Hilsman, 1967, pp. 217–19.)

Although some analysts have described this letter as "hysterical," in Schlesinger's view "it displayed an entirely rational understanding of the implications of the crisis" (1965, p. 827). Unlike the earlier messages to Kennedy from the Soviet leader, however, this one was very emotional. It spoke of the inability of both leaders to stop the course of war, should it break out; for such, Khrushchev pointed out, is the "logic of war." It emphasized that the Soviets had no intention of provoking war. "Only lunatics or suicides, who themselves want to perish and to destroy the whole world before they die, could do this," Khrushchev said. The chairman urged the president to exercise caution and self-control in order to prevent dangerous incidents from occurring and subsequently escalating into world conflict. We "ought to be jointly concerned," the Soviet leader wrote, "with saving the peace, because war in modern conditions would be a world war, a catastrophe for mankind." Finally, the chairman noted, the necessity for a Soviet presence in Cuba would disappear if the United States would assure the Soviet Union that it would not invade Cuba and if it would recall its fleet from the quarantine. In short, since his missiles were there to defend Cuba against invasion, Khrushchev seemed prepared to withdraw them if the United States agreed not to invade. (The public text of Khrushchev's letter may be found in Abel, 1966, pp. 180–83.)

Robert Kennedy reported that he "had a slight feeling of optimism" while driving home from the State Department that evening, for "the letter . . . had the beginnings perhaps of some accommodation, some agreement" (1971, p. 68). Particularly when the letter was read in conjunction with the Fomin proposal, there seemed ample grounds for optimism.

This mood was quickly dispelled on Saturday, when a second Khrushchev message, very different in tone from the first, arrived.

It proposed that American missiles in Turkey be removed in exchange for the dismantlement of Russian missiles in Cuba. The
Soviets seemed intent on testing the will of the Americans.
McCone noted that a single Russian ship was now heading for the
quarantine line in an apparent attempt to test the American response. It was reported that work on the missile sites was being
accelerated. Some Ex-Com members began to feel that the
Khrushchev letters were being used as a means of stalling, pending
the operational capacity of the missiles. Most disconcerting of all,
however, a U-2 reconnaisance plane had been shot down over
Cuba. This showed that SAMs were now apparently operational,
and that the Soviets were not at all reluctant to use them (or at least
to agree to their use).

Since it had been decided earlier in the week to act against the
SAM sites if any U-2 were shot down, elements within Ex-Com
began to press for a retaliatory attack. Robert Kennedy noted that
"there was almost unanimous agreement that we had to attack early
the next morning . . . and destroy the SAM sites" (1971, p. 76).
The president, however, was reluctant to act until the implications
of all possible courses of action had been reviewed carefully. The
decision to take military action was therefore postponed another
day.

It was decided to follow Robert Kennedy's suggestion to "ignore [Khrushchev's] second letter, respond to the terms of the first
letter as refined by Fomin's inquiry, and propose the following: an
American pledge not to invade Cuba in return for the Soviet withdrawal of missiles in Cuba" (Allison, 1971, p. 227). Since the first
letter was obviously more favorable to American interests, this ploy
enjoyed wide support among the members of the Executive Committee. To ensure that the message was clearly understood, Robert
Kennedy delivered the note himself to Soviet Ambassador Dobrynin, along with a verbal warning. "Time [is] running out," Kennedy
told Dobrynin. "We [have] only a few more hours—[and] we need
an answer immediately from the Soviet Union." (Kennedy, 1971,
p. 87) The United States was no longer prepared to remain on
"dead center."

The president was not at all optimistic. "Saturday night,"
Schlesinger recalls "was almost the darkest of all" (1965, p. 830).

The Ex-Com was preparing itself for the momentous decisions to be made on Sunday. Finally, early Sunday morning Chairman Khrushchev relented. He indicated that work on the missile sites would stop, that the missiles described as "offensive" would be crated and returned to the Soviet Union, and that he would undertake negotiations at the United Nations immediately to bring about a final liquidation of the crisis. Analysts offer varying explanations for the Soviet decision to remove the missiles. Although some reasons are more plausible than others, most observers agree that the blockade, by itself, did not compel the Russians to withdraw their missiles from Cuba. The blockade may have prevented the Russians from delivering further military shipments, but it did not force them to remove the missiles already there. Rather, Khrushchev's decision was a response to an explicit threat of an air strike or invasion. As Hilsman noted, "The Soviets backed down in the face of a threat that combined both conventional and nuclear power" (1967, p. 227).

The decision-making process in the Cuban missile crisis reveals features which may characterize all crisis decision making. First, the major elements of strategy were not developed in the regular organs of government. As collective entities, the cabinet, the Joint Chiefs, and the National Security Council, were not involved in the deliberations. Rather, policy was developed in an ad hoc group that was set up by the president especially for the occasion. And although the major policy decisions obviously passed through the president's hands, they were not simply *his* decisions. Rather, both "the definition of the issue and the choice of the U.S. response emerged from deliberations of the group" (Kennedy, 1971, p. 121).

Second, the role of Congress in the entire affair was marginal. As our account has shown, Congress was ignorant of the Soviet missiles in Cuba during the first week of Ex-Com deliberations, and no member of Congress was invited to this first week of meetings. Nor was any member of Congress deeply involved in decisions that were made during the following week. Moreover, despite the opposition of some congressmen to the blockade decision when they were informed of it, the president chose to ignore their advice.

Third, the weight of public opinion in shaping decisions was negligible during the crisis period. Lacking information beyond that which the administration was willing to offer, the American people often appeared unusually confused and uninformed. The administration made every effort, however, to exploit public opinion in its behalf. The president, by emphasizing the serious threat posed by the Cuban missiles to the United States, was able to "structure opinion rather than merely respond to it" (Dolbeare and Edelman, 1971, p. 294). The administration was also generally successful in preventing the disclosure of information that they sought to conceal from the public. Thus, although James Reston of the *New York Times* knew about the missiles by Saturday, the president was able to prevail upon his editor to delay the story until after the White House announcement on Monday (Sorensen, 1966, pp. 786–87).

Finally, Kennedy made every effort to keep the specific decisions and the control over their implementation in his own hands. He determined what ships were to be boarded, and under what circumstances. He determined the level of military action to be used in the anticipated boardings. He opened up channels of communication with the Soviet leader, and he negotiated the final terms of the settlement that ended the crisis. In short, in this particular crisis "the many arms of the American government and all their multiple activities were directed through a single mind" (Hilsman, 1967, p. 214). All of these features suggest that the decision-making process in this case came very close to what many consider the ideal, "rational" model of foreign-policy making.

REFERENCES AND BIBLIOGRAPHY

ABEL, ELIE, *The Missile Crisis.* Philadelphia: Lippincott, 1966.

ACHESON, DEAN, "Dean Acheson's Version of Robert Kennedy's Version of the Cuban Missile Affair," *Esquire*, February, 1969.

ALLISON, GRAHAM T., *Essence of Decision: Explaining the Missile Crisis.* Boston: Little, Brown, 1971.

BELL, CORAL, *The Conventions of Crisis.* New York: Oxford University Press, 1971.

DOLBEARE, KENNETH M., and MURRAY J. EDELMAN, *American Politics: Policies, Power and Change.* Lexington, Mass.: Heath, 1971.

HALPER, THOMAS, *Foreign Policy Crisis: Appearance and Reality in Decision Making.* Columbus, Ohio: Charles E. Merrill, 1971.

HILSMAN, ROGER, *To Move a Nation.* Garden City, N.Y.: Doubleday, 1967.

KENNEDY, ROBERT, *Thirteen Days.* New York: Norton, 1971.

KOENIG, LOUIS W., *The Chief Executive.* New York: Harcourt, Brace & World, 1964.

SCHLESINGER, ARTHUR, *A Thousand Days.* Boston: Houghton Mifflin, 1965.

SORENSEN, THEORDORE, *Kennedy.* New York: Bantam, 1966.

STONE, I. F., "The Brink," *New York Review of Books,* April 14, 1966. pp. 12–16.

WEINTAL, EDWARD and CHARLES BARTLETT, *Facing the Brink.* New York: Scribner's, 1967.

The Nuclear Test Ban Treaty
1963

Like the Cuban missile crisis, the Nuclear Test Ban Treaty which outlawed nuclear testing in the atmosphere, under water, or in outer space, was motivated by a concern over the dangers posed by the widespread development and availability of nuclear weaponry. Unlike the Cuban crisis however, this concern translated itself into a coordinated, comprehensive and long-range effort to curb the arms race, to limit the testing of nuclear weapons, and to achieve a measure of security through cooperation. For our purposes, it is useful to divide the decision-making process leading to the Nuclear Test Ban Treaty into two major phases: drafting and ratification. Although the drafting of the treaty raised some political issues, the principal questions in this phase were military, scientific and technical. By contrast, the ratification process generated a number of significant and hotly-disputed political issues. As a result, we chose in our analysis to focus primarily on an examination of the process of ratification.

During the five years from 1958 to 1963, the United States and the Soviet Union discussed the issues of arms control and disarmament in a variety of forums such as the formal setting of the United Nations or in Geneva at the meetings of the Eighteen-Nation Disarmament Committee, or informally through the transmission of letters or messages between heads of state.

Throughout the Eisenhower administration these initiatives, whether undertaken through formal contacts or informal routes, had for the most part produced little progress. Thus, when the Kennedy administration assumed power on January 20, 1961, American policy in test ban negotiations seemed to have become fruitless. Talks in Geneva were clearly deadlocked, and the United States disarmament policy in the United Nations, appeared to be commanding little sympathy or support (Jacobson and Stein, 1966).

During his campaign for the presidency, Kennedy had been sharply critical of Eisenhower's policy on disarmament and arms control, declaring it to be inconsistent and lacking in direction. "The most gaping hole in American foreign policy," he declared to a student audience at the University of New Hampshire, "is our lack of a concrete plan of disarmament" (For complete speech, see *Congressional Record*, 1963, pp. 4707–10). As president, Kennedy sought to develop such a plan. Shortly before his inauguration he appointed John J. McCloy, a prominent Republican who had served in a variety of governmental posts since 1945, his personal advisor on disarmament and arms control. The appointment of such an advisor appeared to demonstrate that the president considered these matters both serious and urgent. Next, McGeorge Bundy was appointed Special Assistant for National Security. Bundy had been an active participant in the Harvard-MIT seminar group that had been established in 1959 to study the problems involved in securing an acceptable test ban treaty. Jerome Wiesner, a former director of the Electronic Laboratory at MIT and a well-known critic of past American disarmament and arms control policies, was appointed science advisor to the president. It was apparent, therefore, that Kennedy intended to reappraise the nature and direction of American policy regarding disarmament and arms control, and his new appointees were to play a leading role in this task.

The Kennedy administration's early efforts proved fruitless, however. The Soviets continued to object to the American position that "international inspection and control systems" had to be treated as "vital parts of any disarmament agreement" (Lepper, 1971, p. 40). Although little progress was achieved, talks with the Soviet Union continued between March and August, 1961. Meanwhile, pressure mounted within the United States for a resumption of testing, which had been suspended since 1958. On August 30 Moscow radio announced the Soviet decision to resume the testing of nuclear weapons. Minimizing the importance of the test ban as a sole measure of arms control, and citing the French nuclear tests and the tensions surrounding the Berlin problem as the reasons for the Soviet resumption of nuclear testing, the Soviet Union tested its first nuclear device of the new series on September 1, 1961.

The United States responded quickly by issuing a statement condemning the Soviet actions. Although some of his advisors urged him to announce immediately America's intention to resume testing, Kennedy was reluctant to do "anything that might deflect the opprobrium of public opinion from the Soviet deed" (Jacobson and Stein, 1966, p. 281). On September 3 the United States and Great Britain proposed to the Soviet Union an agreement aimed at preventing nuclear testing in the atmosphere. When this proposal was quickly rejected by the Soviets, Kennedy announced his decision to resume nuclear testing underground, as well as through laboratory experiments. And on April 24, 1962 he indicated that the United States would conduct a series of atmospheric tests. Even then, he stressed that "our ultimate objective is not to test for the sake of testing. Our real objective is to make our own tests unnecessary, to prevent others from testing, to prevent the nuclear arms race from mushrooming out of control, to take the first steps toward general and complete disarmament . . . " (quoted in Lepper, 1971, p. 41).

Although the testing of nuclear weapons had been resumed by the two major powers, discussions continued at Geneva until

January, 1962. Then, between January and July, Kennedy and British Prime Minister Macmillan exchanged thoughts about the idea of a test ban and the form and timing of a new approach to Moscow. By the end of July, an ad hoc committee under the sponsorship of the newly created Arms Control and Disarmament Agency, proposed that the United States present a simplified treaty banning nuclear weapons tests in the atmosphere, and also in outer space and under water. Such a treaty would not require control posts or on-site inspections on Soviet territory. The committee also offered alternatives, including a modified comprehensive treaty that would bar testing in all environments, including the underground.

On August 27 the United States introduced these proposals in treaty form at Geneva. The Soviet Union responded negatively to both of these treaties. It accused the United States of seeking to mislead world opinion. The limited test ban, the Soviets noted, was inadequate because it "legalized" underground nuclear tests, did not impede the proliferation of nuclear weapons, and imposed no brake on weapons development. The Soviets argued that a partial ban would, despite Western claims to the contrary, "be likely to increase the threat of nuclear war" rather than reduce it, because it "would lead to an intensification of the arms race" (Jacobson and Stein, 1966, p. 414).

Despite this not unanticipated reaction by the Soviets, discussions continued within American governmental circles, both at the staff level and within a specially constituted interagency group called the Committee of Principals. Beginning in the early fall of 1962, a subcommittee drawn from this group "was told to examine all possible alternatives—complete ban, partial ban, or no ban —with a view to presenting a detailed plan in each case" (Lepper, 1971, p. 43). Throughout the remainder of 1962, however, little progress was made.

By December there were signs of a softening in the Soviet position on a test ban. At the Eighteen-Nation Disarmament Committee, which had reconvened in November, the USSR proposed that "control over underground nuclear explosions could be established through the use of automatic seismic recording stations in the territory of the nuclear powers and in adjacent countries"

(Jacobson and Stein, 1966, p. 428). This proposal was followed by a letter on December 19 from Khrushchev to Kennedy dealing exclusively with the nuclear test ban issue. "It seems to me, Mr. President," Khrushchev wrote, "that the time has come now to put an end once and for all to nuclear tests, to draw a line through such tests" (quoted in Schlesinger, 1965, p. 895). Although Khrushchev questioned the need for on-site inspections, he indicated the willingness of the Soviet Union to permit two or three such inspections to be carried out each year in order, the Soviet premier noted, to help the president obtain congressional support for the agreement to suspend tests.

Kennedy, though gratified at the Soviet initiative, was dissatisfied with those portions of the message dealing with inspections. In his response of December 28, Kennedy stated that three inspections were clearly inadequate but that despite these differences he was "encouraged," and he urged Khrushchev to agree to technical discussions between the two governments. These meetings of experts opened in January, 1963. Although they too produced little progress, and led to considerable partisan domestic sniping by the Republicans, Kennedy continued to pursue his plan for a nuclear test ban agreement. In March and April, he and Macmillan sought to develop new ways to approach Khrushchev. But the Soviet premier remained unmoved by these efforts. To *Saturday Review* editor Norman Cousins Khrushchev revealed that he "felt betrayed by the Western powers, since he thought that they would accept his offer of three on-site inspections annually. He could not ask that the USSR make still one more concession to the West, since he had asserted that the first would be sufficient" (Jacobson and Stein, 1966, p. 433).

On April 24 the British and American ambassadors to Moscow conferred with Khrushchev in an effort to break the impasse in negotiations. The ambassadors delivered Khrushchev a letter penned jointly by Macmillan and Kennedy in which the two leaders indicated their readiness "to send to Moscow very senior representatives empowered to speak for them directly with Khrushchev" (Schlesinger, 1965, p. 898). This note touched off another round of correspondence between the heads of government in May and June.

In late May Senator Thomas Dodd of Connecticut, along with thirty-three other senators, urged the Senate to approve a resolution calling upon the United States to "offer the Soviet Union an immediate agreement banning all tests that contaminate the atmosphere or the oceans," since such tests could be detected without on-site inspection (*Congressional Record*, 1963, pp. 9483–85). At the same time, Dodd indicated the skepticism shared by a number of senators concerning the feasibility and advantages of a comprehensive test ban. This doubt appeared to confirm a view expressed earlier by Senator William Proxmire that "it was unlikely that the Senate would ratify the comprehensive treaty [then] being proposed by the Administration" (Jacobson and Stein, 1966, p. 448).

By the end of May, Soviet intransigence was beginning to concern the president greatly. The Geneva discussions were stalemated. Khrushchev appeared unwilling to moderate his position. "I am not hopeful," Kennedy said in May, 1963; "if we don't get an agreement this year . . . I would think [that] the genie is out of the bottle and we will not ever get him back in again" (Sorensen, 1966, p. 822). Despite this growing pessimism, Kennedy persisted in his effort to obtain an agreement with the Soviets. He joined Macmillan in proposing new talks on the test ban treaty by new high-level emissaries. He decided, once the then current series of nuclear tests were concluded, to suspend nuclear testing in order to reduce tensions further. And on June 10 he delivered a major foreign-policy address on the cold war.

In that speech, described by Sorensen as an effort to reach "beyond the cold war" (1966, p. 822), Kennedy sought to redefine and reassess the whole national attitude toward the cold war. He began by defining the American concept of peace. "[It is] not," he asserted, "a Pax Americana enforced on the world by American weapons of war. [Neither is it] the peace of the grave or the security of the slave. I am talking about genuine peace, the kind of peace that makes life on earth worth living. . . ." (*Ibid.*) He pointed to the mutuality of interests shared by the United States and the Soviet Union, and in particular their mutual abhorrence of war. He disputed the thesis of those who argued that war is inevitable. "We need not accept that view," he maintained. "Our problems are man made—therefore, they can be solved by man." (*Ibid.*) He urged a fresh start on discussions of problems of common concern, and he pointed specifically to the question of a nuclear test ban treaty as a fruitful area for negotiations. Then he announced that he, Prime Minister Macmillan, and Chairman Khrushchev had agreed to initiate high-level discussions that would begin shortly in Moscow on a nuclear test ban treaty.

The speech was generally received favorably by the media, and interest groups favoring a test ban warmly welcomed it. The *New York Times* gave the speech major coverage. The European press was even more enthusiastic. Britain's *Manchester Guardian*, for example, called the address "one of the great state papers of American history" (*Ibid.*, p. 825), and an editorial in the prestigious London *Times* noted that "the broad foundations of President Kennedy's speech should have done something to reduce the suspicion which has so far inhibited agreement" (Lepper, 1971, p. 80).

On June 12 Kennedy announced that Averell Harriman, former ambassador to Moscow and then undersecretary of state for political affairs, would head the American delegation to Moscow. Harriman was appointed by the president because of his considerable skill and experience in dealing with the Russians, and because his appointment as head of the negotiating team in Moscow would fulfill Kennedy's agreement with Congress that discussions with the Soviets on a test ban would be undertaken by the Department of State rather than by the newly created Arms Control and Disarmament Agency. The staff chosen to accompany Harriman was "small and brilliant" (Schlesinger, 1965, p. 905). It included most of the key individuals working on disarmament problems within the Kennedy administration: Carl Kaysen (White House staff), John McNaughton (Defense Department), William Tyler (State Department), and Adrian Fisher (Arms Control and Disarmament Agency). No professional military men were included in the negotiating group.

The mandate given the Harriman group was broad and without specific guidelines. Before their departure Kennedy informed them of the gravity of their mission, of the necessity to keep him regularly apprised of their activities, and of the need to "prevent their prospects of success from being ruined by any premature leak of their position" (Sorensen, 1966, p. 827). The overall direction of the negotiations, however, was to remain in his hands. Throughout the meetings in Moscow, for example, Kennedy insisted that all communications to the Harriman group be cleared through him.

In East Berlin on July 2, Khrushchev responded to the president's speech of June 10. Most of his address consisted of an analysis of past negotiations on arms control and disarmament. Although Khrushchev reverted to the traditional Soviet opposition to on-site inspections, his call for the conclusion of an agreement banning nuclear tests in the atmosphere, in outer space, and under water was encouraging. For the first time, the Soviets had apparently abandoned their former position that a moratorium on underground tests accompany a partial ban. In the past this had been a major stumbling block to a partial test ban agreement.

On July 15 negotiations between the three nuclear powers opened in Moscow. By July 25 the discussions had been concluded, and a "Treaty Banning Nuclear Weapons Tests in the Atmosphere, in Outer Space and Under Water" was initialed. The treaty prohibited any signatory state from carrying out any type of nuclear explosion in the atmosphere, in outer space, or under water. The parties to the treaty would not conduct any nuclear explosion in any environment if such testing would scatter radioactive debris beyond the territorial confines of the testing state. The treaty was to be open to all states for signature. Finally, it would be possible for instruments of ratification and instruments of accession to be deposited with any of the three original parties. This provision was inserted in order to obviate the problems of diplomatic recognition and, in particular, to prevent the United States from indirectly extending recognition to such states as Communist China and East Germany, were they to decide to sign the pact.

Even before the treaty was initialed in Moscow, administration forces were organizing for the struggle to obtain senatorial approval. Kennedy regarded the test ban treaty as the most serious congressional issue he had faced since his inauguration, and he was "determined to win if it cost him the 1964 election" (Schlesinger, 1965, p. 910).

On July 26, the day after the initialing of the treaty in Moscow, Kennedy appeared before the nation to plead for prompt senatorial ratification of the treaty. He sought to place the treaty in its proper perspective and to recognize its limitations. He was aware, he noted, of the risks involved in the treaty, but he observed that "such risks in this treaty are small," particularly beside the "far greater risks [to] our security [from] unrestricted testing, . . . a nuclear arms race, . . . nuclear pollution and nuclear war" (see Lepper, 1971, p. 136). He concluded by urging the public to support him in what he called the "first step" toward peace.

Less than two weeks after his July 26 address, Kennedy sent a strongly worded message to the Senate officially requesting ratification of the treaty. The administration carefully planned the presentation of the pact to the Senate. Witnesses were carefully screened before selection. Efforts were made to schedule the presentation of testimony so as to strengthen the administration's case. Thus, the congressional testimony of the Joint Chiefs of Staff, who were skeptical about the treaty, was delayed purposely until friendlier witnesses, such as Secretary of Defense Robert McNamara and General Maxwell Taylor, had had a chance to present their views (see Sorensen, 1966, p. 832). Futhermore, an interagency group was established to maintain contact with individual senators.

Seeking to obtain the broadest possible support from the Senate, the president exploited every opportunity to emphasize his concern and hope for prompt, favorable Senate action. He worked directly and indirectly through unofficial as well as official channels. At every press conference he urged approval of the pact. Whenever he could, Kennedy spoke individually with uncommitted or wavering senators. He encouraged the creation of a private "Citizens' Committee for a Nuclear Test Ban," a bipartisan group of prominent civic, industrial, educational, and labor leaders whose function was to mobilize support for the treaty. In off-the-record meetings, Kennedy "advised [this group] which Senators should hear from their constituents, approved their newspaper and TV advertisements, counseled them on their approach to the unconvinced, and suggested particular business and other leaders for them to contact" (Sorensen, 1966, p. 833).

When the treaty ran into rough waters before the Senate Armed Services Preparedness Investigating Subcommittee, Kennedy sent letters of assurance to Senators Mike Mansfield and

Everett Dirksen, the majority and minority leaders of the Senate, respectively, informing them that "the Administration was willing to abide by certain safeguards which he hoped would allay the fears of the Senators" (Lepper, 1971, p. 85). One leading opponent, Senator Henry Jackson, announced his support of the treaty shortly after being informed of the president's assurances. According to Mary Lepper "Senator Jackson's shift . . . made it possible for the treaty to pass with the large margin registered" (*Ibid.*).

Congressional discussion of the measure was more than ample. On August 8 the Nuclear Test Ban Treaty was referred to the Senate Committee on Foreign Relations for study. The hearings, at which the Committee on Armed Services and the Joint Committee on Atomic Energy were also represented, began on August 12 and continued for eleven days. Forty-four witnesses were invited to testify. In addition, the Joint Committee on Atomic Energy had earlier heard testimony on the scientific and technical problems related to a test ban. Meanwhile the Senate Preparedness Investigating Subcommittee of the Armed Services Committee also held closed hearings, in some cases concurrently with the hearings before the Foreign Relations Committee.

A debate on the benefits and disadvantages of a partial test ban had been conducted periodically on the Senate floor throughout 1963. In March and again in May, for example, a wide variety of opinions were expressed by Senators Hubert Humphrey, Craig Hosmer, Joseph Clark, William Proxmire, and Thomas Dodd on the merits and drawbacks of a test ban treaty (see *Congressional Record*, 1963, pp. 3663, 4614–26).

Though speaking in support of ratification, administration witnesses appear to have been quite candid in their evaluation of the treaty. As Secretary of State Dean Rusk observed on the first day of the hearings, "This is a limited treaty. The President [is aware of] the things it does not do, and we must keep them in mind in judging its significance" (U.S. Senate, 1963, p. 19). Secretary of Defense Robert McNamara sought to assess the risk of clandestine Soviet testing, the possibility of a surprise abrogation of the treaty, and the impact of the treaty on the proliferation of nuclear weapons. He argued that the Soviets would be unable to test secretly "without incurring a high risk of detection and a high risk of identification" (*Ibid.*, p. 105). He pointed out that as long as the United States maintained the vitality of its weapons laboratories and the logistic capability to undertake tests in any environment, "surprise abrogation does not pose a serious threat to our national security" (*Ibid.*, p. 107). And he noted that the treaty would have the "effect of retarding the spread of nuclear weapons" (*Ibid.*, p. 108). On balance, the secretary concluded, "the risks under the treaty are either small or under our control, and the values of the treaty are substantial. . . . The scales are clearly tipped in favor of the treaty." (*Ibid.*, p. 109.)

Other administration witnesses defended the treaty in like manner. The support of the Joint Chiefs of Staff, particularly that of U.S. Air Force Chief Curtis LeMay, was far from enthusiastic, however. Arguing that the decision of the Joint Chiefs to approve the treaty had been based on political factors and not exclusively on military grounds, LeMay noted that he probably would have opposed the treaty if it had not already been initialed (*Ibid.*, p. 372). LeMay also observed that he was far more pessimistic about the treaty than his colleagues (*Ibid.*, p. 355).

Kennedy was, of course, aware that ratification would be impossible without the support of the Joint Chiefs of Staff. He therefore reassured them that all the safeguards they desired, including a vigorous continuation of underground testing, a readiness to resume atmospheric testing on short notice, the strengthening of detection capabilities, and the maintenance of nuclear laboratories, would be provided. As Schlesinger notes, "the President was prepared to pay this price to commit the nation to a treaty outlawing atmospheric tests" (1965, p. 913).

Despite Kennedy's efforts to blunt the arguments of the test ban's opponents, there remained considerable opposition in some quarters to the partial test ban treaty. Elements within the military were hesitant about certain aspects of the treaty. Major General A. W. Betts of the army, for example, in testimony before the Senate Preparedness Investigating Subcommittee, asserted that a test ban of the sort proposed was clearly not in the national interest. Atmospheric testing, he argued, was necessary in order to protect American security (U.S. Senate, 1964, p. 241). General Thomas Power was even more blunt, stating categorically that he was opposed to the treaty, which he judged not to be in the interests of the United States (*Ibid.*, p. 779). Of the nine commanding officers in the field, however, seven favored the treaty.

Although the scientific community as a whole supported the treaty, there were some notable dissenters, the most significant of whom was physicist Edward Teller. A member of what Lepper calls the "infinite containment school," Teller "believed that the nuclear arms race would necessarily continue and that there would be no control of the arms race until the underlying political differences were settled" (1971, p. 58). Teller believed, therefore, that the development of new weapons should continue unabated. In masterful testimony before the Senate Foreign Relations Committee, Teller expressed his opposition to the treaty, claiming that it was "a step not toward peace but rather a step away from safety, possibly a step toward war" (U.S. Senate, 1963, p. 418). The treaty, he noted further, would "not have the direct effect of slowing down the development of aggressive weapons. What it [would] do is prohibit [the United States] from acquiring the knowledge about effects of weapons, those effects which are of vital importance in ballistic missile defense." (*Ibid.*, p. 422)· He therefore urged the United States to "immediately bend every effort to prepare the needed atmospheric tests . . . and [to] continue to make them until [it] has the information that [it] needs" (*Ibid.*, p. 430).

Teller's arguments clearly impressed the senators. According to one committee staff member, however, an article by Mary McGrory of the *Washington Star*—in which she claimed that Teller's testimony had "mesmerized" the senators—appears to have lessened the impact of his presentation considerably. Moreover, Dr. George Kistiakowsky's identification of Teller's "extraordinarily single-minded . . . devotion to one project, namely, bigger and better nuclear weapons, and specifically the H-bomb," served to stiffen Senate resistance to Teller's case (*Ibid.*, pp. 860–61).

A substantial proportion of the scientific community not only supported the treaty but sought to mobilize support for it. Scientists were frequently asked by the administration to supply technical assistance in the preparation of arguments to be presented to the Joint Chiefs of Staff. In magazines with a wide circulation, they published essays supporting the treaty, and bringing the debate concerning the issue to public attention. And on September 16, during the Senate debate on the treaty, fifty-two scientists sponsored a full-page advertisement in the *New York Herald Tribune* and the *Washington Star* calling for a favorable vote (Lepper, 1971, p. 60).

Opposition to the treaty was expressed by Republican forces, although the issue was certainly not a partisan one. Even while the negotiations were underway in Moscow, some Republicans were quick to state their disenchantment with Kennedy's "fuzzy-thinking disarmament advisors" (Sorensen, 1966, p. 829). The president was concerned that "enough Southern Democrats might combine with Republicans to prevent the necessary two-thirds vote, required for ratification" (*Ibid.*, p. 830). The final vote, which approved the treaty, revealed that Kennedy's assessment of the situation was not far off the mark: eleven of the nineteen senators who voted against ratification were Democrats, and eight were Republicans. All of the Democrats except Frank Lausche of Ohio were Southerners.

On this issue, as in most matters of foreign policy, public opinion played at best a marginal role. Some significance, however, must be attributed to a major shift in public opinion in favor of the idea of a test ban that occurred between June and September, 1963. (Table 3 on p. 172 and Figure 1 on page 173 display the results of diverse surveys conducted on the issue of nuclear test cessation between 1954 and 1963. Special attention should be paid to the responses between January 1962 and August 1963.)

Specifically, a July Louis Harris Poll revealed that 47 percent of those interviewed gave unqualified approval to the test ban negotiations about to begin; 20 percent expressed qualified approval; 17 percent expressed qualified disapproval; 17 percent opposed the negotiations; and 10 percent were not sure. But by September 1, 1963 a Harris Poll found that 81 percent of the respondents approved of the test ban treaty, and only 8 percent disapproved; the balance gave the treaty their qualified approval. Crucial to this shift in public opinion were the efforts of the Kennedy administration to mobilize support for the test ban treaty. President Kennedy —whose skill at exploiting the mass media was, according to some observers, unmatched by any of his predecessors except perhaps

Franklin Roosevelt—took a leading role in this campaign. In press conferences, in private meetings with the press, and in public statements he emphasized the importance of the treaty and appealed openly for broad public support.

In addition to the administration's efforts, the activities of concerned interest groups undoubtedly contributed to the growth of public support between June and September. Among the most active of these groups were the Friends Committee on National Legislation, the United World Federalists, and the Committee for a Sane Nuclear Policy. But the most significant burden in this task was assumed by the Citizens' Committee for a Nuclear Test Ban. Hiring an advertising agency to help prepare and coordinate mass media materials, the Citizens' Committee diligently "set about attempting to create a favorable domestic political climate for the negotiation [and] subsequent approval . . . of such a treaty" (Lepper, 1971, p. 62).

The activities of the interest groups favoring a test ban treaty were not confined solely to the mobilization of mass public opinion. These groups also sought to affect the attitudes and opinions of key elements of the policy-making community. Under the umbrella organization of the Citizens' Committee, each of the major interest groups with an interest in the ratification of the test ban treaty, such as the United World Federalists and the Friends Committee, sought to maintain contact with favorably disposed senators, organize letter-writing campaigns to wavering congressmen, sponsor advertisements in local newspapers, and help draft speeches for supporting congressmen. Running tallies of the anticipated votes by senators were kept by the Friends Committee and "were made available to those persons who were responsible for contacting the Senators to urge a favorable vote on the treaty" (*Ibid.*, p. 63). Speeches by administration officials and congressmen who strongly endorsed the treaty were distributed widely within the policy-making community. The campaigns undertaken by these interest groups were to have a considerable impact. According to some observers, the success of all these efforts was reflected in the final, lopsided vote for ratification by the Senate.

Efforts by interest groups opposed to the treaty were neither as effective nor as well organized as those of the treaty's proponents. Only a few organized interest groups, such as the Air Force

The Politics of American Foreign Policy: The Social Context of Decisions

TABLE 3   National Opinion on Test Cessation, 1954–63 (in percent)

Date	Unilateral American[a]				Multilateral[b]			
	For	Against	DK	(N)	For	Against	DK	(N)
4/6/54[c]	21	72	7	(1,435)				
1/21/55[d]	11	84	5	(1,209)				
3/11/55[d,e]	15	80	5	(1,225)	65	28	7	(1,225)
1/26/56[d,e]	12	83	5	(1,238)	62	29	9	(1,238)
10/16/56[c]	28	53	19	(1,049)				
11/15/56[d]					42	52	6	(1,286)
4/23/57[c]					64	28	8	(1,602)
6/25/57[c]					64	22	14	(1,515)
7/16/57[c,f]								
1/22/58[c]					49	36	15	(1,543)
4/14/58[c]	28	61	11	(1,433)				

Date	For	Against	DK	(N)
11/10/59[c,g]	77	10	13	(1,636)
6/21/61[c,h]	27	53	27	(1,625)
11/15/61[c,i]	44	42	14	(1,523)
1/9/62[c,i]	45	45	10	(1,618)
3/6/62[c,i]	25	67	8	(1,600)
8/13/63[c,j]	61	18	21	(1,246)

[a]Most questions asked something like "Should the United States stop nuclear (atomic hydrogen bomb) tests?" or "continue tests?"
[b]Most questions asked something like the phrase in footnote a, but added, "if all other nations, including Russia, stop."
[c]Date sent out by the American Institute of Public Opinion (AIPO).
[d]Date sent out by the National Opinion Research Center (NORC).
[e]This question first asked if the United States should continue tests, then asked those who wished tests to continue if they favored an agreement by all countries, including the United States and Russia, to stop tests. The total in favor of the multilateral ban here includes those who stated their approval first of unilateral American cessation, the assumption being that they would also approve of an agreement.
[f]This ambiguous question did not specify multilateral or unilateral cessation; the results: 40 percent for (5 percent qualified); 43 percent against (3 percent qualified); 17 percent DK.
[g]The testing moratorium was misleadingly called an "agreement" in this question.
[h]". . . should the U.S. resume tests at this time?"; responses reversed.

i". . . U.S. should or should not start tests in the atmosphere"; responses reversed.
jThose who heard or read about "the agreement with Russia to have a partial ban on the testing of nuclear weapons" (78 percent of the sample) were asked, "Do you think the Senate should vote approval of this ban or not?"
Source: From Eugene J. Rosi, "Public Opinion and National Security Policy: The Nuclear Testing Debate," in Rosi, ed., American Defense and Detente, Dodd, Mead, 1973, p. 369. By permission of Harper & Row, Publishers, Inc.

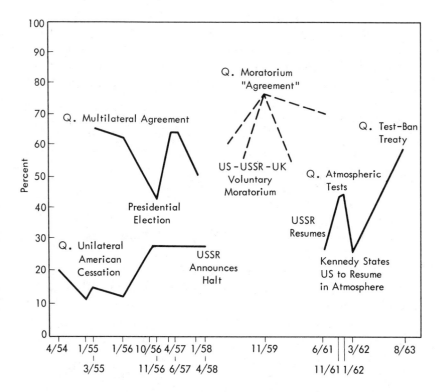

Figure 1.   Proportions of national samples approving test cessation, 1954–63. Based on AIPO and NORC surveys. For the complete data, see Table 3. Responses to "resumption" questions in 1961-62 have been reversed.
Source: From Eugene J. Rosi, "Public Opinion and National Security Policy: The Nuclear Testing Debate" in Rosi, ed., American Defense and Detente, Dodd, Mead, 1973, p. 368. By permission of Harper & Row, Publishers, Inc.

Association,[1] the Liberty Lobby, the Americans for National Security, and the Young Americans for Freedom, publicized their opposition, and apparently no effort was made to coordinate their activities. Two of the organizations, the Americans for National Security and the Young Americans for Freedom, chose to testify before the Senate Foreign Relations Committee, but the testimony of the latter was considerably vitiated by what appeared to be a clear case of faulty and inadequate preparation by its witness (see U.S. Senate, 1963, p. 715).

On August 27 public hearings on the treaty were concluded. These were followed by hearings in executive session, and on September 3 the Committee on Foreign Relations filed its report on the Moscow treaty. By a vote of sixteen to one, the committee recommended that the Senate give its advice and consent to ratification.

Floor debate opened on September 9. The administration followed the debate closely, for ratification was by no means assured at this point. Kennedy maintained close contact with developments on the floor and with key senators. Senator Fulbright assumed the management of the debate, and Senator Humphrey was always available to assist when needed. The debate was far from perfunctory. Significant speeches supporting the treaty were offered by Senators Dirksen, Kuchel, and Humphrey (Congressional Record, 1963, pp. 16788–91, 16884–95). Some senators announced their enthusiastic and unqualified support of the treaty, but others endorsed the treaty in more guarded tones. Senator Jackson noted that he "would vote for the treaty not with enthusiasm but because the alternative of refusal was less acceptable" (quoted in Lepper, 1971, p. 110). Some senators seemed to feel that there was little need to justify their position in support of the treaty. Others sought to defend their preference with carefully constructed arguments. And some alluded to the extraordinary difficulty of making a choice. Notable in this regard was Senator Margaret Chase Smith's explanation for deciding to cast what she called "a very troubled vote against the treaty" (Ibid., pp. 17831–32). Finally, on Sep-

---

[1]This organization is composed of officers, active and retired, and defense contractors. The major result of their stand was the shunning of their annual dinner by the administration (Sorensen, 1966, p. 832).

tember 24 the Senate approved the test ban treaty by a vote of eighty to nineteen.

In virtually every stage in the history of the Nuclear Test Ban Treaty—whether in its drafting, the negotiation phase, or the ratification period—the role of the president is readily apparent. Virtually from the outset of his administration, Kennedy had demonstrated a major interest in the area of disarmament and arms control. Sparked by the president's interest, a wide-ranging debate on the feasibility of a nuclear test ban was conducted regularly within a variety of governmental agencies and at diverse levels. By late 1962, a number of possible options had emerged from discussions within the newly created Arms Control and Disarmament Agency. Despite regular Soviet rebuffs, Kennedy urged that these discussions be continued.

The president personally attempted to engage the Soviets in serious negotiation on a test ban agreement. A regular, almost institutionalized channel of communication, one that relied largely on written messages, was established between Kennedy and the Soviet premier. In these exchanges the president made every attempt to convince Khrushchev of the seriousness of both American motives and objectives in bringing about a test ban. When negotiations finally opened in Moscow, Kennedy personally selected the negotiating team, regularly monitored their progress, and assumed broad direction and responsibility for the overall development of the accord.

The president's central role in the agreement had just begun, however. After the drafting had been concluded, Kennedy played a leading role in the legislative struggle for ratification. This campaign was carefully orchestrated by administration forces under the general supervision of staff advisors to the president. Arguments in support of the administration's case were developed, organized, and coordinated by this same small group, who maintained regular contact with Kennedy. Witnesses were selected with care, their testimony was prepared by administration forces, and the order in which they appeared before the Senate Foreign Relations Committee was designed to bolster the persuasiveness of the administration's position. Every effort was made to obtain optimal tactical advantage.

Kennedy's personal role in the legislative process was no less dramatic than that of his staff. The president arranged private meetings with reluctant senators in which he sought their support. He also made personal telephone calls as part of this endeavor. Kennedy made every effort to ensure that the administration was united in favor of the test ban accord in order to preclude any opposing strategy based on the exploitation of internal dissension. Thus, when the Joint Chiefs balked at some provisions of the treaty, Kennedy made a concerted effort to satisfy their demands and soften their opposition, especially because he considered their support critical for ratification.

As we have seen, the president also attempted to mobilize broad public support in favor of the test ban agreement. He employed every possible forum in a campaign stressing the importance of the treaty and the need for its rapid ratification. The private Citizens' Committee for a Nuclear Test Ban was established with strong presidential support and encouragement. Privately, the administration, and Kennedy himself, provided broad assistance to this group in its educational and promotional activities. Other relevant interest groups were invited to join in this extensive program aimed at enlightening the public regarding the merits of the proposed test ban. Overt appeals for support were made especially to the scientific and technical community, whose expertise seemed particularly relevant in the area of disarmament and arms control. Finally, the mass media was openly solicited, and favorable editorial comment was given broad public distribution.

In short, the president played a pivotal, indeed a central, role in every stage of the policy-making process that culminated in the ratification of the Nuclear Test Ban Treaty.

REFERENCES AND BIBLIOGRAPHY

GILPIN, ROBERT, American Scientists and Nuclear Weapons Policy. Princeton, N.J.: Princeton University Press, 1962.

HILSMAN, ROGER, The Politics of Policy Making in Defense and Foreign Affairs. New York: Harper & Row, 1971.

JACOBSON, HAROLD K., and ERIC STEIN, Diplomats, Scientists and Politicians. Ann Arbor, Mich.: University of Michigan Press, 1966.

LEPPER, MARY MILLING, *Foreign Policy Formulation: A Case Study of the Nuclear Test Ban Treaty of 1963.* Columbus, Ohio: Charles E. Merrill, 1971.

SCHLESINGER, ARTHUR M., JR., *A Thousand Days.* Boston: Houghton Mifflin, 1965.

SORENSEN, THEODORE, *Kennedy.* New York: Bantam, 1966.

U.S., Congress, *Congressional Record,* 1963.

U.S., Congress, Senate, Committee on Armed Services, Preparedness Investigating Subcommittee, *Hearings, Military Aspects and Implications of Nuclear Test Ban Proposals and Related Matters,* 88th Cong., 1st sess., 1964.

———Committee on Foreign Relations, *Hearing, Nuclear Test Ban Treaty,* 88th Cong., 1st sess., 1963.

10

The Dominican Intervention 1965

In the post–World War II era American policy in Latin America appears to have rested upon the conviction that social and economic change should occur gradually, without fundamentally disrupting existing structures or institutions and without endangering American economic, political, and strategic interests. Thus the Castro revolution in Cuba, with its potential for exporting social and economic turmoil throughout Latin America, presented American policy makers with a grave threat to the prevailing pattern of relations between the United States and Latin America. Many countries throughout Latin America shared Cuba's poverty. With significant uneasiness, American officials contemplated the possible development of similar revolutionary movements aimed at eradicating poverty, eliminating large landed estates, and confiscating foreign properties or ending large-scale foreign investment. Government officials were especially concerned that such movements might be readily infiltrated by Communists or their sympathizers and exploited by them for their advantage and to the detriment of American interests.

In April, 1965, certain developments in the Dominican Republic presented the Johnson administration with a set of problems of this order. On April 24, a military revolt aimed ostensibly at restoring former Dominican President Juan Bosch to power broke out at the headquarters of the Dominican army. Bosch, the first legally elected president in thirty-two years in the Dominican Republic, had been overthrown in a military coup led by Brigadier General Elias Wessin y Wessin in September, 1963. In the intervening period, between 1963 and April, 1965, a civilian government led by Donald Reid Cabral exercised power, though with the participation and critical support of the military. For a variety of reasons, military support for the Cabral government deteriorated, particularly during the early months of 1965. In April the military, disturbed by the government's effort to reduce military allocations as part of a general economy drive, withdrew its support. As a result, on April 24 Reid was forced to resign.

Opposition to the Reid regime was not confined exclusively to the military. Efforts by the government to control runaway inflation through an austerity program had proved immensely unpopular with the citizenry. Dissident groups regularly attacked Reid's policies and demanded his resignation. The United States, however, appeared firm in its commitment to the regime. When Reid was finally forced to resign, a *New York Times* editorial noted, "For the United States, this is an unhappy development, since Washington was helping the Reid government as much as it could" (April 26, 1965).

On the day of Reid's resignation, Molina Urena was sworn in as provisional president of the Dominican Republic. Because Molina was clearly identified with the Bosch faction within the military, Wessin y Wessin announced his opposition and quickly organized an anti-Bosch element within the armed forces. A series of minor military skirmishes ensued between these groups, but these proved inconclusive.

On April 26 Chargé d'Affaires William Connett, who had been left in charge of the American embassy in Santo Domingo during the absence of the ambassador, Tap Bennett, dispatched a telegram to Washington requesting technical assistance (radios, communications equipment, and so forth) for Wessin y Wessin's forces. Calling Washington's attention to the "serious threat of a Communist takeover," Connett warned that a "U.S. show of force might be needed" (Barnet, 1968, pp. 169–70).

Distracted by the growing problem of Vietnam, Washington was relatively indifferent to the Dominican situation until April. However, a growing number of intelligence reports telling of the deteriorating situation awakened the attention of the Washington policy making community. In early April, this 'cryptic" message from the American ambassador was received in Washington: "Little foxes some of them red are chewing at the grapes. It is impossible to guarantee a good harvest in view of many unfavorable aspects of the local scene. It is, however, fair to say that a diminution of our effort or failure to act will result in a bitter wine." (*Newsweek*, May 17, 1965, p. 49) Subsequent messages warned Washington of a possible bloodbath and pointed to the increasing fragility of the Reid government. Toward the end of the month, in a personal message to Undersecretary of State Thomas Mann, Bennett wrote, "We are almost on the ropes in the Dominican Republic" (*Ibid.*).

In light of these gloomy assessments, the United States had moved the aircraft carrier *Boxer*, with its contingent of 1,100 marines, to a point within easy reach of the island. This occurred two full weeks before direct American intervention. Despite all of the warnings, however, on April 24, the day the rebels struck, Tap Bennett was in Georgia visiting his mother, and eleven key members of his staff were attending a conference in Panama. Bennett flew immediately to Washington for consultations, but his absence from Santo Domingo added to the policy confusion surrounding the president.

As the Dominican situation dramatically unfolded, Washington's "crisis machinery" shifted into full gear. In the Pentagon, maps and charts of Vietnam were replaced by information about the Dominican Republic. Meetings were scheduled between the president and officials of the CIA, the Pentagon, and the State Department.

On April 27, the Eighty-second Airborne Division was placed on full alert. Upon his return to Santo Domingo from Washington, Bennett arranged logistical support for the antirebel forces. This action was taken even though virtually every analysis, including that of the State Department, claimed that non-Communists were in the forefront of the revolt.

The same day, a delegation of Dominican rebel leaders arrived at the American embassy in Santo Domingo in an effort to enlist Bennett's aid in arranging talks as a preliminary to a cease-fire. Convinced at that moment that the revolt was failing, Bennett flatly refused assistance. Instead, according to an account by Juan Bosch, the American ambassador informed the rebels of his intention to request American military intervention to end the revolt.

The following day, Bennett dispatched a cable to Washington in which he recommended that "serious thought be given to armed intervention to restore order beyond a mere protection of lives" (Szulc, 1966, p. 54). In a later message that day, Bennett noted, "I regret that we may have to impose a military solution to a political problem . . . the issue is really between those who want a Castro type solution and those who oppose it" (Draper, 1965, pp. 45–46). Finally, after obtaining support for military intervention from top governmental officials, including Secretary of State Rusk and Defense Secretary McNamara, Bennett requested that American troops be dispatched to the island to safeguard and protect the lives of Americans and other foreign nationals.

By the end of that day, the first marines had landed and were deployed. President Johnson then based his decision to intervene on the need to protect the lives of both Americans and other foreign nationals. As he would note later, "In this situation, hesitation and vacillation could mean death for many of our people as well as many of the citizens of other lands, [so] I thought that we could not hesitate. Our forces . . . were ordered in immediately." (U.S. Department of State, *Bulletin*, May 17, 1965, p. 745) At that stage, no opposition to this decision was voiced by any member of the administration.

In the following days, the marine contingent on the island was reinforced and paratroopers from the Eighty-second Airborne Division were dispatched to complement them. By May 6, the entire Eighty-second Division plus a contingent of 7,000 marines were engaged in military operations. And although a truce was declared on May 22, it was not until September, 1966 that the last remnants of the American military left the Dominican Republic.

The Organization of American States (OAS) convened on April 29 and immediately asked for a cease-fire. On May 1, a five-man commission was sent by the OAS to the island in an effort to terminate hostilities. Finally, on May 5 the OAS voted to create an Inter-American Peace Force, which in conjunction with the American military contingent ensured the maintenance of the cease-fire.

President Johnson's decision to intervene reflected a variety of considerations. For one thing, his view of the Dominican situation was strongly affected by the reports of the intelligence and diplomatic community. In fact, the embassy reports from Santo Domingo were a major factor in his decision. One reporter noted that although Washington acted with the best of intentions, it was "stampeded into unfortunate decisions by a panicky, ill-informed embassy" (Draper, 1965, p. 34). For Senator Fulbright, hardly an enthusiastic supporter of the administration, the "principal reason for the failure of American policy in Santo Domingo was faulty advice given to the President by his representatives in the Dominican Republic at the time of acute crisis. . . . On the basis of the information and counsel he received the President could hardly have acted other than he did." (Congressional Record, 1965, p. 23858)

Despite the frequently faulty and often contradictory intelligence reports, Johnson apparently relied upon them throughout the crisis. Looking back on the Dominican situation, Johnson told an assembled group of congressmen on May 4,

> We had anticipated difficulty there. The intelligence reports each morning indicate difficulties in dozens of spots throughout the world. We immediately alerted the forces . . . and continued our discussion. When another wire came in at 5:16—almost two hours later—and said that there is firing in the streets, there is great danger to all personnel in this area, [I decided to] land troops immediately to protect our people. It was a rather strong and compelling and almost distressed message. . . . (U.S. News and World Report, May 17, 1965, p. 43)

At no point during the crisis did Johnson choose to challenge the intelligence reports, either on grounds of incompleteness or because of insufficient substantiation. On the contrary, he endorsed many of their recommendations despite what we now know to be their obvious shortcomings and inadequacies.

Johnson's concern for protecting American lives did not appear completely unfounded at the time, however. During April and early May the island was in a state of virtual anarchy. Military clashes, though of limited scope, occurred regularly. On April 27 President Johnson received a report of rebel harassment of 1,000 American citizens who were preparing for evacuation at the Hotel Embajador. Such incidents were reported regularly, but often, it should be noted, with little documentation. For instance, a *New York Times* editorial supporting Johnson's decision maintained that "there was a valid reason for the United States to put a marine landing force into Santo Domingo. This reason was to protect Americans and evacuate those who desire to leave." (April 30, 1965).

Undoubtedly, Johnson's decision was also affected by economic considerations. According to Richard Barnet, the American intervention merely revealed that "the political and economic relationship on which the United States preferred to base its dominant influence in the economy and politics of the Dominican Republic had broken down . . ." (1968, p. 153). Around 1960 the Dominican Republic had become very important to the American sugar industry because of the faltering relations between the United States and Cuba. Other sectors of American industry were attracted to the island, and an effort was made to restructure the Dominican economy as part of a drive to open up investment opportunities for the United States. By 1962, the American presence completely dominated both the politics and the economy of the island. During the shortened rule of Juan Bosch alone, the United States made foreign-aid grants of 84 million dollars to the Dominican Republic. Private American investments in the Dominican Republic increased substantially during the Reid regime. Between 1964 and mid-1965, these investments neared 200 million dollars.

When rebellion broke out, the Constitutionalists (rebels) moved into the business districts of Santo Domingo. *Time* reported that "rebel mobs sacked the new Pepsi Cola plant, set fire to the offices of a pro-Reid newspaper and destroyed Reid's auto agency" (May 7, 1965, p. 32). It should also be noted that on the day of decision in Washington, Ambassador Bennett had received no assurances that the hundreds of millions of dollars of American property and investments could be protected. Surely these material considerations played a large role in Johnson's decision.

Another factor in Johnson's decision was rooted in ideology. As one writer stated, "When the current crisis in the Dominican Republic erupted, Mr. Johnson had no larger political idea to refer to than simple anti-Communism" (Shannon, 1965, p. 279). Senator Fulbright later noted that this reliance on the symbol of anti-Communism was "not in the national interest; foreign policy must be based on prospects that seem probable, hopeful and susceptible to constructive influence rather than on merely possible dangers" (Congressional Record, 1965, p. 23858). Nevertheless, from the onset of the crisis Johnson viewed the situation through the prism of anti-Communism, albeit the announced purpose of intervention was to protect American lives. Those upon whom Johnson tended to rely—in particular, Dean Rusk—also concluded that a rebel victory carried an unacceptable risk of Communism. Rusk was unable to view the Dominican Republic in isolation. Instead, he saw it as a part of a global Communist conspiracy that affected the American position everywhere else in the world, particularly in Vietnam. In short, Rusk felt that the Dominican revolt was a test of American resolve that the Communists would exploit should the United States fail to act forcefully. Others in the administration agreed with Rusk's assessment, and such advice served only to reinforce Johnson's views.

Ideological commitments were downplayed in the early announcements of American policy regarding the Dominican rebellion. But while maintaining publicly that the sole mission of the marines was to protect American lives, Johnson began shortly after the onset of the revolt to brief congressmen and others privately that the marines were needed to prevent a Communist takeover. When the president finally informed the public of this, his previous lack of candor not only served to handcuff him in implementing his decision but created a great credibility gap as well.

On May 1, Johnson was forced to admit,

> Our goal in the Dominican Republic is the goal which has been
> expressed . . . in the treaties and agreements which make up the inter-
> American system. It is that the people of that country must be permitted to
> freely choose the path of political democracy, social justice and economic
> progress. We intend to carry on the struggle against tyranny no matter in
> what ideology it cloaks itself. This is our responsibility . . . and the . . .
> values which bind us together. (U.S. Department of State, *Bulletin*, May
> 17, 1965, p. 743)

This new rationale for intervention would be persistently reiter-
ated and at times glorified in some quarters of the mass press.
Newsweek, for instance, credited the marines with "the perfor-
mance of precisely the same political mission that sends U.S.
Marines at Da Nang out on patrol against the Viet Cong guerillas"
(May 10, 1965, p. 35).

When Johnson spoke of Communist influence in the revolution, he referred to it as a "tragic turn" of events. What began, he
was to argue, as "a popular democratic revolution, committed to
democracy and social justice, very shortly moved and was taken
over and really seized and placed into the hands of a band of
Communist conspirators. . . . The American nations cannot, must
not, and will not permit the establishment of another Communist
government in the Western Hemisphere." (U.S. Department of
State, *Bulletin*, May 17, 1965, p. 745) Johnson's use of the "tragic
turn" phrase in describing the developments in the Dominican
Republic was to create further difficulties for him. Opposition elements on the left, intellectuals, and the press thought the phrase
misleading and inappropriate. As Theodore Draper suggests, its
use seemed to draw attention to American opposition to revolution
of any type, anywhere on the globe.

> How "tragic" could the revolution's turn have really been to an administra-
> tion which had never made the slightest effort to support it in the first
> place? If words have any meaning, if it was tragic that the revolution took a
> Communist turn, was it not equally "tragic" that the United States did not
> support—if nothing worse—the revolution before it took that turn? (1965,
> p. 42)

During the crisis, Johnson often compounded his problems by saying things that made him seem rash and undiplomatic as well as a proponent of gunboat diplomacy. Consider, for instance, this remark of his: "What is important . . . is that we know, and that they know, and that everybody knows, that we don't propose to sit here in our rocking chair with our hands folded and let the Communists set up any government in the Western Hemisphere" (quoted in Geyelin, 1966, p. 238).

The fear of another Cuba was another major factor in the Johnson administration's response to the Dominican rebellion. This "Cuban syndrome" exerted a profound influence on American policy from the start of the rebellion, both from the bureaucratic organization up and from the presidency down. Johnson was determined to make it clear that the United States would not withhold power in a crisis. This attitude was strengthened by the bold efforts then being undertaken by Communists all over Latin America. The president was viewed as expanding the Monroe Doctrine to bar the emergence of a Communist government by any means, anywhere in the hemisphere. This new "Johnson Doctrine" gave a claim of legitimacy to armed intervention in the civil strife of another country.

Officials in Santo Domingo and Washington were badgered regularly by the American press for evidence of Communist conspiracy. The facts had to be found or created, and the administration, "in a desperate effort to prove what was apparently unprovable, sank even more deeply into a morass of McCarthyism that compounded whatever errors it may have originally made" (Kurzman, 1965, p. 193).

The ideological dilemma faced by Johnson was twofold. On the one hand, democracy was sought as an alternative to Castroite Communism. On the other hand, the United States feared the development of democratic regimes, particularly in the "third world" countries, since inexperienced democracies had often proved less resistant to Communism than rightist military regimes. In the face of a Communist threat to advance, therefore, American policy supported almost by reflex the strongman rather than the democrat. Johnson's repudiation of the revolt was thus an eminently predictable response. As Kurzman stated bluntly, "Ironically, this country, conceived in revolution, could not look with approval on revolution elsewhere, particularly near its shores. For in this modern era, no revolution could be free of Communist influence in one degree or another. Coups d'etat could be tolerated for they were always perpetrated by anti-Communist militants." (*Ibid.*, p. 167)

The key role played by Bennett and other embassy personnel in shaping the president's actions has already been mentioned. Apparently, Johnson reached his decision to intervene after the urgent appeal for troops by the ambassador. Significantly, Bennett was a man who was conditioned, both by his general background and by previous American policy, to take a certain course of action. The prototype of a State Department career ambassador and the possessor of a deeply inbred sense of caution, Bennett was not the type of man who could understand or respond realistically to any situation of broad socio-political change.

Despite indications of widespread discontent, the American embassy in Santo Domingo appears to have been unprepared for the disorder. Many rumors were either ignored or not taken seriously. The embassy failed to realize either the extent to which the Dominican people desired constitutionalism or the latent support existing for Juan Bosch. This failure of intelligence was to undermine the effectiveness of the American response to the rapidly shifting developments that occurred throughout the crisis. Bennett's important mistake was his failure to realize that after the rule of Juan Bosch, it was no longer possible for any Dominican to pursue power blindly with complete disregard for the population.

Bennett was selective both in his dealings with people and with the broad range of ideological positions on the island. Tad Szulc quotes an administration official as saying, "Tap didn't seem to know anyone who was to the left of the Rotary club" (1966, p. 67). Bosch described Bennett as "a Southern aristocrat who can't abide any faction that isn't 'his kind of people' " (quoted in Rodman, 1965, p. 24). Bennett appears to have lacked the training and the temperament to succeed as the Dominican ambassador no matter how much he may have wanted to. It simply wasn't in character for him to meet with the rank and file: "He wouldn't know how to dress for the occasion or what to say to a poor farmer or worker. On the other hand he felt perfectly at home with the upper classes . . . and politicians. Inevitably they molded his thinking." (Kurzman, 1965, p. 304) When the revolt broke out, the ambassador almost instinctively gave his full support to the people he knew. He was later to find himself at the mercy of the powers he had completely ignored.

From the outset, Bennett and his fellow diplomats assumed that the rebel movement was Communist-controlled. They refused to establish contacts in the rebel area in order to investigate the validity of their views. Bennett's messages to Washington make it clear that his major concerns were political and not humanitarian. The political leanings of the rebel movement seemed to be a principal consideration for all policy makers but especially for the embassy personnel. Thus, although Washington appeared publicly confused and noncommital and Johnson delayed action, the embassy had clearly cast its lot. Washington was advised that "the embassy military attachés had given loyalist leaders a go ahead to do everything possible to prevent what was described as a 'Communist takeover' " (*Ibid.*, p. 39).

The president's handling of the crisis was intensely personal and, as is so often the case in a crisis situation, revealed the great importance of "presidential style" in the decision-making process. Congressional leaders were summoned and told of Johnson's decision, but in no way did they help make it. Johnson claimed that "he had acted on his own and was not asking the congressional leaders for authority." (*New York Times*, May 1, 1965). As Johnson himself said, "I make the decisions here." He rarely reached deep down into the bureaucracy for advice and expertise: "I talk to Dean Rusk, not to some fifth desk man down the lines. If Rusk doesn't know more than the fifth desk man, he shouldn't be Secretary of State." (quoted in Geyelin, 1966, p. 258)

Johnson devoted an inordinate amount of time to the Dominican crisis, and in many ways his mark was etched indelibly on the decision making that accompanied it. Many observers felt that the president was determined to demonstrate how he intended to react to future crises in Latin America. According to Draper, "Whatever the role of his advisors may have been, [the Dominican intervention] seems to [have been] the President's show, and [this] may have been the reason why he found it so difficult to back away from his original decision and professed motivation" (1968, pp. 84–85). Johnson's determination was revealed further in a series of statements he made during this period. These are remarkable both for their pungency and for their expression of implacable determination.

> When you duck, dodge, hesitate and shimmy, every man and his dog give you a kick. I expect to get kicked but I don't expect to duck . . . (*Time*, May 14, 1965, p. 23).
> If a choice must be made, we would rather that men quarrel with our actions to preserve peace than to curse us through eternity for inaction that might lose both our peace and freedom . . . (*Newsweek*, May 24, 1965, p. 25).
> What can we do in Vietnam if we can't clean up the Dominican Republic? I know what the editorials will say but it would be a hell of a lot worse if we sit here and don't do anything and the Communists take over that country. (Martin, 1966, p. 661)

Johnson's values undoubtedly affected his view of the Dominican crisis. A supreme value for Johnson was consensus. Ironically, evidence would suggest later that Johnson probably had the consensus with him all the time. Yet he constantly sought to demonstrate its existence. Consequently a foreign-policy crisis dissolved rapidly into a crisis of confidence in Johnson himself as the difference between what he said and what was done became increasingly visible. "It produced, in short, what was probably the lowest ebb in Lyndon Johnson's standing as a world statesman in all of the first two years or more of his Presidency." (Geyelin, 1966, p. 237)

Some observers asserted that Johnson, as a Texan, believed he had a special competence in dealing with Latin American affairs and in understanding Latin thinking. According to this viewpoint, Johnson felt that the Latins respected strength and decisiveness. In the view of Walter Prescott, "Partly the key to Johnson's conduct in the days just after the Dominican upheaval may lie in the Texas hills. The very absence of rich history and long tradition in that region encourages a talent for taking something small and blowing it up to giant size. . . . They write of cowboys as if they were noble knights and the cowmen kings." (Quoted in *Ibid*.) To Lyndon Johnson it was "just like the Alamo. . . . Hell, it's just like you were down at that gate, and you were surrounded, and you damn well needed somebody. Well by G——d, I'm going to go—and I thank the Lord that I've got men who want to go with me, from McNamara right on down to the littlest private who's carrying a gun." (*Ibid.*)

Johnson's principal advisors in all of his Dominican decisions were Thomas Mann, McGeorge Bundy, John Bartlow Martin, Robert McNamara, Dean Rusk, George Ball, William Raborn, Jr., Cyrus Vance, Jack Hood Vaughn, Kennedy Crockett, and Bill Moyers. Interestingly, Vice-President Hubert Humphrey was not invited to any of the meetings or top-level discussions.

Johnson and his advisors felt that the choices before them were to (1) do nothing and accept the possibility of another Cuba, (2) go to the OAS, realizing, though, that it was a very slow-moving body, or (3) act and shape the situation.

When the crisis became full-fledged, the number of talks became quite large. Johnson noted that between April 25 and May 2 he held 42 meetings with his top advisors and made 225 phone calls, including 86 to Bundy, 31 to McNamara, 15 to Rusk and 10 to Raborn.

Despite the frequency of Johnson's meetings, it was obvious that the advice that had the greatest impact on the president was the communications he received from Santo Domingo. Describing his reaction to a plea for assistance on the day of the decision to intervene, Johnson wrote,

> When the cable arrived, when our entire country team in the Dominican Republic made up of nine men—one from the Army, Navy, and Air Force, our Ambassador, our AID man, and others—said to your President unanimously: Mr. President, if you do not send forces immediately, men and women will die in the streets, well I knew there was not time to talk, to consult, to delay. (U.S. Department of State, *Bulletin*, May 17, 1965, p. 745)

When the "full country team" recommends immediate emergency action, even an action as drastic as military intervention, the recommendation will likely be accepted. By all standards this was the obvious advice to follow. It was especially obvious to Lyndon Johnson, a president who was famed for his reliance on consensus. For

Johnson to have acted differently than he did in the early days of the crisis, he would have had to invent his own alternatives and ignore his principal advisors, as well as discount his intelligence reports from the scene. Above all, Johnson would have had to change the reality that the weight of the American presence in Santo Domingo had committed the United States to block the rebellion a full four days before the president ordered in the marines.

Johnson appears to have relied heavily on the advice of two persons: Thomas Mann and John Bartlow Martin. Mann was Johnson's choice for assistant secretary of state for inter-American affairs. Johnson stated, "We expect to speak with one voice on all matters affecting the hemisphere. Mr. Mann, with the support of the Secretary of State and the President, will be that voice." (Draper, 1965, pp. 34–35) It appears that Mann served as somewhat of an alter ego to Johnson. Mann held a hard line on Communism and could accept military governments in Latin America. His preference for authoritarian solutions to problems in that area therefore mirrored closely the president's own inclinations.

John Bartlow Martin was a former American ambassador to Santo Domingo. On April 30 Johnson sent Martin to Santo Domingo to assess the crisis. Martin's judgment, which influenced Johnson greatly, was one of the more unfortunate aspects of the Dominican affair. Ostensibly, Martin had been sent to open contacts with the rebels. Yet shortly after he arrived on the scene, he openly committed himself to the Communist-conspiracy thesis. His views gained added credence inasmuch as he was a man not known to be paranoid about Communism. According to Tad Szulc,

> Martin's reporting to Washington during the weekend played an important role in subsequent developments in the Dominican situation. His assessment that the revolution had gone over to the Communists was the final element in convincing the Administration that this was the case and that there was no way out except to help the military leaders at San Isidro to liquidate the Communist danger in some manner. (1966, p. 50)

Johnson's hope for an objective appraisal of the situation by Martin dissolved quickly as the presidential aide rapidly identified himself with the anti-Bosch faction: "It was odd [that] since Bosch's fall, I had become identified publicly with Bosch, and I think President Johnson sent me to the Republic partly for that reason, but I had as many friends, perhaps more, on the other side" (Martin, 1966, p. 682). It is quite clear from Martin's own statements that in the end he became merely another voice reinforcing Johnson's views. He refused to consider the possibility that the revolution would be successful or might lead to a popular government. In some instances his views were even more extreme than Bennett's. Of Colonel Caamano, the rebel leader who, at worst, was thought to be allowing Communists into his movement, Martin said, "In all my time in the Dominican Republic I had met no man whom I thought might become a Dominican Castro—until I met Caamano. He was winning a revolution from below. . . . it makes little difference when Castro 'became a Communist.' It would make little difference when Caamano became one. (*Ibid.*, pp. 661–62) These words came from the man Johnson sent to begin talks with Caamano.

Besides personal preference, embassy reports, and advisors' opinions, other factors shaped the president's decision to intervene. It is important to note the often undercover role played by the CIA and the military attachés in the Dominican intervention. Their activities during the first two days of the uprising present us with the best view of early American policy regarding the intervention. While the diplomats and Johnson were making up their minds, the attachés acted. A journalist on the scene reported the following conversation, which occured after the marines were dispatched to protect the evacuation of Americans:

> A message from Lt. General Bruce Palmer, Commander of U.S. forces in the Dominican Republic, to his troops referred to "the revolution . . . between the Communists and the government of the Dominican Republic." When I asked the general about these statements, he declared that they simply reflected what President Johnson had said. Embassy officials were highly embarrassed by the "message to the troops," which they said did not reflect U.S. policy. They would try, they said, to improve the coordination of military and diplomatic information. (Kurzman, 1965, pp. 240–41)

Later on, however, when the United States began thinking in terms of a coalition government, the military was still acting to prevent a Communist takeover.

The Dominican intervention brought to the forefront the inadequacy of the principle of nonintervention, and the role—or nonrole—of the OAS in Johnson's decision making. Johnson's action threatened the hemispheric unity that had been a major influence on American policy in the area. On the morning of Johnson's decision, the OAS met and discussed the situation. They took no action, and Johnson decided he could wait no longer. In the televised address in which he informed the country of the Dominican intervention, his only reference to the OAS was this: "The Council of the OAS has been advised of the situation by the Dominican Ambassador and the Council will be kept fully informed." In reality, Johnson relied little on the OAS as a decision-making body, and that institution didn't have much influence on his decisions: "He had a low opinion of that organization. 'The OAS couldn't pour ———— out of a boot if the instructions were written on the heel,' he said scathingly." (Geyelin, 1966, p. 254) The only importance of the OAS for Johnson lay in its role in maintaining the American posture of regional defense. Johnson wanted the legitimacy of the multilateralism that the OAS represented. He felt that he could secure the two-thirds majority vote of the OAS to support any de facto move by the United States, and this allowed him to make any decisions he wanted.

In viewing the Dominican situation, it is important to note the role of the press in aiding or obstructing the president's decision making:

> It is difficult, if not impossible, in a country like the United States to separate what anyone, even the President, says U.S. policy is and how that policy is transmitted to and through the press. The way our Dominican policy was transmitted to and through the press in the last week of April 1965 indicates that what this country needs as much as anything else is a pure news law. (Draper, 1965, p. 44)

Newsmen were continually misled during the Dominican affair. An important reason for this was that their briefings were supplied by the military in the absence of the propaganda and information specialists from the U.S. Information Agency. The explanation of what the United States was doing and what it was trying to do was left entirely in the hands of military men. This was reflected in the news reports back home. General Wessin appeared on the cover of *Time* and in the early part of the revolution was termed a Dominican national hero.

Inaccurate reporting was widespread, and in much the same manner that Johnson's representatives in the Republic influenced the reporting, the reporting, in turn, influenced Johnson. References were made to "organized Communists" who had been "given arms and roamed the streets." The United States was reported to be involved in action against "ragtag gangs of armed toughs." It was reported that "Communists backed by Castro's Reds in Havana were out to take over the country" and that "Communist plotters were on the verge of seizing power." Other dispatches asserted that hundreds of armed rebels "stormed into the Ambassador Hotel," where Americans were awaiting evacuation, seized them, "separated the men from the women and children, marched them off out of sight of their families, [and] fired shots over their heads." (These remarks were made in *U.S. News and World Report*, May 10, 1965, pp. 32–34.) The conclusion reached from this "information" was that intervention was unavoidable if the slaughter of Americans was to be prevented. This was reinforced by Bennett's tales of atrocities and mass executions. Thus, the news stories inspired by Bennett played an important role in shaping Johnson's view of the Dominican situation and justifying his decision to intervene. The fictions and myths communicated from the Dominican Republic were even repeated by Johnson long after they had been proved false. For instance, "many weeks later [the president] referred to a sacked and burned embassy in an accounting of the events that led to his decision to intervene in the Dominican Republic" (Szulc, 1966, p. 73).

The errors in the press cannot really be blamed on the newsmen because most of them had arrived on the scene just recently and were thus totally dependent on Bennett for information. "As the versions in *Time* and *U.S. News and World Report* show, the worst offenders were precisely the 'news' organs that most crudely took their lead from the Ambassador" (Draper, 1968, pp. 93–94).

Soon, many newsmen became aware of what was happening. Serious objections to American policy began to be raised by some journalists. "It is not often that journalists can be said to have saved the honor of their country," wrote Theodore Draper. "This was, I believe, one of those very rare occasions." (1968, p. 146) And as Tad Szulc commented, on LBJ's reaction to the press during this period,

> I would like to say respectfully that it was not the fault of that small band of American newsmen reporting from Santo Domingo in what they believed were the traditions of the free American press, that [the president] faced such difficulties in solving the Dominican crisis. We were, I believe, nothing more and nothing less than the Greek chorus of that tragedy. The tragedy was not ours as newsmen, though it was ours as Americans. (1966, p. 306)

The Dominican intervention clearly illustrates the inconsequential role played by Congress in the foreign-policy decision-making process. When Johnson decided to intervene, he informed congressional leaders of his decision. They, in turn, expressed their support. In essence, Johnson told the leaders that he was not asking for their authority but merely wanted to inform them of his decision before they read about it in the newspapers. Arthur Krock asserted that Johnson was using Congress to assure the widest possible publicity and support for his decision: "It was an example of the technique the President employs in his constant search for consensus. By the time the leaders reached the White House they were psychologically conditioned to go along with whatever was the objective." (*New York Times*, May 2, 1965)

Senator Fulbright also noted the congressional nonrole in the president's decision: "We were not asked as to what action should be taken. We were told what had been done." (*Congressional Record*, 1965, p. 23861) The major role of Congress in the Dominican intervention turned out to be its use as a sounding board for any and all post-mortems about the entire affair. In September the House overwhelmingly passed a resolution vindicating the American actions in the Dominican Republic, but the resolution was ambiguous and could have meant anything or nothing at all.

Whatever one's opinion about American policy in the Dominican Republic, one cannot deny that the entire operation was disproportionately expensive. What was done is impossible to separate from the manner in which it was done and how it was presented to the American people. As Szulc summarized the situation, "If, as I believe, the Dominican events were symptomatic of an American crisis, or more exactly, a crisis in the conduct of foreign affairs in this area, the crisis is primarily one of Presidential power and policy, inasmuch as the President and the men around him are almost wholly responsible for the conduct of our foreign affairs" (quoted in Draper, 1965, p. 33).

Events in the Dominican Republic during the crisis broke rapidly, and the American policy makers were caught in a flux of events that made mistakes almost inevitable. Some observers claim, however, that "the final product of crisis diplomacy is more important than all events between the beginning and the end" (Evans and Novack, 1966, p. 527). Such writers maintain that the American policy was successful inasmuch as the Dominican Republic has not become Communist. Yet this is a vast oversimplification, for who can safely say whether the final product of the crisis would have been unacceptable had events been left to play themselves out. As Senator Clark quoted from a *Washington Post* editorial, "[arguing] that all is well in the Dominican Republic is like insisting that because a broken leg ultimately heals it somehow is good for you." (*Congressional Record*, 1965, p. 24245)

Who was responsible for American policy during the Dominican crisis? Research reveals an absence of a fully articulated, comprehensive, and unified policy in Washington. Policy was generated in a variety of policy-making quarters, frequently with minimal coordination. This was true particularly during the implementation of the policy. Confusion became so abundant that Martin Arnold of the *New York Times* finally exclaimed at one point, "You know, I think that all this is just one great insane asylum and all of us are the inmates here" (quoted in Szulc, 1966, pp. 200–201). The method by which the decision to intervene was reached reflects this state of general confusion. As in several of our other case studies, it is clear that this decision was an executive decision made in some haste. Public opinion and interest groups played no discernible direct role, although they did, of course, contribute to the background of the decision: the executive branch was conscious of widespread anti-Communist sentiments among the public, especially regarding the "Red menace" in Latin America; and the administration was fully aware of American business interests in the Republic. Congress, as is normal in crisis situations, was consulted only perfunctorily. Thus, the decision to intervene centered in the executive, and more specifically, in the White House. What is far from certain is the weight the president gave to the advice of the State Department, the embassy in Santo Domingo, the CIA, and his own assistants.

Many analysts of the decision-making process that underlay the Dominican intervention would have us believe that Johnson was remarkably at the mercy of the advice and the activities of his subordinates. Much of the evidence presented here substantiates the view that Johnson did rely heavily on his men in Santo Domingo, Ambassadors Bennett and Martin. Yet the image of an innocent president is not entirely correct, because a Johnson who did not share the inflexible anti-Communist perspective of these two men would surely have discouraged the kind of advice they gave him. Choices were present in the Dominican decision-making process, but many of them were not noticed by Johnson. Above all, Johnson failed, in Richard Neustadt's terms, to overcome the limits of his expertise through his personal power perspective. Johnson did not have the "feel" of his role, and never realized that "nobody and nothing helps a President to see, save as he helps himself" (Neustadt, 1960, p. 145).

REFERENCES AND BIBLIOGRAPHY

BARNET, RICHARD J., *Intervention and Revolution*. New York: World Publishing, 1968.

BERLE, ADOLPH A., "A Stitch in Time," *The Reporter*, May 20, 1965, pp. 22–23.

DAVIES, JOHN PAYTON, JR., "Yankee Go Home? Stay Home? Intervene?" *New York Times Magazine*, May 23, 1965, p. 201.

"Dominican Post-Mortem," *The Economist*, September 18, 1965, pp. 1100–1101.

"Dominican Rewrite," *Commonweal*, December 9, 1966, pp. 280–81.

DRAPER, THEODORE, "The Dominican Crisis: A Case Study in American Policy," *Commentary*, 40, no. 6, (December 1965). pp. 33–68.

———, *The Dominican Revolt*. New York: Commentary, 1968.

EVANS, ROWLAND, and ROBERT NOVACK, *Lyndon B. Johnson: The Exercise of Power*. New York: New American Library, 1966.

The Politics of American Foreign Policy: The Social Context of Decisions

FULBRIGHT, J. W., *Old Myths and New Realities*. New York: Random House, 1964.

GEYELIN, PHILIP, *Lyndon Johnson and the World*. New York: Praeger, 1966.

HANDLEMAN, HOWARD, "After the Battle in the Carribbean," *U.S. News and World Report*, May 17, 1965.

HOOPES, TOWNSEND, *The Limits of Intervention*. New York: McKay, 1969.

KURZMAN, DAN, *Revolt of the Damned*. New York: Putnam's, 1965.

MARTIN, JOHN BARTLOW, *Overtaken by Events*. New York: Doubleday, 1966.

NEUSTADT, RICHARD, *Presidential Power*. New York: John Wiley, 1960.

PETRAS, JAMES, "Dominican Republic: Revolution and Restoration," in *Great Society Reader*, ed. Marvin Gettleman and David Mermelstein. New York: Random House, 1967.

"President's Days of Crisis and Decision: In His Own Words," *U.S. News and World Report*, May 17, 1965, p. 43.

RODMAN, SELDEN, "A Close View of Santo Domingo," *The Reporter*, July 15, 1965, pp. 20–27.

SHANNON, W. V. "The Marines Have Landed," *Commonweal*, May 21, 1965, pp. 278–79.

SMITH, GORDON CONNELL, "The OAS and the Dominican Crisis," *The World Today*, 21, no. 6, (June 1965), 229–40.

"Sugar, Tourists, Dollar Aid and Unrest on U.S. Doorstep," *U.S. News and World Report*, May 17, 1965, pp. 49–50.

SZULC, TAD, *Dominican Diary*. New York: Delacorte Press, 1966.

U.S., Congress, *Congressional Record*, 1965.

U.S., Department of State, *Bulletin*, May 17, 1965.

"The U.S. Steps into Another Hornet's Nest," *Business Week*, May 8, 1965, pp. 28–29.

"War Steps Up: Where It's Headed," *U.S. News and World Report*, May 10, 1965, pp. 31–35.

WELLS, HENRY, "Turmoil in the Dominican Republic," *Current History*, 50, no. 293 (January 1966), 14–22.

"Who Will Rule Now in the Dominican Republic?" *U.S. News and World Report*, May 17, 1965.

11

The Foreign Assistance Act
1967

A perennial issue in American politics, foreign aid has been a major item on the political agenda since the close of the Second World War. From the inception of the program for European economic recovery in 1948, total American foreign aid has exceeded $130 billion. Paralleling the increase in annual expenditures for foreign assistance has been a notable expansion of the geographical scope of international aid programs. Although Europe has continued to be a major recipient of American foreign aid, the United States has made an effort, at least since 1955, to provide support for the underdeveloped areas of the globe. (See Table 4 and Figures 2, 3.)

TABLE 4   Percent of foreign assistance program 1950–69 represented by military assistance ($ millions)

Fiscal Year	Total Foreign Assistance Program	Economic Assistance	Military Assistance	% of Program for Military Assistance
1950	$ 5,042.4	$ 3,728.4	$ 1,314.0	26.1
1951	7,485.0	2,262.5	5,222.5	69.8
1952	7,284.4	1.540.4	5,744.0	78.9
1953	6,001.9	1,782.1	4,219.8	70.3
1954	4,531.5	1,301.5	3,230.0	71.3
1955	2,781.5	1,588.8	1,192.7	42.9
1956	2,703.3	1,681.1	1,022.2	37.8
1957	3,766.6	1,749.1	2,017.5	53.6
1958	2,768.9	1,428.9	1,340.0	48.4
1959	3,448.1	1,933.1	1,515.0	43.9
1960	3,225.8	1,925.8	1,300.0	40.3
1961	4,431.4	2,631.4	1,800.0	40.6
1962	3,914.6	2,314.6	1,600.0	40.9
1963	3.928.9	2,603.9	1,325.0	33.7
1964	3,000.0	2,000.0	1,000.0	33.3
1965	3,325.0	2,195.0	1,055.0	31.8
1966	3,933.0	2,463.0	1,545.0	39.5
1967	2,935.5	2,143.5	792.0	26.8
1968	2,295.6	1,895.6	400.0	17.4
1969	1,974.1	1,599.1	375.0	19.1
Total	$78,777.5	$40,767.8	$38,009.7	Avg. 48.6

Data from: 1950–1968 in *Military Assistance Facts*, October 1968, Department of Defense, Office of the Assistant Secretary for International Security Affairs, 1968, p. 25. 1968 in *U.S. Code Congressional and Administrative News*, 90th Congress, 2nd Sess., 1968, Vol. III, p. 3973.
Source: From Adam Yarmolinsky, "Military Involvement in Foreign Policy," in Eugene J. Rosi, ed., *American Defense and Détente: Readings in National Security Policy*, Dodd, Mead, 1973, p. 493.

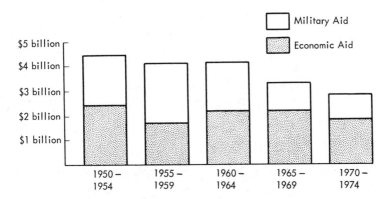

Figure 2 Agency for International Development: Military and economic assistance (yearly average). (*Source: Statistical Abstract of the United States.*)

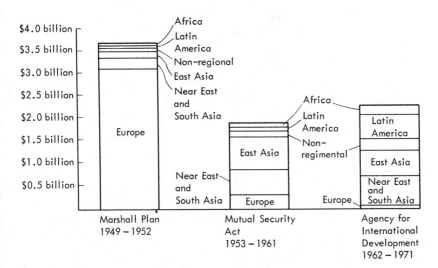

Figure 3 Regional Distribution of Foreign Aid (Yearly Average). (*Source: Statistical Abstract of the United States.*)

However, as John Montgomery has pointed out in his study of foreign aid, "No aspect of American foreign policy has consistently aroused more controversy [in the United States] than foreign aid" (1967, p. 6). Montgomery's view was undoubtedly true in 1967, and it is even more apparent today. The press reports regularly on the bitter debate surrounding the American foreign aid program. Major congressional figures have openly expressed their displeasure: some urge a major overhaul in the direction of the program, and others press for its complete abandonment.

Although dissatisfaction with the nature and operation of the American foreign aid program has been a staple of American political discourse virtually since the inception of the program, the 1960s witnessed the most violent denunciations. Efforts undertaken by the Kennedy and Johnson administrations to reorient the program and to tighten up its administrative procedures have done little to silence such criticism.

The outlook for the proposed foreign aid bill in 1967 was decidedly bleak. Most congressional insiders and informed executive officials were convinced that any request for increased appropriations would encounter serious obstacles, particularly in view of the mood and the composition of the 90th Congress. As the *New York Times* noted, "The larger Republican membership in the Senate and a revived coalition of Republicans and Southern Democrats in the House, where they constitute a working majority, add up to the gloomiest Congressional outlook for foreign aid in many years" (January 16, 1967).

Though undoubtedly sensitive to this opposition, President Johnson was clearly far from deterred. After all, his presidency had been marked by mounting congressional dissatisfaction, at least since 1965, and he was therefore familiar with the threat of opposition. Moreover, as a highly skilled persuader and bargainer the president was reasonably confident of his ability to construct a bipartisan congressional coalition that would support his foreign aid program. He certainly would not seek to avert a conflict with Congress over this issue, either by significantly cutting back on American programs of international assistance or by abandoning them altogether. The latter course of action was, as Johnson noted, "unthinkable." Even so, in anticipation of an inhospitable congressional reception Johnson sought to devise a foreign aid program that would maintain intact the American commitment to foreign assistance and that would also serve to blunt the arguments of his principal opponents.

First, Johnson asked in the 1967 Foreign Assistance Act for the smallest appropriation for foreign aid in twenty years. By paring down his request for funds—to the dismay of some executive officials, particularly those in the Agency for International Development (AID)—the president sought to disarm those congressional critics who had frequently labeled the foreign aid program as wasteful and extravagent. This country, Johnson argued, "can well afford to devote less than seven-tenths of one per cent of its national income" to foreign assistance (*New York Times*, February 10, 1967).

Second, the president stressed the central role of foreign aid in the fulfillment of American foreign policy objectives. In particular, he emphasized its importance, as he put it, in "reducing the chances of future Vietnams" (*Ibid.*). Here, Johnson echoed the viewpoint of those congressmen who perceived foreign aid essentially as a tool in America's cold war competition with Communist China and the Soviet Union.

To those who were concerned about mismanagement and inefficiency, Johnson offered a plan to improve the overall administration of the foreign aid program. His bill called for strengthening the role of AID in planning development projects, ensuring closer supervision of field activities, and providing for closer coordination of all foreign assistance programs.

Finally, in response to those who charged that the foreign aid program was merely a "giveaway," Johson included a set of provisions by which development assistance to a country would be extended in relation to that country's efforts to increase its food production, provide a more favorable environment for private enterprise, increase popular participation in the development process, and engage in internal economic, social, and political reforms, such as land reform or improved tax-collection administration. These "self-help" provisions of Johnson's bill would specify the criteria to be taken into account by American policy makers in furnishing development aid. William Gaud, newly appointed administrator of

AID informed Congress that these provisions would ensure that "all countries receiving our aid . . . recognize the basic obstacles blocking their own progress and [would] require of them . . . a sincere and sustained effort to overcome these obstacles" (U.S. House, 1967, p. 68).

In reality, however, the self-help criteria had been inserted into the bill in order to pacify those in Congress who had criticized the foreign aid program in the past. The *New York Times* was therefore right when it noted that the criteria were probably prompted by "a desire to satisfy Congressional demands for a 'get tough' policy" that might "achieve some quick development results" (April 2, 1967).

Although Johnson was most interested in offsetting conservative opposition to his bill, he was not unmindful of the viewpoints of the liberal forces in Congress, which under normal circumstances could be relied on to favor foreign aid legislation. Due to increasing discontent over the escalation of the war in Vietnam, coupled with growing concern about urban unrest, liberal support for the president's program could not be assured in 1967. Liberals were also upset over what they considered to be Johnson's refusal to abide by congressional guidelines—which had been inserted into the Foreign Aid Bill of 1966—regarding the allocation of technical assistance. This was particularly true in the Senate, where, for example, Senator William Fulbright, normally a supporter of foreign aid, had protested as early as February Johnson's extension of technical aid to twenty-six more countries than had been specified by Congress (*New York Times*, February 15, 1967).

Johnson's attempt to mollify liberal opponents in Congress included two essential strategies. On the one hand, his bill called for the increased employment of multilateral institutions for the dispensation and distribution of international assistance. And on the other, it pleaded for a two-year authorization so that the flexibility and planning procedures of the foreign aid program could be improved. Both these provisions had been favored by liberal elements within Congress for many years. Of course, as Johnson's legislative campaign evolved it became apparent that his strategy would permit him to abandon the positions favored by the liberal camp in order to ensure conservative support in Congress. The president was undoubtedly convinced that in the crunch, liberal supporters of foreign aid, although unhappy with certain provisions of his bill, would not permit foreign assistance to be buried permanently.

The most significant opposition to the foreign aid measure in 1967 developed in the Senate. Here, opposition clustered principally around two or three elements of the president's program. A perennial issue of senatorial concern, and one that was particularly evident in 1967, concerned the effect of foreign aid on the manner in which power is shared by the legislative and executive branches of government. A substantial number of senators, many of them liberals, expressed dissatisfaction with the trend toward executive domination in foreign policy matters, including foreign aid, and urged Congress to reassert its constitutional status as a coordinate branch of government. The difficulty "that has developed with the foreign aid bill," claimed Senator Wayne Morse of Oregon "is the growing recognition in this country that we [that is, Congress] ought to do a better job of exercising our constitutional checks, and particularly the purse strings, at the legislative level" (U.S. Senate, 1967b, p. 180). Whoever got the idea, Morse asked rhetorically, that the "President has unchecked authority in the field of foreign policy" (Ibid., p. 178)?

Some senators were quick to criticize the administration for what they considered to be its unnecessary secrecy. Commenting upon the military aid program, for example, Senator Frank Church of Idaho pointed out that "secrecy that shrouds . . . military aid forces the public to accept on faith the well-worn litany of phrases about the importance of this program." "A democratic system," he noted, "does not survive on faith—it survives on freedom of debate and freedom of information." (Congressional Record, 1967, p. 22644) Of course, not all senators were willing to endorse congressional limitations on presidential authority in order to correct an alleged executive-legislative imbalance. For example, John Sherman Cooper of Kentucky argued that "if the Congress considers foreign assistance a worthwhile instrument of our foreign policy, then it ought to provide the President some flexibility for its effective conduct" (Ibid., p. 22560).

Other senators objected to the foreign aid program because of their dissatisfaction with American policy in Vietnam. America's expanding role in Vietnam, some felt, demanded a reappraisal of the scope of the foreign assistance program. "I am not convinced," said Senator Church, "that we can conduct a $25 billion war in Vietnam, then go ahead with foreign aid as usual as though the war did not exist . . ." (U.S. Senate, 1967b, p. 202). The escalating costs of American actions in Southeast Asia therefore required a reduction in foreign assistance appropriations and expenditures.

Some senators claimed that the Vietnam crisis called for a reevaluation of national priorities in the distribution of American resources that were decidedly not limitless. It was more important, Senator Fulbright argued, to relieve the crisis of the cities than to continue foreign assistance at current levels. "There is something wrong with a system of priorities," Fulbright noted, "that proposes to continue foreign aid as usual, under the circumstances facing our nation today" (*Congressional Record,* 1967, p. 22550; see also U.S. Senate, 1967b, p. 166). Others pointed to America's expanding commitment in Vietnam as the principal threat to badly needed domestic programs. As a result of the taxing burden of Vietnam on our limited resources, we are far from accomplishing the goals of the Great Society in our own country, claimed Senator Church. Moreover, he expected Congress to make further cuts in planned domestic programs.

Despite a strenuous educational campaign by administration forces, a number of senators denied the administration's claim that foreign aid would prevent "future Vietnams." As Morse noted, "Much [of foreign aid], particularly its military aspects, is conducive to war, and not to peace . . ." (U.S. Senate, 1967b, p. 20). In addition, as some senators pointed out, foreign assistance often served as a convenient pretext for American involvement and intervention throughout the globe. Fulbright asserted that he could not "dissociate what we are doing in Vietnam, [and] what we did in the Dominican Republic, from what appears to be our tendency to intervene on the slightest provocation on the basis of an aid program" (*Ibid.,* p. 119).

Traditionally, foreign aid did gain support insofar as it was promoted and accepted as a powerful anti-Communist weapon. By 1967, however, many senators were beginning to question seriously the validity of this claim. Such a rationale, Senator Edward Kennedy of Massachusetts noted, tended to divert foreign assistance from those nations having the greatest potential for economic development. (*New York Times*, May 3, 1967) Sharing Kennedy's position, Church urged that American foreign aid be based upon the obligation of the United States as a rich nation to help bridge the gap between the poor and the wealthy nations and to improve living standards throughout the world (U.S. Senate, 1967b, p. 201.)

The image of aid as a direct anti-Communist tool has also led, at least in the recent past, to congressional support for military assistance. But by 1967, even that formerly most sacrosanct component of the foreign aid program was being criticized severely. Senator Morse was perhaps the most outspoken critic of American military-aid policy. During the congressional hearings on the Foreign Assistance Act, he pointed to the distribution of American military assistance throughout the globe as the "greatest cause of the spread of Communism," and warned of a military takeover of the foreign policy of our country. "The American people," Morse asserted, "are going to have to decide whether they will have a form of military takeover in this Republic by putting more and more unchecked power in the Pentagon [and thus substituting] the military mind for the civilian mind in determining the policy of our Government" (*Congressional Record*, 1967, pp. 22631–32).

The administration's case was presented most succinctly by Secretary of State Dean Rusk before the House Foreign Affairs Committee. He argued that "the military assistance program is a necessary complement to the economic assistance program; and it is a small insurance policy against the growth of situations around the world which might require far greater commitments of our resources, perhaps even including our military manpower" (U.S. House 1967, p. 836). Although most senators agreed that military assistance could not be abandoned wholly without jeopardizing American national security, several objected to the administration's reluctance to reveal either the nature or the extent of such aid to recipient countries. A report by the Senate Foreign Relations Committee, for example, labeled as "unfortunate" the policy of the executive branch in "shroud[ing] the names of the countries [receiving military assistance], the amounts and the details involved, from public scrutiny, so that it is virtually impossible to establish a meaningful dialogue on the question of whether, and to what extent, the military assistance program, as constituted, is vital to our current interests" (U.S. Senate, 1967a, p. 14).

Most senatorial critics of military aid policy, however, chose to focus their opposition on a Johnson proposal that would have permitted the Pentagon to employ a special revolving fund in order to finance arms sales throughout the world. From the outset, military arms sales by the Pentagon had been a source of controversy. The Johnson administration's intention to expand the operation of the revolving fund converted the question of military aid, and more particularly the issue of arms sales by the Pentagon, into a major subject of legislative debate.

As early as January, 1967 it was becoming apparent that forces within the Senate were organizing themselves for an attack against the prevailing pattern of military sales policy. On January 29 Senator Eugene McCarthy of Minnesota labeled the arms sales program a "vested interest of the Pentagon and the United States armaments industry" and expressed agreement with the results of a Senate staff study that described military sales policy as "marred by a lack of information, by weaknesses in interdepartmental coordination at highest levels and, finally, by a lack of serious attention to the problems of reconciling an active arms control policy with an arms sales program" (*New York Times*, January 30, 1967). The United States, McCarthy warned, seemed to be "drifting into a policy of preemptive selling" rather than pursuing the more difficult alternative of arms denial.

The action taken by the Senate Foreign Relations Committee to curb arms sales by abolishing the Pentagon's revolving fund was therefore not unexpected. The committee reported that it did "not believe that military assistance should be used as a kind of Public Law 480 surplus disposal program for the Pentagon" (U.S. Senate, 1967a, p. 13). Moreover, as Committee Chairman William Fulbright argued, the committee action would not eliminate the role of the Defense Department in the distribution of military aid, but it would exclude the Pentagon from the "banking business" (*Congressional Record*, 1967, p. 22639).

Meanwhile, other critics of American military sales policy were attacking it from slightly different perspectives. Wayne Morse, as we noted, perceived the issue in terms of civilian supremacy over the military. Others claimed that the fundamental question at stake in the issue of the revolving fund was the role and responsibilities of Congress. The continuation of the revolving fund, these senators maintained, would seriously weaken Congress's political control. Senator Albert Gore's objection to the revolving fund, for example, stemmed from his conviction that "Congress should exercise its oversight function and annually review these programs, rather than permit the continuation of a huge revolving fund, for all practical purposes solely within the power of the Executive Branch" (*Congressional Record*, 1967, p. 22567). Still others pointed with dismay to the consequences of military sales policy in the past, a policy that had subsidized "weapons manufacturers to a dangerous and undesirable extent," and these senators favored the abolition of the revolving fund as a necessary step in challenging the military-industrial complex (*New York Times*, January 30, 1967). Finally, some senators charged that arms sales policy, particularly in the underdeveloped world, served merely to heighten international tensions and to divert scarce resources in those areas from the immediate tasks of economic development. Fulbright claimed, "The true interests of this nation are not served by a policy which encourages the spread of sophisticated United States weapons in the hands of poor, unsophisticated people who should be using their meager resources to grow more food and in building . . . schools and houses, not in buying tanks and jet fighters" (*Congressional Record*, 1967, p. 22550).

The administration's supporters in the Senate sought to rally their forces behind an amendment proposed by Senator Henry Jackson of Washington aimed at restoring the provisions in the administration bill regarding credit sales for military equipment (in other words, the revolving fund). Major congressional figures within the legislative hierarchy, particularly those with unimpeachable credentials on defense matters, were enlisted in behalf of the administration's cause. Senator Richard Russell, chairman of the powerful Armed Services Committee, unqualifiedly endorsed the administration's position. In the legislative debate, Russell produced a letter from the Joint Chiefs of Staff expressing their belief that any "serious reduction of military aid caused by the lack of . . . provision for credit availability . . . would . . . raise world tensions rather than reduce them" (*Ibid.*, p. 22563). Support for the president's position was also offered by Senators John Tower of Texas and Jacob Javits of New York (*Ibid.*, pp. 22643, 22647). Senator John Stennis of Mississippi, a specialist on military matters, delivered a sharp rebuke to the Foreign Relations Committee, calling its decision to outlaw credit sales "a unilateral disarmament move by the United States alone." The "cessation of our selective credit sales to developing countries will [not]," Stennis argued, "prevent their purchase of arms elsewhere" (*Ibid.*, p. 22547).

During the Senate hearings, major administration spokesmen sought to defend the arms sales policy. Although Secretary of Defense Robert McNamara admitted that the "general run-of-the-mill military sales do not come to the attention of the President" (U.S. Senate, 1967b, p. 264), he claimed that the overall arms sales policy was scrutinized at the interdepartmental level to ensure its conformance with the general policy of the State Department. As he elaborated before the House Foreign Affairs Committee, "every military sale made is either consonant with overall policy established by the Department of State, or is specifically subjected to a careful . . . review within the U.S. Government before a negotiation is instituted. The review is concerned with the military legitimacy of the requirements, the recipient's ability to pay, [and] the potential effect on peace or stability in the area" (U.S. House, 1967, p. 119). According to McNamara, the purpose of the revolving fund was to reduce the threat of an arms race and to avoid what he considered "destabilizing relationships among nations" or a power imbalance (U.S. Senate, 1967b, p. 312).

Angered by this flurry of activity on behalf of the administration, critics of the American arms sales policy redoubled their efforts. Responding to Senator Stennis's charge that any restriction on credit sales was tantamount to unilateral American disarmament, Senator Gore argued that the liquidation of the revolving fund "is an effort to check the United States lead in the armaments race," a race in which America finances "the dumping of armaments into countries which do not need them and [taxes] the American taxpayer for it" (*Congressional Record,* 1967, p. 22567). Fulbright forthrightly condemned the Armed Services Committee for its position favoring the Jackson amendment. The Arkansas senator indicated his intention to vote against the bill should their effort succeed. Criticizing the intensive efforts of administration lobbyists to obtain legislative support for the foreign aid program, Fulbright observed disparagingly that "in recent years nearly every agency of the Executive Branch has vastly expanded the number of people charged with responsibility for getting legislation passed in a form satisfactory to the Executive" (*Ibid.*, p. 22551). (Despite this extensive effort by the administration to restore the credit sales provision, the Jackson amendment was ultimately defeated.)

Even before the administration had formally presented its foreign aid program to Congress, it was clear that the opposition in the Senate was stiffening. Hearings before the Senate Foreign Relations Committee were convened on June 12, fully a month before administration witnesses were available to testify. Moreover, the Senate committee had already decided to cut military aid, reduce the number of countries eligible for technical assistance, and eliminate the revolving fund even before hearing administration officials. Most administration spokesmen, as a result, were put in the difficult position of merely urging the committee to reassess its earlier actions, a position that the hostility within the committee simply exacerbated.

Even after obtaining what appeared to be a substantial victory in cutting back military aid and in defeating the Jackson proposal, the liberal contingent of the Foreign Relations Committee was far from enthusiastic in its support of the foreign aid measure. On July 27, Senator Fulbright announced that he would not manage the bill on the Senate floor and would probably vote against it. Indeed, at one point the committee was evenly divided over the question of reporting the bill to the floor without committee recommendation. Of course, had such action been approved, it would have seriously jeopardized the fate of the measure. The tie was eventually broken and the measure was reported on August 9. "The most common attitude among members," noted the committee report (U.S. Senate, 1967a, p. 4) "was the feeling that foreign aid policy has not kept pace with a changing world, and that all too often dollars were applied in an attempt to serve as a substitute for sound policies." Despite this dissatisfaction, the committee reasoned that the world leadership position of the United States demanded that it do something to close the gap between more- and less-developed countries. As the report concluded, "The question at issue in this bill . . . is not 'Should we provide aid?'; it is, rather, 'How, what kind, and how much?' " (*Ibid.*, p. 15)

Unhappy with the Foreign Relation Committee's actions, the administration hoped that it could convince the Senate to reverse the committee's decisions. It managed to obtain support from the *New York Times*, which described the Senate committee's action as "more spite than selectivity" and claimed that traditional supporters of foreign aid were "using the bill as a whipping boy to vent their ire over Administration policies in other areas, namely Vietnam" (July 30, 1967). In addition, General Earl Wheeler, chairman of the Joint Chiefs of Staff, was called upon to plead with the Senate for a restoration of cuts in military aid. On the whole, however, such administration efforts in the Senate were not as extensive as one might suppose. The president, for example, chose not to intervene directly in the legislative struggle. Instead, the administration shifted its efforts to the House. Since the House was clearly more favorably disposed toward Johnson's foreign aid program than the Senate, the administration may have reasoned that some of the essential elements of that program might be salvaged when the differing provisions of the measure were reconciled in conference.

Hearings on the foreign aid bill before the House Foreign Affairs Committee were opened on April 4. Committee Chairman Thomas Morgan was a staunch supporter of the administration's proposals. Administration officials, therefore, found a much more hospitable environment than they had found in the Senate. In their testimony before the House committee they defended the program on the grounds that it would help prevent future Vietnams, as well as fulfill the responsibilities of the United States to decrease the gap between the developed and underdeveloped areas of the globe. In particular, they stressed that the inclusion of the self-help provisions in this act marked a departure from the previous patterns of American foreign aid policy. As AID administrator William

Gaud noted, "The legislation before you stresses the importance of self-help by specifying criteria to be taken into account in furnishing development aid . . ." (U.S. House, 1967, pp. 67–68).

On August 11, four months after the opening of hearings, the House committee concluded its deliberations and sent the bill to the floor for House action. Despite considerable support for the measure within the House as a whole, a number of congressmen were decidedly less than enthusiastic about the Johnson program. Some congressmen, expressing concern about rising government expenditures, objected to the magnitude of the economic aid provisions (*Congressional Record*, 1967, p. 23681). Even many of them, however, were perfectly willing to go along with the administration's request for military assistance. As John Buchanan of Alabama said, "I would urge support for the amendments which will be offered to trim down economic aid. Cuts in military assistance, however, should be made with great caution" (*Ibid.*, p. 23666). This economy-minded group within the House was successful in trimming $100 million from the development loan provisions of the bill, despite Chairman Morgan's claim that the loan program "is not a giveaway program," and that the "loans are being repaid" (*Ibid.*, p. 23915).

Another group of congressmen objected to the potential for presidential abuse of the technical assistance provisions of the measure. A leading spokesman for this group, E. Ross Adair of Indiana, questioning the effectiveness of foreign aid programs in the past, observed that "one of the failures in our foreign aid program is the lack of selectivity in determining the nations to whom we give aid" (*Ibid.* , p. 23602). He then offered an amendment that would have reduced technical assistance. Leonard Farbstein of New York responded that such reductions might undermine efforts to stimulate private foreign investment, particularly in underdeveloped nations. "If you are going to decrease those moneys that are necessary in order to assist the various underdeveloped countries to help themselves," Farbstein claimed, "you are defeating not alone the question of foreign aid, but you are defeating the basis for all efforts that we are expending in order to get private interests to go into foreign countries" (*Ibid.*, p. 23919). By an extraordinarily close vote, the Adair amendment was defeated.

The request for a two-year authorization for the foreign aid program was also opposed by many in the House. Most of these individuals viewed the proposal as yet another effort by the executive to curb legislative power. Should the House accept the two-year authorization, said Robert Taft, Jr. of Ohio, "would it not be a recognition of the fact that the Executive and not the Legislative Branch is to make policy in this area?" (*Ibid.*, p. 23612) Obviously, a majority in the House agreed with this view, because the proposal was voted down.

Opposition of a broader nature, opposition that involved a general repudiation of the principles and purposes of foreign aid, was also evident in the House. This stemmed primarily from more conservative and less internationally minded quarters among whom a brand of neo-isolationism was the major theme. This group had existed in the past, but dissatisfaction with American policy in Vietnam and with what appeared to be the government's growing insensitivity to domestic problems enlarged it considerably. Even so, efforts by this faction to shelve foreign aid legislation for 1967 proved abortive. H. R. Gross of Iowa, a leading figure within this faction, offered an amendment that would have referred the bill back to committee for a removal of its enacting clause, thus effectively terminating further consideration of the measure. This amendment failed to pass by a wide margin (*Ibid.*, pp. 23930–31), and a recommittal motion sponsored by Gross at a later stage of debate was also defeated, although by a closer vote.

As subsequently enacted, the House bill differed considerably from the Senate version. On August 28, a few days after the House bill had been approved, the Senate announced its disagreement with the House measure and moved for a conference on the bill. At this point, leading opponents of Johnson's program in the Senate expressed their pessimism about reconciling the differing versions of the measure. Fulbright indicated his intention to let "the bill languish in conference indefinitely if we cannot reach a satisfactory agreement on the major proposals" (*Ibid.*, p. 2296).

Amidst a decidedly less than optimistic atmosphere, the Conference Committee deliberated for a period of seven weeks. Initially at least, little progress appeared to be made. Efforts by the State Department to facilitate negotiations proved fruitless. By late

October it appeared that the committee was deadlocked. The most intractable problem before the conferees proved to be the issue of arms sales, in particular, the status of the Pentagon's revolving fund. Unlike the Senate bill, the House measure had retained the revolving fund. In conference, both sides appeared reluctant to budge from their respective positions in order to work out a mutually acceptable formula. On October 30, Fulbright noted that a resolution of the deadlock in conference did not "look good" (*New York Times*, October 31, 1967). The public interest, he observed, might be better served by no foreign aid bill than by the House measure, "which would . . . encourage . . . a continuation of the policy of arming poor and underdeveloped countries" (*Congressional Record*, 1967, p. 3068).

Aware of the notable lack of progress in negotiations, the Democratic leadership in the House, with White House support, developed a plan of action that involved going directly to the Appropriations Committee for approval of the foreign aid program, thereby eliminating completely the need for a preceding foreign aid authorization measure. Such a strategy, if pursued successfully, would have bypassed the Foreign Relations Committee, hence excluding a major center of opposition (*New York Times*, October 25, 1967). Such a step proved unnecessary, however, since on November 3 the Conference Committee announced that its members had resolved their outstanding differences. The House conferees agreed to the termination of the Pentagon's world-wide arms sales program on June 30, 1968 in exchange for a Senate commitment to increase the level of military aid spending.

On November 8 both the House and the Senate approved the Conference Committee report, and the bill was adopted. In signing the bill into law, President Johnson said that "it reduced the margin of hope to the danger point."

Despite this evident discontent, Johnson had made only limited gestures to ensure the enactment of his measure. At no point during debate on the measure in either the House or the Senate did the president choose to intervene directly. For example, Chairman Morgan's request to release a letter from the president affirming support for the foreign aid program was refused by the administration. Undoubtedly, a clear-cut, forthright position by the president on the measure would have improved its chances for passage without significant amendment. Moreover, his silence on the bill was perhaps interpreted by many congressmen as indifference to the fate of the program (*New York Times*, August 24, 1967).

Johnson obviously preferred to rely upon the Democratic leadership in Congress and certain key agencies within the executive branch, including the Department of Defense, AID, the Joint Chiefs, and the Department of State, to mobilize support for the measure in Congress. Confronting serious domestic crises and an escalating involvement in Vietnam, which were producing a growing budget deficit and necessitating serious consideration of a tax increase, Johnson concluded that his optimal course of action under these circumstances was to refrain from overt participation in the legislative process. Moreover, even under the best of circumstances, as many commentators have noted, a strong presidential commitment to foreign aid programs does not necessarily guarantee a high degree of congressional conformance with executive requests (see, for example, O'Leary, 1967, p. 123).

In the case of the 1967 foreign aid bill, however, both the leadership provided by the executive branch agencies and the Democratic congressional leadership faltered badly. The leadership in the Senate was badly divided, and even the measure's supporters were far from enthusiastic. Although they were more united than their counterparts in the Senate, the House leaders too often pursued an unwise and untimely strategy. For example, the decision by the House Democratic leadership to hold the House in a marathon fifteen-hour session in the closing days of debate in order to battle through more than forty-five amendments was a singularly ill-advised tactic that angered some of the bill's strongest advocates. But perhaps the most significant measure of the failure of the House Democratic leadership was that critical support for the successful enactment of the measure had to be delivered by the Republican leaders. As the *New York Times* observed, "[It was] the G.O.P. high command in the House that prevented a complete disaster for the Administration" (August 26, 1967). In the final House vote on the measure, 52 Republicans joined 150 Democrats to provide the margin of victory. Republican support in the Senate was no less significant.

The impact of public opinion and interest groups on the Foreign Assistance Act of 1967 was, on the whole, marginal. As in the past, the public in 1967 was generally not interested in the issue of foreign aid. Moreover, Johnson's apparent indifference to the fate of his foreign aid measure served only to reinforce this lack of interest. Little effort was made by the administration to educate the public on the elements of the foreign aid program, or to mobilize broad community support for its enactment.

Despite this indifference of the general public, most interest groups and associations testifying on the measure indicated their approval of the program. Testimony before the House and Senate committees was offered by a wide variety of interest groups, including the National Farmers Union, the National Association of Home Builders, the Friends Committee on National Legislation, and the International Economic Policy Association. Although most of these groups supported the foreign aid program, there were one or two notable exceptions. The Citizens Foreign Aid Committee denounced foreign aid for "entangling the United States in the military, economic and psychological affairs of recipient countries" and "for failing to do what it is supposed to do" (see U.S. House, 1967, p. 914; U.S. Senate, 1967b, p. 357). Despite the preponderance of organized opinion in favor of Johnson's program, such opinion appears to have had little impact on the legislative deliberations on the measure. The statements by these groups before the Senate and House committees evoked little response or reaction from the congressmen. Thus, O'Leary's claim that "in the case of foreign aid, . . . groups tend to observe rather than influence the policy-making process" (1967, p. 47) seems to be born out in this instance.

Our examination of the decision making involved in the Foreign Assistance Act of 1967 reveals the extent to which the legislature was able to mount a successful challenge to the traditional pattern of presidential domination in the field of foreign policy, and to substantially revise a proposal of the executive branch in the process. Congressional dissatisfaction with presidential supremacy in foreign-policy making, discontent that was due to a growing frustration over the administration's policy of escalation in Vietnam and growing concern about urban unrest and domestic crises, provided the immediate context for independent legislative action. The president's unwillingness to support actively his program, a badly divided leadership and faulty planning in both the House and the Senate, and a close partisan division in both houses also bolstered legislative initiative. Although these situational factors were undoubtedly important in deciding the fate of the 1967 foreign aid bill, one has to remember the context within which foreign aid policy is made. As we indicated at the beginning of this chapter, there has been a history of congressional opposition —from a variety of political stances—to foreign aid. Furthermore, this policy area is especially susceptible to congressional intervention since (1) foreign aid is a continuing program requiring regular legislative action, and (2) it involves very directly that congressional holy of holies—control of the purse strings. Thus, it is not surprising that in the case of the 1967 foreign aid bill, as with the Trade Expansion Act, the foreign-policy making process—and in particular the relations between the executive and legislative branches that are a part of that process—bears a stronger resemblance to the domestic-policy making process than in most of the other cases discussed in this book.

REFERENCES AND BIBLIOGRAPHY

BANFIELD, EDWARD C., *American Foreign Aid Doctrines*. Washington: American Enterprise Institute for Public Policy Research, 1963.

MONTGOMERY, JOHN D., *Foreign Aid in International Politics*. Englewood Cliffs, N.J.: Prentice-Hall, 1967.

NELSON, JOAN M., *Aid, Influence and Foreign Policy*. New York: Macmillan, 1968.

O'LEARY, MICHAEL KENT, *The Politics of Foreign Aid*. New York: Atherton, 1967.

U.S., Congress, *Congressional Record*, 1967.

U.S., Congress, House, Committee on Foreign Affairs, *Hearings, Foreign Assistance Act of 1967*, 90th Cong., 1st sess., 1967.

U.S., Congress, Senate, Committee on Foreign Relations, *Foreign Assistance Act of 1967*, Report no. 499, Serial no. 12750—3, 90th Cong., 1st sess., 1967a.

——Hearings, *Foreign Assistance Act of 1967*, 90th Cong., 1st sess., 1967b.

12

The Decision
to Cut Back the Bombing
in Vietnam
1968

President Johnson's decision on March 31, 1968 to declare a partial
halt to the bombing in Vietnam amply illustrates the complexities
of the interior processes of presidential decision making. This
momentous decision was reached after an intensive month-long
debate within the top circles of the Johnson administration, a debate that involved most of Johnson's key advisors.

Since much has been written on the early history of American
involvement in Vietnam, there is little need to recount this period
in detail. (See, among others, Kahin and Lewis, 1967; Eidenberg,
1969.) Instead, it is sufficient to identify and highlight a number of
major stages in the escalating military policy which replaced the
cautious approach of the 1950s (see Chapter 4).

During the Kennedy administration, American involvement was limited largely to civilian technicians and military trainers. By the time of Kennedy's death, however, the American military presence in Vietnam had grown from a few hundred to about 16,000. In the early months of 1964, fully six months before the Tonkin Gulf incident of August, covert military activities were undertaken by the United States against North Vietnam. These operations ranged from flights over North Vietnam by U-2 spy planes to kidnapings of North Vietnamese citizens for intelligence information to commando raids from the sea designed to destroy rail and highway bridges. It was also during this period that the Joint Chiefs of Staff drew up a list of ninety-four potential bombing targets in the North.

By the time of the Tonkin Gulf incident in August, plans for expanding military actions were well advanced. At a strategy session held early in June at Honolulu, high governmental and military officials considered carefully how to prepare the American public for the contemplated escalation. Later in the month, "State and Defense Department sources made repeated leaks to the press affirming U.S. intentions to support its Allies and uphold its treaty commitments in Southeast Asia" (Sheehan et al., 1971, p. 252). Widespread publicity was also given in June and July to American military prepositioning moves. Meanwhile, key Johnson aides met during June to consider a congressional resolution authorizing the use of military force in Southeast Asia. Although the president appeared reluctant to employ military force at this time, he pushed his administration "to plan energetically for escalation" (Ibid., p. 245).

On the evening of August 4, North Vietnamese torpedo boats apparently launched an attack against two American destroyers in the Gulf of Tonkin. (A full account of this disputed incident is provided in Goulden, 1969.) Shortly after news of the interception had been transmitted to Washington, the Joint Chiefs began selecting possible targets for reprisal air strikes from the target list that had been prepared earlier. Although this was not the first attack by the North Vietnamese on American military forces it precipitated a round of discussions within key governmental circles. Within a few hours the president convened the National Security Council, which in turn recommended immediate retaliatory actions. It was also decided that Johnson would seek prompt congressional support for further military steps.

A retaliatory strike consisting of sixty-four bombing missions was ordered against the North. The administration perceived this action as the initial step of a possibly broader bombing campaign against North Vietnam. This longer-range aspect became apparent on the following day when Defense Secretary Robert McNamara announced during his press conference the transfer of an attack carrier group from the Pacific Coast to the Western Pacific, the movement of interceptor and fighter-bomber aircraft into South Vietnam and Thailand, and the transfer of interceptor and fighter-bomber squadrons from the United States to advance bases in the Pacific. The press was also informed that selected army and marine forces had been alerted and readied for movement (Sheehan et al. 1971, p. 264).

Shortly after the decision for retaliatory strikes had been made, sixteen congressional leaders were summoned to the White House by the president. They were informed both of the decision and of Johnson's intention to request a congressional resolution supporting further military action. According to *The Pentagon Papers*, however, the congressmen were not told of the broader purpose behind the military deployments, which McNamara was to announce at his press conference.

The president's decision was supported unanimously by the congressional delegation. Not a single congressman objected to the retaliatory raids. It was decided that Senator William Fulbright, as chairman of the Foreign Relations Committee, would assume the task of guiding the resolution through the Senate, and Representative Thomas Morgan, Fulbright's counterpart in the House, would perform a similar service in that institution. In an address to the nation later that evening, Johnson defended the air strikes as "limited and fitting" and declared his expectation that the desired congressional resolution would "be promptly introduced, freely and expeditiously debated, and passed with overwhelming support" (quoted in Halper, 1971, p. 83).

The next day, August 5, the president submitted a formal request for a congressional joint resolution that would "approve and support the determination of the President . . . to take all necessary measures to repel any armed attack against the forces of the United States and to prevent further aggression" (Kalb and Abel, 1971, p. 173). This resolution, as Hoopes was later to write, was to become "the principal constitutional instrument by which [the President] radically altered the character of U.S. involvement in Vietnam six months later" (1969, p. 25). At that time, however, there were few dissenting voices either in the country at large or in Congress. Few congressmen realized that they would be surrendering much of their influence over the future course of policy in Vietnam by passing the joint resolution in the form requested by the administration. As one observer remarked later, the resolution "was subsequently parlayed into a blank check to rationalize the President's unwillingness to have Congress play a meaningful role in his Vietnam policy" (Cooper, 1970, p. 243).

In an atmosphere marked by grave urgency, closed-door hearings on the resolution were held in each chamber on August 6. Defense Secretary McNamara and Secretary of State Dean Rusk testified in support of administration policy. Except for Wayne Morse of Oregon, no congressman attempted to scrutinize the testimony. Chairman Fulbright asked no questions at all. On the following day, after an inconsequential floor debate, the House by a vote of 416 to 0 and the Senate by a vote of 88 to 2 adopted the joint resolution.

Despite the magnitude of congressional support for the resolution, there remained considerable confusion in Congress regarding its meaning. Congressional opinion varied as to its policy implications and substantive meaning. Most congressmen viewed the measure as demonstrating both support for the president's actions and a determination to oppose future aggression. Beyond these central beliefs, however, there was little consensus. As the authors of *The Pentagon Papers* observed, "Several spokesmen stressed that the Resolution did not constitute a declaration of war, did not abdicate Congressional responsibility for determining national policy commitments, and did not give the President carte blanche to involve the nation in a major Asian war" (Sheehan et al., 1971, p. 268). Despite these disclaimers, one cannot deny that the "Tonkin

Gulf Resolution set U.S. public support for virtually any action" (*Ibid.*, p. 269).

A "general consensus" to conduct a series of air attacks against the North was reached by the Johnson administration as early as September, 1964. There was disagreement, however, over the timing and the extent of these raids. In a memorandum to McNamara on August 26, the Joint Chiefs advocated an immediate decision to conduct an air war against the North, which they viewed as "essential to prevent a complete collapse of the U.S. position in Southeast Asia" (*Ibid.*, p. 312). A "provocation strategy" was then outlined in which an effort would be made to "provoke the [Hanoi] government into taking actions which could then be answered by a systematic U.S. air campaign" (*Ibid.*, p. 313). In a separate memorandum from the civilian side of the Defense Department on September 3, Assistant Secretary of Defense John McNaughton recommended a similar policy of provocation. McNaughton, however, called merely for reprisal attacks, and suggested postponing the decision to escalate the bombing until a series of provocatory acts could "culminate in a sustained war" (*Ibid.*, p. 313). Despite this tactical disagreement, it was apparent that by the end of 1964 a consensus in favor of bombing the North had developed.

By early March, 1965 the president had approved Operation Rolling Thunder, a program of sustained air attacks against the North. This decision followed Vietcong attacks in early February on American installations in Vietnam. It was felt that these guerrilla actions could serve as the pretexts sought by the administration to initiate its bombing campaign. Referring to the Vietcong attack at Pleiku, McGeorge Bundy observed, "Pleiku's are [like] streetcars, i.e., if one waits watchfully, they come along" (quoted in Hoopes, 1969, p. 30). After initial reprisal attacks, the "air strikes," Townsend Hoopes observed, "were almost imperceptibly transformed into a systematic program of bombing the North . . ." (*Ibid.*). Thus, by the end of February the whole concept of reprisal had been wholly abandoned, and the chosen policy of a "slow squeeze"—that is, gradual escalation of a modest bombing campaign to weaken the North's ability to support the insurgents in the South—was put into effect.

By the end of March it was apparent that the bombing had not, in the words of *The Pentagon Papers*, "staved off collapse in the South" (Sheehan et al., 1971, p. 382). On April 1 Johnson decided to deploy American ground troops for offensive action in South Vietnam, despite CIA warnings that this action was not likely to succeed. The president agreed to send approximately 20,000 troops and two additional marine battalions. It was also decided that the marine units guarding major American installations would be permitted to engage in active combat. The dispatch of the marines and the extension of their mission beyond passive security operations marked an important and perhaps irreversible step in the escalation of the war.

In the ensuing months, the American military presence expanded markedly. In large part, the American build-up occurred as a result of the abandonment by the administration of the enclave strategy in favor of the Joint Chiefs' search-and-destroy policy. Unlike the enclave strategy, the object of which was the involvement of the United States forces at relatively low risk, the search-and-destroy strategy sought to "take the war to the enemy, denying his freedom of movement anywhere in the country . . . and deal him the heaviest possible blows" (*Ibid.*, p. 403). Johnson endorsed this strategy fully, although it obviously entailed an "open-ended commitment," since "force levels for the search-and-destroy strategy . . . depended on the enemy's response" (Clotfelter, 1973, p. 222).

The results of this strategy can be seen in the following figures. By October, 1965 there were 150,000 American soldiers in Vietnam. By March, 1966 this figure had increased to 215,000. Toward the end of that year there were 389,000 troops in Vietnam, and by June, 1967, 463,000.

The war continued unabated through 1966. Efforts were made to reduce American involvement, but these proved largely abortive. In March, after months of pressure by the Joint Chiefs, McNamara recommended the bombing of North Vietnamese petroleum, oil, and lubricant supplies. These were ordered by the president in May. Despite the growing apprehension shared by some elements in the Johnson administration in late 1966 regarding the effectiveness of American policy in Vietnam, the president refused to alter his position. In February, 1967 a "spring air offensive" involving attacks on power plants, the mining of rivers, and the relaxation of restrictions on air raids near Hanoi and Haiphong were approved.

As the spring of 1967 passed, however, a small group in the Pentagon and State Department earnestly set about to develop a proposal with potentially important implications for the course of the war. This proposal centered in a recommendation to cut back all bombing of North Vietnam to points south of the twentieth parallel. Pitted against this group of "disillusioned doves," who were led principally by McNamara, were the military, who pressed for an extension of the conflict. The president, along with civilians in the White House and the Air Force and some State Department officials, took a middle position.

In a memorandum to the president on October 14, 1966, McNamara had for the first time called for sharp cutbacks in military requests for reinforcements. Previously, such requests had been approved almost routinely in Washington. Now, McNamara was recommending that the administration should be "girdling openly for a longer war" rather than pursuing General Westmoreland's strategy of attrition (Sheehan et al. 1971, p. 549). Despite prevailing United States policy, McNamara seemed willing even to contemplate a role for the Vietcong both in the peace negotiations and in the postwar life and government of Vietnam. Then in mid-March, in response to a request by Westmoreland for 200,000 more troops, a broad-ranging examination of the prevailing military strategy and the effectiveness of the air war was initiated. The conflict between the advocates of a greatly expanded air campaign against North Vietnam and the "disillusioned doves" urging relaxation was now joined by Westmoreland's request for additional military manpower.

In early May the president was presented with a paper drafted by McNaughton, in which the assistant secretary specifically urged a cutback in bombing to the twentieth parallel. This recommendation departed significantly from McNamara's proposal the previous October, which had vaguely urged a "narrowing of the bombing campaign as a possible step toward negotiations" (*Ibid.*, pp. 532–33). Then on May 19, in a climactic statement penned jointly by McNamara and McNaughton, the case against the strategy of widening the war and in favor of curtailing the air assaults was presented to the president. The two men recommended a cutback to the twentieth parallel and an allotment of only 30,000 more troops for General Westmoreland. Perhaps more significantly, the memorandum also advocated a considerably more limited overall American objective in Vietnam, a suggestion that "amounted to . . . a recommendation that we accept a compromise outcome" (*Ibid.*, p. 535). The prevailing policy in Vietnam was being seriously challenged, and by no less prominent a person than the secretary of defense. As the authors of *The Pentagon Papers* were to note,

> Let there be no mistake, these were radical positions for a senior U.S. policy official within the Johnson Administration to take. They would bring the bitter condemnation of the Chiefs and were scarcely designed to flatter the President on the success of his effort to date. (*Ibid.*, p. 584)

The response of the Joint Chiefs to McNamara's proposals was not long in coming. Within four days they had submitted three memorandums to the defense secretary renewing earlier requests for 200,000 troops, for air attacks to mine North Vietnamese harbors and their approaches, and for raids on eight major North Vietnamese airfields and on railways leading to China. On May 31 the Joint Chiefs delivered their sharpest rebuttal to McNamara, contending that his proposed changes in policy "would undermine and no longer provide a complete rationale for our presence in South Vietnam, or much of our efforts over the past two years" (*Ibid.*, 538). They expressed grave reservations about the proposal for a bombing cutback, since they doubted that such a step would induce Hanoi to move toward negotiations. In late June, just prior to the president's meeting with Soviet Premier Kosygin at Glassboro, New Jersey, the bombing-cutback proposal was briefly revived within the Department of State. However, when the White House gave it a cool reception the idea was dropped. Not until March, 1968 would the defense secretary's proposal for a reduction of the bombing reemerge.

By July, the president was confronted with a genuine policy dilemma: he "faced a situation where the Chiefs were in ardent opposition to anything other than a significant escalation of the war, with a call-up of Reserves" (*Ibid.*, p. 538). This was clearly opposed by McNamara. It was apparently at this juncture that the defense secretary decided to take his opposition to the air war to Congress. The forum for the first public disclosure of his policy differences with the Chiefs was provided by the Senate Preparedness Sub-committee, which had decided in late July to schedule hearings on the conduct of the air war. Here, after ten military leaders had called for more and heavier bombing with fewer civilian-imposed bombing restrictions, McNamara sought to defend the administrations's past policies and to justify their continuance. The gist of his statement was

> that unless the United States shifted to an indiscriminate bombing cam-
> paign aimed at annihilating the population of North Vietnam, the air war
> against the North could not be expected to accomplish more than "to con-
> tinue to put a high price tag on North Vietnam's continued aggression." He
> saw nothing in the record to indicate that Hanoi "can be bombed to the
> negotiating table." (Hoopes, 1967, p. 87)

Arguing that the bombing had only a negligible effect on North Vietnam's capacity to prosecute the war, McNamara concluded by announcing his firm opposition to any further expansion of the air war: "However tempting, such an alternative seems to me illusory. To pursue this objective would not only be futile but would involve risks to our personnel and to our nation that I am unable to recom-mend." (quoted in Kalb and Abel, 1971, p. 198)

The subcommittee's reaction to McNamara's arguments was bitter and negative. Viewing the bombing restraints as irrational, the subcommittee "unquestionably set out to defeat" the defense secretary (Sheehan et al., 1971, p. 540). The president's reaction was even less restrained. McNamara's public denigration of the bombing of the North outraged the president, who felt that such remarks might benefit Hanoi's bargaining position. From that point on, McNamara's influence in the administration began to wane. Hence, the November 28 announcement that McNamara would be leaving the administration to become president of the World Bank should not have been unexpected. By committing himself clearly to a policy of de-escalation, McNamara had become a political liability to the president. "That military genius, McNamara, has gone dovish on me," Johnson was to complain bitterly to one senator (Hoopes, 1969, p. 90). The president could not readily tolerate opposition within the bosom of his own official family, particularly on a matter as sensitive as that of Vietnam, and he apparently "could not stomach the idea that McNamara, of all officials, should be venting his doubts in public, perhaps encouraging others in the Administration to follow his example" (Kalb and Abel, 1971, p. 199). Internal dissent, Johnson believed, was highly contagious.

While public criticism of the Vietnam War mounted in the autumn of 1967, the basic thrust of American policy continued intact. Sensitive to the rising criticism, however, Johnson attempted to counter it. The Senior Advisory Group on Vietnam, an informal assemblage of distinguished former officials, retired generals, and ambassadors who had been meeting at least once or twice a year since 1965, convened in November, announced that the war was going well, and, with the single exception of George Ball, endorsed the president's Vietnam policy. Despite this glowing assessment, Gallup Polls continued to reveal a growing public disaffection with this policy. (Figure 4 illustrates this trend in all age groups.) The president therefore decided to call home Westmoreland and Ambassadors Robert Komer and Ellsworth Bunker from Vietnam in a special effort to persuade "an increasingly skeptical public that the war was going well" (Kalb and Abel, 1971, p. 20).

Bunker contented himself with an expression of quiet optimism, but Westmoreland was far less restrained. Before the National Press Club, the general reported significant gains and stated that the war had been turned around. A few days later he predicted that Communist strength would be sufficiently sapped by 1969 to permit the withdrawal of some American troops.

On New Year's Day General Westmoreland asserted, "We should expect our gains of 1967 to be increased many-fold in 1968" (Cooper, 1970, p. 384). At this time, Washington exuded confidence that the end of the war was in sight. This mood of optimism was broken on January 31, when the Communists launched a surprise offensive consisting of a series of powerful, simultaneous attacks against dozens of key cities and towns. Saigon was attacked and partially occupied by several thousand enemy troops. A tiny band of Vietcong seized parts of the supposedly impregnable American Embassy and held them for over six hours. A second squad nearly succeeded in occupying the heavily fortified Tan-sonhut airport. American bases throughout Vietnam—in the north, south, and central highlands—were also attacked. On February 4 the *New York Times* wrote that "the guerrillas, with apparently only minor assistance from North Vietnamese units, had made major assaults on twenty-six provincial capitals and uncounted numbers of district towns and American and Vietnamese airfields and bases."

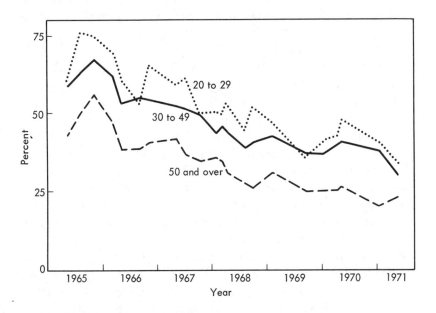

Figure 4   Trends in support for the war in Vietnam, by age.
Source: John E. Mueller, *War, Presidents and Public Opinion* (New York: John Wiley & Sons, 1973), p. 139.

In an effort to dispel any belief that the Tet offensive had been psychologically or militarily damaging, the administration moved quickly to bolster its public position. Claiming in early February that the "enemy's well laid plans went afoul," Westmoreland dismissed the Communist tactics as suicidal and urged that they be seen as a "last desperate push" by Hanoi to redress an increasingly unfavorable military balance. (*New York Times*, February 5, 1968) At his press conference on February 2, Johnson announced his agreement with these views and dismissed the enemy offensive as a "complete failure." The enemy's military and psychological goals had failed, the president pointed out, because they found little or no popular support in the cities. Johnson also sought to dismiss the belief held by some that the Allied Forces had been unprepared for the offensive. Information on the offensive had been gathered well in advance of the event; the enemy action, the president noted, "had been anticipated, prepared for and met" (quoted in Halper, 1971, p. 113). In the weeks that followed, the president's views were echoed by his principal advisors and by a number of very prominent Senate hawks.

Not all observers were as convinced of the president's analysis. Senator Stephen Young ridiculed Johnson's contention that the Allies knew of the Tet offensive beforehand. A *New York Times* editorial noted that "American preparedness for the unexpected" must be considered "a critical failure" (February 4, 1968). Doubts were also expressed about the president's view of the Tet offensive as a psychological and military defeat for the North. There can be no question that the offensive, wrote one reporter on the scene, constituted a "political-psychological setback of unprecedented magnitude" for the United States (quoted in Halper, 1971, p. 116). There was little doubt that a major psychological victory had been achieved by Hanoi, since it had clearly demonstrated to the Allies and the Vietnamese civilians that the Vietcong and North Vietnamese were still strong and could strike at will.

In the aftermath of the offensive, the administration retreated gradually but significantly from its earlier position. As Halper asserts, "It was, after all, difficult to call the offensive a complete failure in the face of the Vietcong's holding parts of Hue for twenty-four days, and forcing the South Vietnamese government's pacification teams to abandon the countryside for a month" (1971, p. 117). The offensive, it was privately admitted, had surprised even the White House and the Joint Chiefs. Its duration and intensity only prolonged that shock. The preparation by the Joint Chiefs in mid February of a proposed "mobilization package" entailing the immediate call-up of two National Guard divisions and some army reserve units clearly indicated that the offensive had shaken the military chiefs. In addition, these proposals, it might be noted, were another effort in a lengthy campaign by the military to force Johnson "a long way toward national mobilization in an effort to win victory in Vietnam" (Sheehan et al, 1971, p. 589). The president, though apparently disappointed and shocked by the intensity of the offensive, made no effort at this point to reconsider or alter his policy. He defended Westmoreland in strong terms. He announced his unwillingness to compromise, and he urged total firmness by the United States in the conduct of the war. Nonetheless, he was cautious about making further manpower commitments.

The Tet offensive was to mark the beginning of a fundamental change in Washington's appraisal of the war. As the dimensions of the offensive became widely known, dissatisfaction with the war within administration circles grew markedly. In late February the *New York Times* noted that "not only had the pool of disenchantment spread to fence-sitters in Congress, to newspaper offices and to business organizations [but] it has also reached the upper echelons of the Government" (quoted in Strum, 1972, p. 99). In recalling this period, Hoopes noted that

> in the Pentagon, the Tet offensive performed the curious service of fully revealing the doubters and dissenters to each other, as in a lightning flash. [Paul] Nitze [Deputy Secretary of Defense] suddenly spoke out on the unsoundness of continuing to reinforce weakness. . . . [Paul] Warnke [Assistant Secretary of Defense] thought Tet showed that our military strategy was foolish to the point of insanity. . . . [Finally] in various ways, the Undersecretary of the Army . . ., the Assistant Secretary of Defense for Manpower . . . and other influential civilians expressed their strong belief that the Administration's policy was at a dead end. (1969, pp. 145–6)

The Tet offensive clearly revealed that the undoubtedly growing number of official doubters and dissenters in the State Department, Congress, the Pentagon, and the CIA were not alone, and prompted them to seek jointly an American disengagement from the war.

In late February, 1968 the president decided to dispatch General Earle Wheeler, chairman of the Joint Chiefs of Staff, to Saigon to confer with Westmoreland regarding his military requirements in the aftermath of Tet. In a series of messages between Westmoreland and Wheeler shortly before this meeting, the stage had been set for a request for additional military manpower. Apparently, if the situation warranted such action, Johnson was prepared to abandon the 525,000 troop ceiling imposed in 1967.

The view of the Joint Chiefs, unlike the more pessimistic appraisals of certain civilian members of the government, was that the Tet offensive offered a great opportunity. Tet would, they felt, encourage the president to look with favor upon their program for a major expansion of American military strength. Wheeler therefore left for Saigon with a "far more ambitious program in mind then merely to restore the pre-Tet stalemate in Vietnam" (Kalb and Abel, 1971, p. 214). Along with the Joint Chiefs, he wanted to rebuild the strategic reserve in the United States, expand the bombing, and stage raids on Haiphong and possibly Hanoi—in short, to pursue a strategy of military victory in Vietnam. In Saigon, Westmoreland was enlisted in this venture. He was encouraged to develop his military strategy on the basis of the new assumptions developed by the Joint Chiefs. As Kalb and Abel observed, "It was a clear case of the Joint Chiefs using a popular Commander to help them sell the President and the incoming Secretary of Defense on a new strategic posture for the United States—one that would go far beyond the predicted needs in Vietnam alone" (Ibid., p. 215). Obviously, the service chiefs believed that their proposals would receive a more favorable reception from the new secretary of defense, Clark Clifford, than from the departing McNamara.

On February 23 Wheeler sent a cable to Washington setting forth his assessment of the situation and of the additional "force requirements" that both he and Westmoreland considered necessary. Claiming that the military situation was improving, Wheeler nonetheless reported that Westmoreland's forces were stretched thin and required prompt and substantial reinforcement. He then divided the "force requirements," which amounted to about 206,000 men, into three time phases: 107,00 by May 1, another

43,000 by September 1, and the final 56,000 by December. Washington appeared stunned at the magnitude of the request. "A fork in the road had been reached," wrote the authors of *The Pentagon Papers*.

> Now the alternatives stood out in stark reality. To accept and meet General Wheeler's request for troops would mean a total military commitment to South Vietnam—an Americanization of the war, a call-up of Reserve forces, vastly increased expenditures. To deny the request [or to reduce its size] would just as surely signify that an upper limit to the U.S. military commitment in South Vietnam had been reached. (Sheehan et al., 1971, pp. 596–97)

Neither alternative was particularly appealing. It was apparent, moreover, that in the absence of McNamara's skills in managing the manpower question, agreement within the administration regarding the level of troop reinforcements would not be reached quickly.

At a breakfast meeting at the White House on February 28, General Wheeler outlined his plans to Johnson and a small group of presidential advisors. The sheer size of the troop request shocked Johnson and most of the civilians. One participant was to recall that "it was a helluva serious breakfast!" (Strum, 1972, p. 98) The president was hesitant about making a massive new commitment. The service-chiefs-inspired request for a substantial military build-up far exceeding immediate military needs had obviously been unexpected. Johnson was particularly wary since the request reflected solely military judgment. With half a million troops already in Vietnam and with no military victory in sight, the president appeared now, perhaps for the first time, to doubt that the United States was on the right military track. The president believed, moreover, that Wheeler's proposal had not come at a particularly propitious time. Concerned with a rapidly declining level of public support for the war, the apparently growing success of Eugene McCarthy's peace campaign in New Hampshire, and an increasingly recalcitrant Congress, Johnson was extremely reluctant to broaden American commitments at that time.

Wheeler's request was to serve as a catalyst for the "disillusioned doves" within the administration, who were now "for the first time able to assert their strong anti-escalation position in a favorable psychological and managerial climate" (Hoopes, 1969, p. 165). Serious reexamination of American policy in Vietnam, they felt, was now unavoidable, and the appointment of Clark Clifford to succeed McNamara opened up new channels of communication for debate.

Later that day, the president named an Ad Hoc Task Force on Vietnam, with Clifford as chairman. The president asked the group to examine the Wheeler-Westmoreland request and to explore its domestic implications. For Clifford, the mandate of the group was not to assess the *need* for substantial increases in men and material, but to "devise the means by which they could be provided" with acceptable domestic consequences (Clifford, 1969, p. 609). Later, in an interview with Walter Cronkite in early February, 1970, the president was to argue that he had given Clifford the much broader mandate of exploring alternatives to the prevailing policy (see Kalb and Abel, 1971, pp. 217–18).

On March 1, the first formal meeting of the Ad Hoc group was convened by Clifford in the private dining room of the secretary of defense. The group was to meet in day and evening sessions through March 6. Rusk also briefly attended the meetings. The regular participants included Nicholas Katzenbach, William Bundy, and Philip Habib for the State Department; Nitze, Warnke, and Assistant Secretary Phil Goulding for the Defense Department; Wheeler for the Joint Chiefs; Richard Helms for the CIA; Walt W. Rostow for the White House; Henry Fowler for the Treasury Department; and Maxwell Taylor, a special advisor.

Clifford, feeling that the president's mandate was too narrow, moved immediately to broaden the scope of the inquiry. At the group's first meeting, the new defense secretary noted that the central problem was "not whether we should sent 200,000 additional troops to Vietnam," but whether, if "we follow the present course in South Vietnam, [it could] ever prove successful even if vastly more than 200,000 troops were sent" (Sheehan et al., 1971, p. 598). During that week of meetings, the central issues of military strategy and policy came to the forefront and were widely debated. By the end of that period, two broad coalitions had emerged within the Ad Hoc group. One, led principally by Rostow, Wheeler, and

Taylor, favored a continuation of Westmoreland's strategy of attrition. They urged prompt and substantial reinforcements for Westmoreland so that an increased Allied military pressure would force Hanoi to the conference table. The other group, led largely by Nitze and Warnke, with Katzenbach's support, challenged the premises of the old strategy and urged instead a less aggressive ground war, new efforts to open negotiations, and an implicit program for political compromise. The Tet offensive had given them, one dissenter recalls, something to "hang [their] arguments on, something to contradict the beguiling upward curve on the progress charts" from Saigon (Strum, 1972, p. 101).

As the debate wore on, Clifford's early concerns about American policy were reawakened:

> After days of analysis, my concern had greatly deepened. I could not find out when the war was going to end; I could not find out whether the new requests for men and equipment were going to be enough, or whether it would take more and, if more, when and how much. . . . All I had was the statement . . . that if we persisted for an indeterminate length of time, the enemy would choose not to go on. (Clifford, 1969, pp. 611–12)

Doubts about the direction of American policy in Vietnam had begun to develop in Clifford's mind as early as August, 1967. At that time, on his return from a trip on the president's behalf to Vietnam and Allied countries to discuss their increased participation in the war, Clifford confessed to Johnson his uneasiness at "having discovered that the American view of the war was not fully shared by Australia, New Zealand, Thailand and the Philippines" (Strum, 1972, p. 101). Later, Clifford was to confess that he had returned home "puzzled, troubled, concerned" (Clifford, 1969, p. 607). Perhaps the United States had inaccurately assessed the danger of a Hanoi victory in Vietnam to the stability of Southeast Asia and the Western Pacific. After all, "if the nations who lived in the area and whose security was more directly at stake were not prepared to make a serious and substantial effort, the United States should very definitely [have reduced] its own commitments" (Hoopes, 1969, p. 171).

Despite Clifford's uneasiness about American policy, he still considered himself in early March, 1968 a staunch supporter of existing Vietnam policy. He had, after all, been chosen by Johnson to succeed McNamara not only because of his personal relationship with the president, but because Johnson evidently viewed him as an eloquent hawk who had no doubts about the war. In *Newsweek* Clifford was described as "loyal, well-seasoned and, more important, determined to hold the line in Vietnam" (quoted in *Ibid.*, p. 150). Obviously concerned about the growing number of dissidents in the administration, the president apparently believed that he could count on Clifford for strong and steady advice and support on the Vietnam issue.

Although Clifford appeared to many observers to be a staunch supporter of administration policy, he was much too independent a thinker to be merely the president's man. After his return from Asia, Clifford had been encouraged by Johnson's public announcement on September 30, 1967 of the San Antonio Formula. This was a proposal to halt the bombing of North Vietnam provided that that action would lead promptly to productive talks and that the adversary would not take advantage of the bombing cessation. Clifford was depressed, however, by later official interpretations of the formula, for these "seemed to insist that North Vietnam must stop *all* resupply of its forces in the South" before the United States would deem Hanoi's response satisfactory (Hoopes, 1969, p. 124). Such a rigid position, he believed, was unreasonable and would virtually assure North Vietnam's refusal to inaugurate negotiations. Later, at his confirmation hearings on January 25 before the Senate Armed Services Committee, Clifford sought to ease the rigidity of the San Antonio Formula in order to render it more acceptable to Hanoi. Asked to interpret the president's formula, the newly appointed defense secretary asserted that Washington would not consider Hanoi to be exploiting a bombing halt if it continued a "normal" resupply of its forces in the South. Thus, in Clifford's view, following the suspension of the bombing the United States did not "expect Hanoi to stop the flow of men and materiel into South Vietnam [provided that] the flow would not go beyond 'normal' current levels" (quoted in Cooper, 1970, p. 385). Clifford apparently had not consulted with anyone before making this statement. Reports indicate that the president was puzzled by the new secretary's interpretation. Rusk was visibly angry, and one source reports that "all hell broke loose at the State Department" (see Strum, 1972, p. 101). Rusk sought to persuade the president to disavow Clifford's statement. In the end he failed, for on January 29 the State Department announced that Clifford's testimony represented the official administration view. Johnson had decided, at least at this juncture, to avoid a public difference with his new cabinet officer.

On March 5 Clifford transmitted the recommendations of the Ad Hoc group to the president. They confirmed existing policy in all essential respects. A brief, unsigned memorandum recommended giving Westmoreland 50,000 more troops in the next three months and outlined a schedule for supplying the balance of the 206,000 men over the next fifteen months. There was to be a repetition of the San Antonio Formula, but no new initiative toward negotiations or peace. Finally, the memorandum simply noted that the group was divided on the question of bombing policy: some favored an extension of targets, and others advocated a step-up of bombing through the spring. There was no mention, in the memorandum or in any of the drafts or papers related to the Clifford group's work, of a proposal to cut back the bombing to the Vietnam "panhandle." Despite its absence from the memorandum, the proposal to cut back bombing to the twentieth parallel was, according to *The Pentagon Papers*, one of the principal ideas then being considered and debated throughout the administration. Clifford was to urge its adoption at a number of meetings he had with the president during the rest of March. The proposal was omitted from the memorandum perhaps as a tactical move by Clifford to deter the opposition. The defense secretary apparently had decided that "to have raised the idea of constricting the bombing below the 19th or 20th Parallel in the memo to the President would have generalized the knowledge of such a suggestion and invited its sharp, full and formal criticism by the Joint Chiefs and other opponents of a bombing halt" (Sheehan et al., 1971, p. 604). Despite its absence from the memorandum, the proposal for a partial bombing halt by mid March had become the main focus of debate and the major air-war alternative within the administration.

Although he passed along the Ad Hoc group's report, Clifford was clearly uneasy about it. He did not challenge the report directly, but he sought to delay implementing its recommendations. The president, along with Rusk and Rostow, also appeared inclined to delay. It was decided that the Task Force should continue to meet for several more days. By March 7 Clifford, reinforced by worried and skeptical members of his own staff—especially Nitze, Warnke, and Goulding—and by other officials in the State Department, had become more convinced about the need for a shift in American policy in Vietnam.

In a conversation with the president on March 8, Clifford conveyed his doubts about the effectiveness of the ground strategy, the efficacy of the air war, and the benefits of further massive military infusions. The president was "less than pleased with Clifford's position" (Hoopes, 1969, p. 181). Relations between the two cooled dramatically thereafter, and the defense secretary, a friend of the president for thirty years, was to have the odd feeling of being shunned by the White House at times during this period.

On March 14 Clifford met with Senator Robert Kennedy and Theodore Sorensen. Kennedy had been under considerable pressure to enter the presidential race. However, he was much more concerned, he claimed, with changing the course of American policy in Vietnam. If there were some way he could do that, Kennedy said, he would not feel obliged to run. He then proposed that a commission be appointed to conduct a thorough investigation of Vietnam policies and report its findings to the president and the American people (Hoopes, 1969, pp. 182–83).

The same day, Clifford conveyed Kennedy's message to Johnson. The president curtly dismissed the offer as unacceptable. On March 16 Kennedy announced his decision to seek the Democratic presidential nomination.

By mid March, public pressure on Johnson had begun to mount rapidly as speculation developed that the administration was considering further escalation. On March 10 the *New York Times* reported General Westmoreland's request for 206,000 troops. Johnson, it was reported, became furious at this leak. The publication of the troop-request figure not only provided a focus for political debate, but intensified public dissatisfaction as well. A Gallup Poll released on March 9 indicated that growing numbers of Americans were convinced the United States was losing the war in

Vietnam (see the *New York Times*, March 10, 1968). Old trusted friends of the president, such as Senator Richard Russell, powerful head of the Armed Services Committee, complained bitterly about General Westmoreland. Other congressmen urged Johnson to proceed cautiously in mobilizing the reserves. On March 12 a House resolution introduced by 21 representatives called for a limitation on further American involvement in Vietnam (see the *New York Times*, March 13, 1968). On March 18, 139 members of the House sponsored a resolution calling for an immediate congressional review of American policy in Southeast Asia.

On March 12, hearings ostensibly on the 1968 Foreign Aid Bill were opened by the Senate Foreign Relations Committee, but Vietnam quickly became the central subject of investigation. For two full days Secretary Rusk was subjected to a scathing examination of American policy in Vietnam. An effort was also made to have Clifford testify, but he refused, arguing in part that his recent elevation to the Defense post would not make him a very useful witness. It was decided that Nitze would testify in his place. But Nitze also declined, refusing to testify in support of a policy with which he completely disagreed by then. He even offered to resign, but Clifford ultimately convinced him to reconsider. This was not the only case of a threatened resignation. Such threats, according to one observer, had become almost commonplace (*New York Times*, March 24, 1968). It was then decided that Warnke would testify for the Defense Department, but Chairman William Fulbright demanded to hear only Clifford or Nitze. This demand was retracted only when Clifford, in a private conversation with Fulbright, revealed his own doubts about Vietnam and indicated the scope of his current reappraisal of prevailing policy.

Johnson's position at this time was far from clear. Publicly, he adopted a stern, firm stance. On March 17, in speeches before the National Alliance of Businessmen and the National Farmers Union, the President attacked the proponents of a less aggressive, less costly ground strategy. "Those of you who think that we can save lives by moving the battlefield in from the mountains to the cities where the people live have another think coming," he said. He derided critics who would "tuck our tails and violate our commitments." Then he called for a total national effort to win the war.

(See Sheehan et al. 1971, p. 608.) Speaking before a State Department group March 19, Johnson introduced a clear note of chauvinism into his address (see Hoopes, 1969, p. 206). Clifford, discouraged by these outbursts and by now clearly pushing for a partial halt to the bombing, feared that he and his supporters had lost out to those favoring a continuation of existing policy. "Those hardnosed speeches," one dissident would later recall, ". . . left me feeling it was all over" (Kalb and Abel, 1971, p. 237).

As the president's public declarations increased in stridency, Clifford and his supporters grew more pessimistic about the ultimate outcome of the Vietnam issue. In the now almost daily meetings on Vietnam at the White House, the new defense secretary found himself regularly outvoted and finally forced to confess that he was "not getting very far with the President" (Hoopes, 1969, p. 207). Convinced, however, that the American course in Vietnam was not only endless but hopeless, he refused to cease his efforts to influence the president. Instead, he began quietly to search for allies close to the president. He found one in Harry McPherson, Johnson's speech writer.

McPherson had also slowly begun to grow disenchanted with the Vietnam conflict. Some time before the Tet offensive, McPherson had recommended that the president make a speech explaining American objectives in the war. When he heard that Clifford was moving toward a different policy on Vietnam, he was elated. The two quickly established an alliance. McPherson sought to keep "hawk stuff out of anything the President said . . . and [to] warn Clifford of bureaucratic ambushes ahead" (Kalb and Abel, 1971, p. 235). Searching for additional allies, Clifford talked to Dean Acheson, McGeorge Bundy, and Douglas Dillon, all of whom were members of the Senior Advisory Group on Vietnam. As we have seen, this group had endorsed the administration's policy in November, 1967, but Clifford was aware that some of its members were reassessing their earlier positions. Acheson, for one, had already expressed his disaffection to the president. Having sensed this shift within the Senior Advisory Group, Clifford managed to convince the president to convene the group for a post-Tet assessment before any final decisions on Vietnam were made. These meetings were scheduled for March 25–26.

By March 20 Johnson seemed to have recovered a measure of calm. Despite his earlier critical outbursts, it now appeared that the president "was weighing what the critics had been saying and was also pondering the mood of the country" (Sheehan et al., 1971, p. 608). On March 20 Johnson met with United Nations Ambassador Arthur Goldberg to discuss the latter's March 15 memorandum proposing a bombing halt. Only five days before, this recommendation had infuriated Johnson. On March 16 the president flatly asserted to his advisors that he would not stop the bombing. The meeting on March 20, however, was cordial and open, and it ended with the president inviting Goldberg to present his proposals to the planned meeting of the Senior Advisory Group on March 25. On March 22 Johnson announced that Westmoreland would be recalled and would return to the United States as Army Chief of Staff. Although these acts were not conclusive and did not commit the president to major substantive change, they appeared to indicate that Johnson was leaning away from any major escalation of the ground war. His views seemed to be in transition, and these actions seemed to demonstrate that the president "was tentatively clearing away the accumulated underbrush and preparing the site for the construction of a possibly different policy" (Hoopes, 1969, p. 208). The president, unknown to virtually all of his advisors, was apparently also considering a return to private life, coincident with the new turn in Vietnam.

On March 22 Johnson's closest advisors were informed of his plans to present a speech on Vietnam, and a meeting was convened at the White House to discuss it. Since the first of March McPherson had, at the president's initial request, made five drafts of the speech. The draft that the group considered on March 22 was essentially a tough and uncompromising reiteration of administration policy. Although McPherson later insisted that it was not "a belligerent, hawkish speech in any conventional use of the word" (Kalb and Abel, 1971, p. 242), it contained no new peace initiative. Clifford was disturbed by the tenor of the speech, and he urged that it be amended to include some serious gesture toward peace. In particular, he pleaded for at least a partial bombing halt as a first step in a process of tacit, mutual de-escalation. After seven hours of exhaustive discussion, Rusk sought to summarize the results of the meeting. Although the consensus seemed to be that some American move toward negotiations were desirable, he asserted, there was considerable doubt that a partial cessation of the bombing would satisfy the North Vietnamese. He ruled out total cessation, arguing that such a step would jeopardize American troops along the Demilitarized Zone.

After a restless night in which he sought to develop a formula that would satisfy both the broad desire to make a gesture toward peace and the fear of its rejection by Hanoi, McPherson proposed to Johnson on March 23 that the president stop all bombing north of the twentieth parallel. Simultaneously, Johnson would offer to stop the bombing entirely provided Hanoi would show restraint at the DMZ and would refrain from attacking Saigon and other major cities. McPherson admitted later that his proposal was not a wholly new idea. McNamara, as we have seen, had advocated such a plan in 1967. But, McPherson noted, now "it just happened to be dressed up in the right way at the right time" (*Ibid.*, p. 244). Johnson's response was positive. Copies of McPherson's proposal were sent to Rusk and Ambassador Bunker, who responded with tacit if unenthusiastic approval.

Although the time for decision was drawing near, the president still hesitated. A former White House official described this time "one of those periods when the President had everybody thinking he was about to make up his mind, when actually he wasn't" (Strum, 1972, p. 110). Clifford was to confide to a friend later that this was a "lonely, stultifying, miserable period" (Brandon, 1969, p. 131). It now appears clear that by March 25, the day the Senior Advisory Group was to meet, the president was still wavering in his decision.

On March 25 the Senior Advisory Group convened in the White House. Its membership consisted of the top figures of the American foreign policy establishment. Present at the March 25 meeting were Dean Acheson, George Ball, Douglas Dillon, McGeorge Bundy, Cyrus Vance, Arthur Dean, Omar Bradley, Matthew Ridgeway, Maxwell Taylor, Robert Murphy, John McCloy, Henry Cabot Lodge, Abe Fortas, and Arthur Goldberg. (For a more detailed list of the group's members, see Strum, 1972, pp. 101–2). After reading a number of background papers, the group went to dinner with the principal cabinet officers, plus Rostow, Harriman, and William Bundy, whom they questioned at length. Afterward, the group was briefed by experts from the CIA, the Pentagon, and the State Department. The discussion continued late into the night and resumed the next morning.

At an early stage of the proceedings, it was readily apparent that the group's unanimity of the previous fall had largely evaporated and that a majority were deeply troubled: "Some were seeking a means of cutting back the war enough to make it politically and economically endurable for an indefinite period; others felt that disengagement was now the only answer" (Hoopes, 1969, p. 215). Only a small minority—Taylor, Fortas, and Murphy—stood firm in advocating a hard line. Acheson, McGeorge Bundy, Dillon, Vance, Goldberg, Ball, and Ridgeway all advocated a change in policy. McCloy, Lodge, Dean, and Bradley stood somewhere in the middle—troubled, doubtful, but less ready to opt for a dramatic shift in policy. The group had reached no consensus on the bombing issue, although Goldberg and Ball advocated a total halt as a way to negotiations.

On the afternoon of March 26 the group met with the president to report on its discussions. McGeorge Bundy summarized the group's views. The group believed, he said, that "present policy had reached an impasse, could not achieve its objective without the application of virtually unlimited resources, was no longer being supported by a majority of the American people, and therefore required significant change" (Hoopes, 1969, p. 216). When some members objected that these positions were not shared by the entire group, Acheson moved to Bundy's defense. Bundy's summary, the former secretary of state declared, represented his views and the great majority of those present.

According to a former aide, Johnson was visibly shaken by this report. To the president and his senior advisors, this shift in views carried "more weight than something like the New Hampshire primary" (Strum, 1972, p. 111). Johnson was more deeply shocked by the apparent defection of such men as Bundy and Vance. Bundy, after all, had in 1965 been a major architect of American intervention in Vietnam, and Vance had served as McNamara's chief deputy at the Pentagon. Perhaps, Johnson thought, the briefers had unduly exaggerated the effects of Tet. Later, Wheeler was to ask what sort of a "jerk" had briefed the Senior Advisory Group (Brandon, 1969, p. 133). The next day, the president invited the briefers to his office to repeat their presentation. After they had finished, Johnson declared, "You aren't telling me what you told them. You must have given them a different briefing" (quoted in Kalb and Abel, 1971, p. 249). Thereafter, Johnson remained convinced that someone had "reached" the briefers, since he was never able to satisfactorily explain the shift of sentiment within the Advisory Group. (Hoopes has suggested [1969, pp. 217–18] that the president's sense of disbelief reflected the extent to which he had become the victim of Rostow's selective briefings and the prevailing climate within the White House of complete agreement on fundamental questions regarding Vietnam.)

Although Clifford was undoubtedly satisfied by the Advisory Group's performance, he felt the struggle was by no means over. The president was clearly upset, but he had not yet given any clear sign of a changing attitude. On March 28 Clifford met with McPherson, Rostow, and William Bundy in Rusk's office to polish the president's speech, which had been scheduled for delivery on March 31. The current draft presumably reflected the White House discussions of March 22. It made no mention, however, either of McPherson's proposal or of the majority views of the Senior Advisory Group. Hoopes described it as "essentially a defiant, bellicose speech, written to be delivered between clenched teeth" (Ibid., p. 219). It clearly reflected the views of Rusk and Rostow. Visibly upset, Clifford immediately launched into an impassioned plea against adopting this approach. "I can't do it—I can't go along with it," he said. "The President cannot give that speech! It would be a disaster!" What was needed, Clifford urged, "was not a war speech, but a peace speech." (Strum, 1972, p. 112)

Rusk listened impassively, making no move to cut Clifford short. Eager to find some way to the negotiating table, the secretary of state now appeared more receptive to alternative proposals than he had been in the past, although he continued to believe that the bombing cutback would not satisfy Hanoi. The crucial moment in the conversation came when Clifford asserted that "the Establishment had turned against the war," obviously referring to the leadership in industry, finance, and commerce. This final argument "seemed to make the deepest impression on those present" (Brandon, 1969, p. 138). By late afternoon, discussion had ranged far beyond the scope of the speech into the very nature and purpose of American policy in Vietnam. When the meeting finally ended, Clifford had achieved a considerable breakthrough. Rusk had agreed that McPherson should prepare an alternate draft so that the president might have two speeches—and thus the benefit of a clear-cut choice—to consider. Rostow raised no objection, presumably because he thought that the president had already decided not to halt the bombing.

Working through the night in a state of exhilaration, McPherson completed the new draft by the next morning. A copy was immediately sent to Johnson. Later that day the president telephoned McPherson to ask him to check a passage on "page three." Johnson did not specify which draft, but after a brief look McPherson was relieved to discover that the president was now working from the alternate draft, the "peace" speech.

From then until March 31, when Johnson delivered his address, the speech went through five more drafts. None altered the essence of the speech, although a Katzenbach proposal modified the bombing-halt provision by stating it in "functional terms." (For an elaboration of this proposal see Kalb and Abel, 1971, p. 251.) On Saturday evening, March 30, after successive drafts had grown progressively more dovish, McPherson turned his attention to the conclusion of the address. He volunteered to draft a new conclusion, but the president spurned his offer, saying, "No need to—I may have one of my own" (Strum, 1972, p. 114). On Sunday Horace Busby, a former presidential aide, was called in to work with Johnson, ostensibly on final revisions. It was he, however, who helped draft Johnson's announcement of withdrawal from the 1968 presidential race. Few of Johnson's advisors, including even his closest ones, knew of this decision beforehand. Clifford, who had been invited to the Executive Mansion to hear the address, learned of the surprise ending only moments before Johnson delivered it to the nation. At 9 P.M. the president began perhaps his most important speech, in which he announced his decisions to cut back the bombing and to withdraw from the upcoming presidential contest.

The turnabout in the president's position on the bombing had occurred in less than a month. It was stimulated by Clifford's forth-right opposition to prevailing policy in Vietnam. Beginning in mid March, Clifford pointedly and continually told the president of his opposition. Clifford was, Hoopes claims, "the single most powerful and effective catalyst of change" (1969, p. 224). To strengthen the persuasiveness of his case, the new defense secretary sought allies in the State Department, in the Pentagon, among the prominent figures of the foreign-policy establishment, and in the White House itself. Johnson's change in position was also prompted by diverse political developments, including the remarkable success of McCarthy's peace campaign, mounting evidence of growing public disaffection with the war (see Table 5), and, perhaps most important, the entrance of Robert Kennedy into the presidential race. Finally, the president's change in position was fueled by the undeniable Communist psychological victory resulting from the Tet offensive, in which the bankruptcy of the prevailing American strategy was pointedly revealed.

The decision to cut back the bombing involved only a small number of participants. This, of course, is not particularly notewor-thy, since such decisions are often made by just a few individuals. However, in this case, much like the earlier Cuban "quarantine" decision in 1962, the president emerged as virtually the sole deci-sion maker and as the focal point of an organized campaign within his administration to reverse the prevailing military strategy. In the effort to alter prevailing policy in Vietnam, central roles were played by Robert McNamara and his successor at the Defense Department, Clark Clifford.

TABLE 5   Rating of Johnson's performance on Vietnam (by percent)

	Latest	Early March	February, 1968	January, 1968
Approve	26	32	35	39
Disapprove	63	57	50	47
No Opinion	11	11	15	14

Question. "Do you approve or disapprove of the way President Johnson is han-dling the situation in Vietnam?"
Source: Gallup Poll; New York Times, March 31, 1968.

Obviously distressed by the notable decline in public support, by the growing visibility of dissent within his administration, and by the increasing restiveness of Congress, the president moved slowly, seeking to conceal his thinking from public view and attempting to bide for time by postponing an immediate decision. The president kept his personal views well hidden virtually until his announcement of his decision to cut back the bombing. By this time, however, the growing persuasiveness of Clifford's arguments, the clear Vietcong success at Tet, the obvious inadequacy of the Joint Chiefs' plea for further escalation, and the apparent evaporation of his cherished consensus and broad public support undoubtedly affected Johnson's outlook. Moreover, although few major interest groups had adopted a public stand opposing the prevailing Vietnam policy, Johnson was undoubtedly aware of the growing dissatisfaction among the business, financial, and educational communities, as well as the mounting opposition of the mass media.

In short, by March, 1968 pressures from a variety of sources favoring disengagement had converged on an increasingly beleaguered president whose few remaining allies could offer little but recommendations for continuing prevailing policy, the repetition of clichés, and promises of a brighter future. For Johnson, however, by now fully chastened by the failure of such advice in the past, the "light at the end of the tunnel" could be reached only by a new path.

REFERENCES AND BIBLIOGRAPHY

BRANDON, HENRY, *Anatomy of Error: The Inside Story of the Asian War on the Potomac, 1954–1969.* Boston: Gambit, 1969.

BRODIE, BERNARD, *War and Politics.* New York: Macmillan, 1973.

CLIFFORD, CLARK, "A Vietnam Reappraisal: The Personal History of One Man's View and How it Evolved," *Foreign Affairs*, July, 1969, pp. 601–22.

CLOTFELTER, JAMES, *The Military in American Politics.* New York: Harper & Row, 1973.

COOPER, CHESTER L., *The Last Crusade: America in Vietnam.* New York: Dodd, Mead, 1970.

EIDENBERG, EUGENE, "The Presidency: Americanizing the War in Vietnam," in *American Political Institutions and Public Policy*, ed. Allan P. Sindler. Boston: Little, Brown, 1969.

GOULDEN, JOSEPH C., *Truth is the First Casualty: The Gulf of Tonkin Affair—Illusion and Reality*. Chicago: Rand McNally, 1969.

HALPER, THOMAS, *Foreign Policy Crisis*. Columbus, Ohio: Charles E. Merrill, 1971.

HOOPES, TOWNSEND, *The Limits of Intervention*. New York: McKay, 1969.

————, "Standing History on Its Head: LBJ's Account of March, 1968," *New Republic*, March 14, 1970, pp. 17–19.

KAHIN, GEORGE M. T., and JOHN W. LEWIS, *The United States in Vietnam*. New York: Dial Press, 1967.

KALB, MARVIN, and ELIE ABEL, *Roots of Involvement: The U.S. in Asia, 1784–1971*. New York: Norton, 1971.

SHEEHAN, NEIL, et al., *The Pentagon Papers*. New York: Bantam, 1971.

STRUM, PHILIPPA, *Presidential Power and American Democracy*. Pacific Palisades, Calif.: Goodyear, 1972.

13

Context and Process in American Foreign Policy

Having presented a number of diverse foreign policy decisions over a twenty-year period, we can now return to some of the general questions raised in Chapter 1 and see how our case studies shed light on them. As we noted there, since foreign policy is a form of public policy and therefore a part of a more general political process, one fundamental issue concerns the extent and manner to which foreign and domestic elements combine to produce foreign policy.

Our cases show that each decision had major domestic components. Even though the decision makers were, by and large, a small group of foreign policy specialists (or, to use Richard Barnet's felicitous phrase, "national security managers"), they inevitably took account of domestic stimuli, needs, and anticipated reactions in formulating their options and choosing among them. In the Trade Expansion Act, the Aswan Dam decision, and the Marshall Plan, domestic considerations were clearly discernible. Domestic political pressures and interests were undoubtedly uppermost in Kennedy's mind in 1962 as he fashioned a coalition of forces to ensure the enactment of his trade bill. And Truman in 1948 was certainly not unmindful of powerful domestic business interests who favored a policy that would ensure them access to a rehabilitated European market as the Marshall Plan unfolded. In the decision to rescind the loan to Egypt for the construction of the Aswan Dam, the Republican policy makers were undoubtedly influenced by their determination to demonstrate Eisenhower's leadership to a Congress that was controlled by the opposition party and that was very reluctant to provide any funds for Nasser's regime.

As for the crisis decisions we have examined—whether Berlin, Cuba, or Vietnam—the domestic factors, though perhaps less explicit, were nonetheless considerably important and in some instances decisive. Consideration of this important impact of domestic factors runs directly counter to conventional wisdom, which tends to depreciate the role of such factors in crisis decision making. But as we have seen, Truman in 1948 was not unmindful of the domestic political ramifications of the various options that he was considering. Johnson's Vietnam policy was shaped in no small way by powerful internal political pressures and interests; some commentators have even gone so far as to claim that the president's apparent penchant for treating the conflict in domestic terms was chiefly responsible for its failure. Although he would have disagreed with this assessment, Johnson evidently saw Vietnam as tied inextricably to the political situation in the United States. But perhaps it was in Cuba—again, contrary to most conventional accounts—that the domestic factors were most evident. Here, as our analysis demonstrated, Kennedy's choice for some form of decisive action was undoubtedly buttressed by his desire to regain his domestic stature after the abysmal outcomes of the Bay of Pigs invasion and Kennedy's meeting with Khrushchev in Vienna. (President Ford's recent action following the seizure of the

Mayaguez may have been motivated by very similar domestic considerations.)

Our examination of crisis decision making, moreover, suggests that decisive acts (such as intervention, quarantines, airlifts, and confrontation) may well be used by a president to mobilize broad popular support, to rally, through patriotic appeals, those segments of the public who are either apathetic or hostile to his actions in other areas, and thereby to enhance the authority of his office. A president confronted with mounting domestic problems might use a foreign policy crisis to convert broad public dissatisfaction or disinterest into popular acclaim, and thereby bolster his domestic status. Even Truman's airlift policy, Eisenhower's intervention in Lebanon, and Kennedy's quarantine decision were not totally free from such considerations. Thus, even the distinction between crisis and noncrisis decisions seems far less meaningful in the context of a general political process, since here too we see a mix of foreign and domestic considerations.

From this analysis it is clear that the *sources* of foreign policy must be sought in the domestic needs and demands generated by the political system, and the process by which foreign policy is formulated can be understood only within the general framework of public policy making. In particular, the foreign policy process requires an understanding of the relationship between individuals and institutions, the impact of the broader social environment on this relationship, and the factors accounting for continuity and change in policy.

Although our case studies are of specific episodes in the post–World War II period, when taken as a whole they reveal a certain ideological continuity. In order to account for this continuity, we must apply our findings about the role of individuals and institutions, on the one hand, and the societal power structure, on the other, to the period under study. Here, the question of the formulation of the national interest becomes crucial, for it is the implementation of different elements of the underlying national ideology, however defined, that ultimately determines the overall structure and orientation of foreign policy.

By themselves, the decisions we have presented can only

begin to answer the questions we have raised. Fortunately, there is a considerable literature that addresses itself to various aspects of these issues. In the following pages we intend to examine this literature in order to see how these questions have been treated by others, and how their insights and observations can help us analyze foreign policy decisions. As will become evident, there is no general agreement among foreign policy analysts about these issues. We believe, however, that the literature we have examined does suggest a general framework that, considered in conjunction with the decisions covered in the preceding chapters, can provide important insights into the foreign policy process. Although we employ this framework to shed light on our case studies, it should also assist the student in any future investigation of other important cases of American foreign policy.

THE RELATIONSHIP BETWEEN INDIVIDUALS AND INSTITUTIONS

In each of our case studies it is clear that the decision reached was a result of the interaction of a limited number of participants, among whom the president played a central part. This is especially true of those crisis decisions, such as Dien Bien Phu and the Lebanese intervention, where the number of participants, whether individuals or institutions, tended to be few and their relationship to the domain of foreign policy tended to be unequivocal. Besides the president, the major participants varied according to the issue and the administration, coming from different positions in the executive agencies and on the White House staff. In the development of the Trade Expansion Act, for example, the participants were drawn chiefly from key personnel on the White House staff but also included a few individuals from certain governmental departments. In the drafting and subsequent negotiation of the Nuclear Test Ban Treaty, important figures from the scientific community joined a wide assortment of officials from the Defense and State Departments and the Arms Control and Disarmament Agency. Only rarely did Congress or interest groups play an important role in the decision making, and in virtually no case was public opinion significant, except perhaps at the implementation stage. Even in the cases that were clearly not of a crisis nature, such as the Aswan Dam, the Marshall Plan, and the Test Ban decisions, the number of participants increased only marginally. This focus on a small group of individuals raises the important question of the influence of personality on decision making: Would different individuals in decision making positions have acted differently? It also raises the equally important issue of organizational affiliation. To what extent does the secretary of state, for example, behave in accordance with his role as head of a major department, and a special assistant to the president in accordance with his role as a staff advisor, regardless of their individual personalities?

Many scholars have approached this broad and complex problem with the aid of two simplifying assumptions:

1. The most important aspect of foreign policy (and international relations) is the interaction among nation-states, and it follows that the focus of analysis should be on the impact that the actions of one state have on the others.

2. Therefore, it is justifiable and most useful to regard the state as the actor, recognize that its decisions are made by groups of individuals, but assume that since all such people are acting in some "national interest," they reflect the common psychological dispositions of all states.

Individual differences, idiosyncracies, and psyches, if not completely unimportant, are at best secondary factors (Wolfers, 1959, pp. 83–106). Thus, the emphasis should be on common dispositions of states, and on existing circumstances and stimuli *external* to the nation whose foreign policy one is studying according to this view.

When early scholars attempted to handle questions of individual influence, they often engaged in a rather sterile debate over the role of "the hero in history." Does the leader have a decisive influence on the course of historical events, as some historians claimed, or does he always function within the rather stringent limits imposed by societal factors, as Marx, for instance, would have asserted? What is more, this problem was often handled by the use of another simplifying notion, which might be termed "the rational actor model." Hans Morgenthau perhaps described this model most succinctly when he suggested that we put ourselves in the position of a statesman facing a foreign policy problem and ask what rational alternatives we have and which of them we are likely to choose under the circumstances (1967, p. 5). Put another way, rational models assume that the individual responds by cool, clearheaded calculation, uses the best information available to him, and chooses the alternative most likely to maximize his goals. The decisions he reaches will have no psychological side effects on him—at least none that are relevant to the outcome (Verba, 1969, p. 218). The implication is clear: one need not worry about individual differences, because as a rule any individual in a position of decision-making power will behave more or less in accordance with the same rational model. However, once we begin thinking of foreign policy as a political process, especially one that has at least as many *domestic* dimensions as international ones, it becomes much more difficult to avoid a close look at the issue of individual influence. (See, for example, Klineberg, 1964.)

During the past twenty years, a variety of efforts have been undertaken to deal with the relationships between individuals and institutions in a more systematic and sophisticated manner by the use of concepts and ideas borrowed from various social science disciplines. Collectively known as the decision-making approach, all these efforts use the outputs of the foreign-policy-making process as their central unit of analysis and attempt to identify the conditions and factors that explain particular decisions. In order to analyze foreign policy decisions, Richard Synder, one of the pioneers of this approach, constructed a broad framework around three sets of variables: *situational factors*, which explain the "occasion for decision"—that is, the immediate circumstances calling for a decision; *organizational practice*, the set of rules and procedures of the institutions involved in the decision making; and *individual factors*, including the personality structure of the decision makers, their socioeconomic backgrounds and experiences, and their personal values. According to Snyder, these three sets of factors interact to shape decision makers' perceptions of their environment and to determine, in large part, foreign policy outcomes. Unfortunately, the ways in which these interactions occur were never specified. (For further details of the decision-making approach see Snyder, 1963; Robinson and Snyder, 1965.)

Graham Allison (1971) attempted to clarify the relationships between individuals, organizations and foreign policy decisions by constructing three models of decision making. According to the *rational-actor model*, which we have already described, decisions are the result of a careful and objective calculation of means to ends, and strategy to action, on the basis of "perfect" information. The analyst who uses this model explains the decision by demonstrating the reasonableness of the foreign policy action, given the goals of the government. In contrast, the *organizational-process model* defines a foreign policy process in which decisions are more often the outputs of large organizations that operate according to standardized procedures and routines, and that in turn define the range of policy choices and structure the situation in which decisions are made. This model differs from the third approach, the *governmental* (or *bureaucratic*) *politics model*. Here, each member of the decision-making group is conceived as a player in a competitive game: politics. This game consists of bargaining with the other players in order to enhance one's own power and government behavior is best seen as the result of these games. It is obvious, then, that to explain why a particular decision was made, it is necessary to identify the game and the players, to display the coalitions, bargains, and compromises made during the games, and to convey the confusion and uncertainty that marked the playing of it. Decisions and actions are, of course, the political results of the game.

Although the decision-making approach attempts to unravel the relationship between the individual and the institutional environments within which he functions, most of its theorists have preferred to ignore or down-grade the role and impact of *personality* in the foreign policy process. Some presumed that the organizational or institutional context would so constrain individual behavior as to make the consideration of personality as an independent factor unnecessary. The preferences of participants in the foreign policy process, they argued, are not individual but stem from the rules of the organizational system, specific routines, and organizational experiences. Others claimed that the personality dimension was not germane in foreign-policy making. Thus, despite the differences among the individuals participating in decision making, including differences in predisposition and motivation, these are somehow less important in foreign-policy making than in decision making in general:

> The foreign policy decisions of national governmental institutions occur in a context which normally minimizes the influence of personal and emotional factors, and make it likely that the collective political decision will embody a more practical wisdom than do most everyday personal decisions of individuals (Dougherty and Pfaltzgraff, 1971, p. 344).

Despite this viewpoint, the analyses of personality-oriented scholars have at times added to our understanding of the foreign policy process by offering us further clues toward identifying the sources of American foreign policy. Studies of the American decisions to stop the bombing in Vietnam, to impose a quarantine in Cuba, and to intervene militarily in Lebanon, for example, all become more comprehensible when they take into account (1) Johnson's obsessive commitment to the basic thrust of his Vietnam policy in the face of mounting evidence of its failure; (2) Kennedy's desire to demonstrate to the Russians both his maturity in international affairs in the wake of his demoralizing meeting with Khrushchev at Vienna, and his "coolness under pressure" during the famous "thirteen days"; and (3) the distinctive character of Dulles's perceptions of the nature and roots of Communist behavior in Lebanon. (For a general treatment of these issues, see de Rivera, 1968.)

An attempt to differentiate presidential styles in policy making on the basis of relationships with parents and a relatively simplistic classification of presidential character resting on predispositional dimensions is found in a recently published book by James Barber (1972). Barber begins his study of presidential character with the statement, that:

> Every story of Presidential decision-making is really two stories: an outer one, in which a rational man calculates, and an inner one, in which an emotional man feels (Barber, 1972, p. 7).

It is the inner story with which Barber is primarily concerned, although he does admit that the two cannot be totally separated.

Presidential character, he asserts, can be best understood as a product of two dimensions. The first of these is what he calls *active-passive*. This category revolves primarily around the amount of energy that is invested in the job. One might rank presidents on a scale from Coolidge, at one end, to Johnson, perhaps, at the other. The second dimension is the *positive-negative*. This is dependent on how much the president enjoys or dislikes the holding and using of power. According to Barber, F.D.R. loved it and Herbert Hoover hated it. Individual presidents combine these characteristics in different proportions, so that an individual president might be active-positive, or active-negative (although this is less likely) and another might be passive-negative, or passive-positive (again this is less likely). It might be useful, in order to understand more clearly how Barber uses these dimensions, to dichotomize them and present them in the following 2-by-2 table, with the presidents that we deal with in this book neatly pigeonholed:

	POSITIVE	NEGATIVE
ACTIVE	Truman Kennedy	Johnson (also Nixon)
PASSIVE	(Madison)	Eisenhower (also Coolidge)

One interesting fact that emerges from this table is that the four presidents who are relevant to the decisions we dealt with fall into three different boxes. It would seem that this should make it fairly simple to explain differences in behavior on the basis of these categories. When one tries to do this, however, this classification seems to fall apart. The active-positive Truman, for instance, dealt with the Korean Crisis—or Berlin, for that matter—in a manner very similar to the way in which the active-negative Johnson dealt with Vietnam and the Dominican Republic, or the passive-negative Eisenhower with Lebanon. The problem seems to lie in the oversimplification of the concept of character and the excessive separation of character variables from situational ones. Barber does admit that presidential character interacts in some way with the political situation. He acknowledges that such factors as public and interest-group support, party balance in Congress, and the necessities of election politics, all intrude on the decision-making process in significant ways. There is even room, he suggests, for the "climate of expectations"—that is, the needs of the public for reassurance, progress and action, and legitimacy. However, all of this is naturally mediated through the character of the president, which then becomes the crucial factor for explaining policy. Unfortunately, Barber's attempt to demonstrate this empirically falters when he omits nonpsychological factors that could make for an equally plausible and more parsimonious explanation of the same events.

The most recent and perhaps the most significant effort to employ psychological insights in the study of foreign policy has been the work of Irving Janis (1973). Although the individual personality does appear in his treatment, Janis chooses to focus on the group, and specifically on the psychodynamics of group activity in the foreign-policy-making process. According to this approach, unlike the earlier psychological approaches, all decisions need not be mediated through the character of any *single* decision maker.

There are, Janis points out, two logical shortcomings in decision making: those resulting from intrapersonal problems, and those resulting from interpersonal or intergroup problems. Intrapersonal shortcomings and their impact on social decisions have been dealt with extensively in the social-science literature. The ways in which temporarily reduced mental efficiency can result from emotional compulsions such as fear, jealousy, and envy—the chronic blank spots of a decision maker that can arise from social prejudice—are common examples of individual shortcomings. The usual way of counteracting individual shortcomings is by relegating decisions to groups, thereby creating, it is supposed, a decision-making environment in which individual shortcomings neutralize one another and individual strengths reinforce one another.

Group decision making has been the characteristic mode of modern society. The literature, however, has neglected the very serious problems that are indigenous to this type of decision making. Janis identifies the following group shortcomings as crucial factors in the failure of many recent political decisions:

1. Mindless conformity, either to please the leader or to preserve the clubby atmosphere of the group.

2. Lack of vigilance, because everyone assumes someone else is responsible for it.
3. The tendency toward excessive risk taking, because members reinforce one another and generate group courage.
4. Types of "group madness," such as collective panic and scapegoating.

All of this Janis calls "groupthink," and he points out that the chances for its occurring are greater when the members of the group have similar social and educational backgrounds. In addition, groupthink is more likely to occur when the group is highly cohesive, both psychologically and in terms of social background; when the group is isolated from the additional and perhaps disturbing expertise of qualified outsiders; and when the leader promotes his own alternative with extreme aggressiveness. Specific defects in group decision making can be clearly identified. Some of them are as follows:

1. The discussion is often limited to only a few alternatives, usually the leader's and its opposite.
2. There is a failure to reexamine the alternative initially preferred by the majority.
3. Little attempt is made to obtain information from a variety of outside sources. "We have all the experts we need in this group" is the characteristic syndrome.
4. Bias exists toward information supporting group predispositions.
5. Little attention is paid to possible obstacles or accidents or to unforeseen developments.

An obvious example of groupthink is, of course, the Bay of Pigs invasion, which demonstrated virtually all of these shortcomings. The process leading to the Marshall Plan decision also displayed these deficiencies. In the Cuban missile crisis, however, there was an obvious attempt to counteract these failings: the consideration of a variety of alternatives was encouraged and the leader attempted to play a less influential role in the decision making, at times temporarily absenting himself from the deliberations of his advisors.

The atmosphere of group decision making in the Johnson administration, especially with respect to Vietnam, also appears to illustrate most of the shortcomings identified by Janis. Further examples of groupthink can be gleaned from our case studies. One can point to the profound resistance to the adoption of a new policy in Vietnam, even after the Tet offensive had so clearly revealed bankruptcy of the prevailing strategy to be symptomatic of the "mindless conformity" so characteristic of groupthink. Or one can see how the fear of ostracism during the debates on the appropriate response to the deployment of Russian missiles in Cuba narrowed the range of viable alternatives, or how, in this same instance, group unanimity seriously underplayed the risks entailed in the imposition of a quarantine. Kennedy himself was to estimate the probability of nuclear war at fifty-fifty, and to justify his action on the need to deter a Soviet threat to the "psychological balance of power." In the face of such a risk, and in the absence of group solidarity and support, it is at least conceivable that the president might have refrained from recommending such a perilous course of action as a quarantine. It is even more certain that few of his advisors would have been willing to recommend such a clearly risky enterprise. Moreover, during the internal executive debate on the Nuclear Test Ban Treaty, the American position on on-site inspections that nearly wrecked the subsequent negotiations with the Soviets stemmed from incorrect data and information. Though congruent with prevailing group beliefs, these data were clearly inconsistent with scientific findings. And during the discussions on a bombing halt in Vietnam, reports from the field, even after the Tet offensive, continued to paint a rosy picture and predict a future victory. In this case, internal group solidarity was once again work-ing to distort information and to turn a major setback of prevailing policy into a resounding reaffirmation of the basic principles of that bankrupt strategy. It was only when group coherence dissolved that a new departure could be seriously entertained and "group madness" successfully overcome. And the price was high: the de-parture of the secretary of defense and the withdrawal of the presi-dent from active political life.

To summarize, most scholars agree that decision making is a process that combines individual and institutional components, but no one knows what the mix looks or tastes like. Some writers emphasize that since we are dealing primarily with public policy made by official decision makers, the psychological perceptions of such decision makers are the chief ingredient. Others argue that the institutional or organizational environment is at least as relevant, if not more so, in that it imposes limitations on these perceptions and corrects erroneous past decisions. It might be argued that the interaction between the institutional and psychological environments is filtered through the personalities of the decision makers. What distorts their perceptions, how much they are distorted, and in what direction are the crucial questions. Moreover, some analysts maintain that decision makers' preferences are not entirely individual, but derive from the rules of the organizational system, shared organizational experiences, and available information. In addition, decision makers' motivations are not necessarily personality-based, or if they are, the personalities are *social* personalities, shaped in part by professional affiliations, by ethnic and cultural background, and, more broadly, by social class and even by national values.

The decision-making approach, even when enriched by a careful treatment of the psychological dimension of decision making, provides at best only a partial explanation of the foreign policy process. It focuses attention on individual decisions, particular strategies, and specific national objectives. Therefore, it tends to see the foreign policy process largely in terms of a series of disjointed outcomes. To be sure, some broad insights can be gained into the respective roles of the participants in the foreign policy process, but little understanding of the principal underlying political relationships is provided. By relying on this approach, political explanation tends to become a by-product of bureaucratic or organizational behavior; the analyst fails to identify not only the major locus of power in foreign affairs, but also the processes by which this power is used to convert resources into action.

Amos Perlmutter (1974, pp. 87–106) has attempted to correct these shortcomings by directing his attention specifically to the political foundations of power. Any attempt to analyze foreign policy, Perlmutter argues, "must begin with an analysis of the locus and degree of power within the American political-behavioral and constitutional context" (*Ibid.*, p. 106). That locus is the "presidential political center," which consists of a small, well-integrated elite of elective party politicians, bureaucrats (both military and civilian), and intellectuals of various types. In the absence of fully coordinated political elites, a highly centralized party system, or a powerful administrative apparatus, this presidential political center "has become pivotal, with almost exclusive control over foreign affairs" (*Ibid.*, p. 97).

Power within this political center is by no means diffused or fragmented. The president is clearly the dominant figure in the hierarchy. Whatever the social background or status of the individuals recruited into the political center, and however much these resources may assist them in gaining access to the "presidential court," their possession does not guarantee these individuals political power. Whatever the merits of this view, power is derived from proximity to the presidential political center rather than from social or institutional sources alone. The fundamental political conflict, then, is reduced to a basic struggle within the elite circles for the "domination of the political center and the center of the center—the Presidency and its most coveted power: the power over foreign affairs" (*Ibid.*, p. 89). Thus, the political struggle over foreign policy is a central institutional-constitutional conflict and not a matter of merely bureaucratic politics.

The case for identifying the presidential political center as the locus of foreign-policy making has much to recommend it. Our case studies amply illustrate the significance of the presidential role in policy making. Whether in instances of crisis, such as in Cuba and in the Dominican Republic, or in the noncrisis situations of the nuclear test ban or the Aswan Dam decisions, the initiating role of the president is striking and clearly identifiable. The president was at the center of virtually all of these decisions. Congress, therefore, played simply a legitimating function on these occasions. As we have seen, this was true of the decisions on Berlin, Dien Bien Phu, and the Dominican Republic. In other instances the president effectively, and apparently without excessive difficulty, mobilized support within Congress for his program. Although the techniques of Presidential pressure on Congress may have varied, and although the president may have had to strike some bargains with Congress to ensure their support, the results were almost universally the same: a presidential victory. It is sometimes forgotten that a strong president has at his disposal a large arsenal of "weapons" with which to create legislative majorities in behalf of his program. There is no doubt, then, that we have witnessed in recent years the emergence of what Arthur Schlesinger (1973) called "The Imperial Presidency."

We have serious reservations about Perlmutter's treatment of the patterns of recruitment into the presidential political center. He chooses to lump the elite surrounding the president into a broad category: the presidential court. If the president has a court, we undoubtedly are encouraged to consider its members as servants to a president-monarch. The relationship between the president and the members of his court is clearly unequal, for despite their training, experience, and skills, they "live under the shadow of his total power" (*Ibid.*, p. 103). They are chosen, Perlmutter continues, "in the knowledge that the President will dominate and manipulate [the court] and use it to create a consensus for his decisions. The members are his creatures, whose course of action he dictates" (*Ibid.*, p. 104). Apparently, the president exercises considerable control over their reputations and credibility.

A different image of the presidential center is offered by Richard Barnet in his book, *The Roots of War* (1973). Barnet describes the decision-making center in terms of a president surrounded by a small group of "national security managers":

> These men exercise their power chiefly by filtering the information that reaches the President, and by interpreting the outside world for him. They structure his choices. . . . The relationship between the President and the national security managers is truly symbiotic. They are engaged in a complex and continuous process of mutual persuasion. The President is as concerned with how to move the bureaucracy as the advisers are concerned with how to convince the President. In the Vietnam War, Lyndon Johnson and Richard Nixon pressed their advisers to formulate plans that would avoid the defeat they could not accept. The advisers, in turn, pressed the President to take the risks and to sanction the homicidal power necessary to achieve victory (pp. 76–77)

Barnet perhaps overemphasizes the autonomy of the bureaucracy and its ability to proceed on the momentum of its own logic, but his description clearly underlines the extent to which Perlmutter has given us only a partial, one-sided, and therefore distorted, perspective of the presidential center.

Perlmutter tends to overlook the degree to which a president depends on his subordinates for information and expertise in setting the basic lines of policy. The basic proposals of the Nuclear Test Ban Treaty, for instance, were developed by a scientific group within the bureaucracy. Permitting the Soviets to reject on-site inspections and prohibiting only atmospheric testing were decisions tied at least as much to technical considerations as to political ones. In the Dominican intervention, Johnson relied heavily upon advice from intelligence and diplomatic services in the Dominican Republic. In Berlin, Truman responded to military advice from both General Clay and the Air Force about the feasibility of an airlift. Even in the formulation of the Marshall Plan, a specially convened coordinating group developed the basic outlines of the program with help from regular State Department personnel as well as a wide variety of Government economic experts. In some ways the Bay of Pigs incident illustrates the classic dilemma of excessive dependence on intelligence or expertise, as Kennedy himself so eloquently testified.

In addition, Perlmutter's comments overlook the role of key personnel in the presidential entourage in specifying the range of issues and options for the president. Would one really claim that Dulles, with respect to both the Dien Bien Phu decision and the intervention in Lebanon, was simply a "creature" of the president, particularly when his role on both occasions as the definer of alternative policies was central to the outcome? Similarly, and so we may not be accused of partisanship in our choice of presidents, did Truman really "dictate" the course of action for Clay to follow on the Berlin question in 1948? Our analysis appears to suggest quite the reverse. And finally, although no single figure dominated the presidential court in 1968, Johnson's decision to cut back the bombing was undoubtedly influenced greatly by the manner in which the options were posed by Rusk, McNamara, and Clifford. We might also add that Johnson's previous decisions to escalate in Vietnam were based on continual estimates of imminent victory offered by his military experts. Perlmutter's case for the president's domination of his court fails, therefore, at a number of points.

We might also note that Perlmutter even fails to consider the limitations on presidential domination that result from a divided, disloyal, or unresponsive bureaucracy displaying the normal bureaucratic disease of inertia. In the Cuban missile crisis, for instance, Kennedy was to be embarrassed by the failure of the bureaucracy to implement an order given early in his administration calling for the removal of missile bases from Turkey. Although Perlmutter might claim that these problems are irrelevant because they fall outside the presidential political center, it seems quite clear that the presidential power to make decisions may be effectively nullified by bureaucratic noncompliance.

Perlmutter's analysis of the nature and structure of consensus within the presidential center provides some interesting insights. Perlmutter defines consensus as the "broadest and most generalized acceptance of specific but universal orientations, beliefs, practices and procedures"; not a program or policy, "it is a collective perception and identification of friends and foes, and of issues" (1974, p. 105). Alternatively, consensus may be thought of as the operative security and diplomatic ideology of the presidential court that serves to integrate the court's elite so that it may in turn inculcate the consensus into the political community. This function, if properly executed, facilitates the performance of the presidential role in foreign-policy making.

We are not told how this consensus is formed, although it is undoubtedly related to political developments and maneuvering within the presidential court. We do know, however, that insofar as the consensus is reflected by the elite, its range of opinions and ideas is limited, since the elite who are recruited to the court must "represent society's centers of values, symbols and beliefs" (Ibid., p. 104). Therefore, elites of unorthodox views—whether of the left or the right—would be systematically excluded from the presidential center: "Elites outside the Presidential political center who are not oriented toward the ideology of the consensus will not join the court" (Ibid., p. 105). Irrespective of the prevailing ideological orientation of the administration in power, there is within any presidential court a substantial uniformity of attitudes, interests, values, and beliefs that contributes to the development and maintenance of the existing consensus. Even so, Perlmutter would choose to assign the president the critical role in the development of that consensus.

There are two things to note with respect to this claim for presidential dominance. First, by any standards a president's personal views can hardly be considered radical. His own recruitment and the elaborate process of selecting a president in the United States assure his adherence to the prevailing ideology of the consensus. After all, presidential nominations do not come easily, and the financial aid necessary to support an extensive campaign would not be forthcoming unless the presidential candidate were acceptable to the major financial and economic interests providing the resources. In addition, party support for the presidential nominee, a crucial asset, might well be withdrawn from a candidate whose views diverged significantly from those of the party leadership. Both the Goldwater campaign of 1964 and the McGovern campaign of 1972 are instructive in this regard. It should also be noted that the party leadership, as well, is dependent on large financial contributions. It should be apparent that these constraints in the American presidential recruitment and nomination process narrow the range of candidate types, views, and philosophies: "A President is a known quantity who was selected to respond within a certain range of predictable ways. He may have certain options in any given situation, but these options are narrowly circumscribed." (Prewitt and Stone, 1973, p. 105).

The second observation to be made in considering the claim for presidential dominance is that the president's role in the formation of the consensus, particularly as that role expresses itself in policy decisions, is, as we have suggested, not wholly determinative. What appears to be presidential autonomy is very often simply a barely concealed and rather profound presidential dependence on advisors and subordinates within the presidential court. In the long run, this issue may well be unimportant. The question is whether the president is the crucial shaper of the consensus, or whether he inherits it from a society whose major values have already been shaped by dominant elites and their control of the socialization process.

For Perlmutter the president and his court constitute a particular consensus that adheres to a specific set of values, beliefs, and orientations, a context within which the basic lines of American foreign policy are discussed, formulated, and justified. What ideas, values, and beliefs does this consensus encompass, and what is its nature? Perlmutter claims that the consensus is broad and diffuse, that it supports policies as diverse as the Berlin Blockade, the maintenance of the balance of nuclear terror, and the encouragement of anti-Communist regimes in Asia and Africa. In our view, consensus also extends to the foreign policy decisions justifying such actions as intervention in the Dominican Republic and in Lebanon, the suspension of aid for the construction of a dam in Egypt, and the expansion of international trade.

The consensus includes such concepts as "cold war," "peaceful coexistence," "polycentrism," "the balance of terror," and "détente." These constitute the initial ideological context for the formulation of foreign policy actions, and may be employed, if necessary, for justificational purposes. They may also be seen as the biases that are built into our value system and our institutional structure. By affecting the identification of issues, the posing of options, and the outcomes of decisions, these biases have a primary impact on our foreign policy decisional system. (In regard to the notion of bias see Bachrach and Baratz, 1969 and 1970, especially Chapters 1–3.)

However one chooses to view them, it is clear that these concepts are not neutral. They affect interests in the society differently, and since foreign policies are founded on them, they will also affect such policies differently. The consensus is therefore by no means impartial: it tends to favor certain interests over others and to distribute benefits and burdens in certain clearly identifiable directions. It is this critical issue that Perlmutter has chosen to downgrade.

Much of Perlmutter's thesis is commendable, and we agree with him on a number of crucial points. We agree that in the domain of foreign-policy making the presidential political center is determinative. We agree that in this policy area the president and his court have been able to virtually ignore such institutions as Congress, political parties, and interest groups. We agree that the recruitment of the elite into the presidential court is selective, that certain elite sectors in society are excluded, and that the resulting court represents a rather narrow range of values and orientations. We agree that the resulting consensus is therefore neither impartial nor representative, but rather selective and restrictive.

Having conceded all this, we repeat two criticisms that are of crucial importance, in our view. First, we differ with Perlmutter on the issue of presidential autonomy within his court on the matters of consensus formation and the determination of foreign policy. The president is much too dependent on his staff and subordinates for information, expertise, and the presentation of options for the thesis of autonomy to be maintained. However, since the president shares the consensus with his court, it is unnecessary to see him as the central determiner of this system of beliefs and orientations.

Second, and of even greater importance, although Perlmutter has provided us with some shrewd insights into the role of consensus in foreign policy, he has added little to our understanding of either the nature of this consensus or its major sources. Unfortunately, what is missing from his analysis is any effort to deal with the matter of the interests that are benefited by the prevailing consensus.

THE ROLE OF THE SOCIAL STRUCTURE

A careful examination of our case studies should provide us with some critical insights into the components of this consensus. But we shall save this discussion for the final chapter. Instead, we again suggest that a proper understanding of the nature and substantive content of this consensus cannot be obtained if the student relies exclusively on the work of the decision-making theorists, that of the bureaucratic-politics school, or even the more recent model proposed by Perlmutter. The shortcomings of these approaches are also manifest when they are employed to shed light on the structure of the foreign-policy-making process. An adequate explanation of this process, as well as of the consensus that underlies it, can come only from understanding the interplay between the structure of power in society and the policies by which societal problems are resolved and societal goals are accomplished. Of course, this observation applies to domestic- as well as to foreign-policy making, since the political process makes no basic distinction between foreign and domestic policy.

At present, there are two major interpretations of the structure of power in American society. These may be identified as the pluralist and elitist interpretations. Each has a considerable history and a body of empirical work upon which it rests. In the postwar years, these two interpretations have constituted the two camps in a continual and bitter struggle for dominance in the discipline of political science.

Pluralism begins with the presumption that power in society is fragmented and diffused throughout the social order. Stemming from this basic proposition is a series of assumptions:

1. Many groups in American society have sufficient power to participate in some significant way in the decision-making process. Final decisions are usually a result of bargaining and compromise between these groups.

2. This, in turn, presupposes a balance of power among significant groups, such that no one group is powerful enough to dictate in any absolute way to other groups—in short, an equilibrium of relative equality.

3. This equilibrium is the natural state of a democratic society, and if it is to endure, there must be some self-corrective mechanism by which it is maintained in the face of fundamental challenges to its continued existence.

American social and political scientists have been particularly adept at positing such mechanisms. (See, among others, Galbraith, 1952; Berle, 1954; Riesman, 1950).

Almost all pluralist theorists have assumed that there is neither a conscious purpose nor a unified power structure behind the making of national policy. They maintain that each policy domain involves distinct problems and separate sets of political actors and forces, so that each outcome is the result of a unique and complicated process of interaction. In order to understand this interaction, pluralists recommend that actual decisions be studied. As one supporter of this school has argued, pluralists should make an "attempt to study specific outcomes in order to determine who actually prevails in community decision-making" (Nelson Polsby in Ricci, 1971, p. 127).

Pluralists also make much of the distinction between potential and actual power. They presume that there is no precise equivalence between potential power and its exercise in particular situations. As a prominent advocate of the pluralist point of view, Robert Dahl, points out, "the mere possession of resources or attributes of power, whether it be wealth, status or occupational position, [is] no clear indicator of power, since an individual need not use such resources to gain direct or indirect influence over officials of government" (Dahl, in Gillam, 1971, p. 28). The recent disclosures of Watergate and the "Rockefeller gifts" have given us a clear indication of the absurdity of this position. If nothing else, these incidents demonstrate the ease and pervasiveness with which wealth is converted into political power. Nevertheless, the unequal distribution of resources provides no clear clue to the distribution of actual power in a society, the pluralists argue, and if this claim is not sufficient to restore faith in the pluralist version of democracy, the pluralists will also claim that resources tend to be noncumulative and dispersed, so that no one person or group is completely without sources of support in his access to power.

Furthermore, the pluralist view rests on the assumption that the political system is sufficiently separate from the economic and social system so that one can understand it by focusing exclusively on the behavior of governmental institutions and the electoral process by which political officeholders acquired their positions. The government has an independent power base that permits it to respond to pressures and to support a more general public interest against the selfish private interest of nongovernmental groups and institutions. The pluralists often see the state as an umpire with an overarching authority to oversee, and at times compel, a settlement among the interests of competing groups. According to this view, the impartiality of government is a consequence of its independent power sources. Groups are also accorded relatively equal opportunities to gain access to the governmental apparatus.

Finally, the pluralists assign an important role to the politician, who not only reflects the interests of the population as registered in the electoral process, but also accommodates diverse and competing interests with one another. The system provides for a set of procedures and institutions to facilitate the bargaining and compromises that lay at its foundation.

Although Dahl never denies the existence of inequality in society, he continues to rail against the thesis of a single unified ruling elite. To be sure, he admits, elites may dominate in various specific issue areas, but in general they do not coalesce into anything that might be remotely described as a national elite.

In contrast, C. Wright Mills, the principal contemporary theorist of the elitist point of view, focuses on a unified, cohesive, national elite. As a sociologist, Mills approaches the study of power from a broader perspective than that of Dahl and other pluralists. Whereas Dahl visualizes power as a personal attribute and makes much of the distinction between power as potential and power in use, Mills chooses to view power in its structural and institutional aspects. For Mills, power resides in those who man the major institutional structures of society. This power displays itself principally in decisions of great import—that is, "whatever decisions men make about the arrangements under which they live and about the events which make up the history of their time" (Mills, in Gillam, 1971, p. 52). At this stage in America's development, Mills argues, the power to make the critical decisions is so "clearly seated in political, military and economic institutions that other areas of society seem off to the side, and on occasion readily subordinated to these" (*Ibid.*, p. 54). For Mills, as well as for other elitists, the ascendancy of this institutional complex is a by-product of historical developments buttressed by powerful technological forces. The elitists maintain that the political division of labor must, under modern industrial conditions and despite democratic institutions, concentrate political power and political competence in the hands of a few. The economic facts of life are such that economic power is concentrated in the hands of expert managers. The international political system of sovereign states—with its eternal possibility of modern warfare—inevitably enhances the power of the military. Moreover, modern life not only increases the number and complexity of decisions to be made, but this very complexity and the increasingly esoteric nature of the information needed to make decisions intelligently serves to concentrate power into fewer and more technically expert hands. This process of concentration is apparent in the seemingly inherent tendency in all major industrial-political systems for power to be centralized in the hands of the executive, or, to put it in another and perhaps more illuminating way, for power to shift from those who are elected to those who are appointed.

As a result of these institutional developments, Mills tells us, there now exists in the United States an extraordinary concentration of power in the hands of a relatively small elite. Moreover, the central institutional domains are interrelated, and their interests often coincide. This interlocking relationship and the increasing coincidence of interests are the foundations of the emerging power elite: "As each of these domains has coincided with the others, as decisions in each have become broader, the leading men of each —the high military, the corporation executives, the political directorate—have tended to come together to form the power elite of America" (*Ibid.*, 55). The power of this elite is profound and far-reaching. It could "overturn the *status quo*, call into question the existing social relationship, and establish a new structure" (Parry, 1969, p. 54). The elite alone decides the truly significant issues of war and peace, or slump and prosperity.

But it is not simply the oligarchical character of this elite that is so significant. Mills also stresses the underlying cohesion and unity of this group, and does so without resorting to a claim of conspiracy. For one thing, this unity has rested on a growing coincidence of interest and on increasing mutual reinforcement among the elites of politics, industry, and the military, particularly during the post–World War II period. This coincidence has occurred for a variety of reasons. The military, for example, was interested in growing and modernizing itself; the corporate elite was concerned with obtaining military contracts and a profitable manufacture of modern weaponry; and the political elite was concerned with the maintenance and defense of the system and with the overriding questions of loyalty and authority. A second reason for the cohesiveness of the elites within the various institutional spheres is that they frequently circulate from a post in one institutional domain to a post in another with considerable ease. This interchangeability of personnel can only serve to strengthen a similarity of outlook among them. Mills identifies a very clear triangular pattern of personnel circulation among top military, economic, and political positions. The cohesion of the elite, Mills maintains, is also bolstered by their similar social experiences, which tend to produce common psychological traits and outlooks. For instance, the prestigious private schools play a crucial role in the training and socialization of the power elite. Through a process of cooptation, Mills argues, norms of institutional behavior are enforced and conformity is encouraged. In fact, conformity is regularly demanded as the price for entrance into the select circle. Thus, even individuals with vastly dissimilar social and economic backgrounds learn to adopt the behavioral styles and outlook of the elite.

On a number of points Mills and the pluralists—especially Dahl—are in basic agreement. Mills is quite willing to accept the pluralist interpretation as a description of what he calls the "middle levels" of power, as distinct from the power elite. At this middle level Mills places the general day-to-day activities of politics; Congress, political parties, and pressure groups are the central actors. Issues at this level tend to be of local or sectional import and of rather narrow and specific scope. Most important, issues and policies at this level never challenge the fundamental nature of the economic, social, or political system. That most pluralistic interpretations of American society emerge from studies of local communities rather than the national system lends support to this point of view. Mills is even willing to concede that balance, equilibrium, and stability do, or could, exist at this level. But in short, "the middle level of politics is not a forum in which there are debated the big decisions of national and international life" (Mills, in Gillam, 1971, p. 58). The power elite is involved only tangentially in the issues of the middle level, because it feels that these are only marginally relevant to its own basic interests.

At the lowest or "mass" level of politics, according to Mills, is the vast bulk of the citizenry. Basically apathetic, uninformed, or disinterested, those at this level play an insignificant role in political affairs. Characteristically, they feel a sense of hopelessness at the enormity and complexity of social problems and at the bigness of institutions, and, consequently, they lose interest in public affairs and privatize their world. Men in authority are considered indispensable and wise, and they use their positions of authority to perpetuate this state of affairs. In a mass society the vast bulk of the population is fragmented, disorganized, and susceptible to manipulation and mobilization by the elite. Moreover, the new technology has placed in the hands of elites instruments of manipulation that were hitherto unimagined. As a result, the public no longer serves as a restraint on elites, and its opinions are shaped more often by elite action than by independent discussion.

On the whole, most American analysts tend to employ, often implicitly, a pluralist framework in their analysis of foreign policy decisions. Thus, much of the work of the decision-making school of thought is clearly within the pluralist camp. Even the bureaucratic-politics theorists—who deploy a more sophisticated decision-making model—reflect, as we have noted, a pluralist persuasion. But this is to be expected, since the adoption of decisional outcomes as the basic unit of analysis tends to favor a pluralist interpretation.

However, a few foreign policy analysts, particularly in the 1960s, have found the elite interpretation more useful in understanding foreign policy. Although he was trained as a social psychologist, G. William Domhoff (1970) was among the first to apply a manifestly elite perspective to the foreign policy process. The elitist interpretation is also reflected in the foreign policy studies of William A. Williams (1959), Gabriel Kolko (1969), and Richard Barnet (1973). In 1973 Prewitt and Stone, in a general work on "elite theory," provided much new empirical support for that theory and urged that an elitist perspective be applied to the foreign policy process in order to broaden our knowledge of it.

Perhaps more interesting is the growing appeal of the elite model to those who were formerly linked clearly to the pluralist school. No less a figure than Gabriel Almond (1960) has provided a description of the foreign policy process that, although pluralist in its general outlines, recognizes elites as the central actors in any foreign policy decisions. The foreign policy process described by Almond may best be seen as a series of concentric circles in which the participants are arranged as follows:

1. The outer circle: the "general public," who are ignorant and indifferent except when aroused on highly visible issues.

2. The middle circle: the "attentive public," who are informed and interested and provide an audience for the discussion among elites.
3. The inner circle: the "policy and opinion elites," who structure the
discussion and give or deny access to various groups.
4. The bull's eye: the official policy leadership, consisting of the authoritative decision makers who are the central actors in any foreign policy
decisions.

Of course, unlike the elites proposed by such men as Mills and
Domhoff, Almond's elites are autonomous and competing rather
than cohesive and unified.

A second major pluralist figure, Theodore Lowi, has seemed
similarly disposed to depart from his earlier position. Turning his
attention to the field of foreign policy in the late 1960s, Lowi
attempted to plot the relationship between issue areas and the
environment in which decision making is conducted. He began his
analysis by postulating three different categories of issues-
—distributive, regulative, and redistributive—and then attempted
to correlate them with different modes of decision making that
"clearly have consequences for American foreign policy" (Lowi,
1967, p. 298). Lowi was most interested in identifying the prevailing structures and patterns of power in the domain of foreign-policy
making. In his view, these are reflections of an underlying set of
conditions that include events, institutions, policies, and types of
policies. Thus, events such as crisis decisions involve only
"command-post positions, with the public and its institutions . . .
far removed, and public and semipublic responses largely ceremo-
nial and affirmative" (Ibid., p. 300). Mills's description of the
power elite and its operations is entirely applicable to these decisions, Lowi argued. Even in noncrisis matters, moreover, a
pluralist interpretation cannot be presumed.

Efforts by Lowi to categorize issues according to policy domain have not proved particularly rewarding. In the field of foreign
policy it is often difficult to differentiate distributive issues or
policies from regulatory ones. The criteria for doing so are too often
obscure or ambiguous. (See Zimmerman, 1973, for an effort to
refine these criteria and develop the categories more fully.) Even a
superficial perusal of the case studies in the present book would
indicate how impossible it is, in our view, to classify such decisions

as the Marshall Plan, the suspension of atmospheric nuclear testing, or trade expansion as regulatory, distributive, or redistributive. Moreover, the effort to segregate the various domains of policy making according to issue seems too rigid and inflexible, and inconsistent with experience.

Obviously, Lowi has never been entirely comfortable with the elitist interpretation of foreign policy. By a series of semantic maneuvers, he sought to limit the scope of its applicability to foreign policy events and decisions. He restricted the power-elite thesis to crisis situations, and then defined "crisis" in such a manner as to insure its rarity in the world of political affairs. Judging from the crisis situations offered by Lowi, his operational definition of a crisis seems confined to instances that involve an immediate and urgent military response to a military threat. Lowi also admits the applicability of the power-elite interpretation to noncrisis situations in which *no* internal resources were involved at all; but he claims that in virtually all noncrisis situations it is *impossible* to conceive of the *absence* of internal resources. By definition, therefore, this noncrisis set would never have any members, and as a consequence an elitist interpretation would never appear.

Recently, however, a flurry of scholarly activity seems to be presaging the growing legitimacy of the elite perspective as a means of deepening our knowledge of the processes of foreign policy. In our view, this is a welcome development in model building for foreign policy analysis. First, an elitist model helps us identify the central political actors in the foreign policy process. Second, it provides us with a more useful description of the process of foreign-policy making, one that is more likely to conform to the "real" world of foreign-policy making than the pluralist conception. Such a perspective, moreover, is not formally inconsistent with the bureaucratic-politics model or earlier decision-making approaches, but rather can build upon the findings and insights of previous analyses. (See, in particular, Barnet, 1973, for illustration of how the bureaucratic politics model might be combined with an elite perspective.) From our viewpoint, the elitist model has the additional advantage of shedding new light on the structure of the foreign-policy making that we examined in our case studies. In comparison with other perspectives, as the reader will discover shortly, an elitist perspective not only permits us to make greater sense of our observations and specific findings, it enables us to generalize about a broader range of cases. Moreover, since it does not prejudge any foreign policy decision, it permits us to use case studies in order to determine how much power elites have with respect to any particular policy, and what goals they are seeking.

We maintain that the greatest step toward developing a fresh perspective in foreign policy analysis would link the *elite* dimension to a *historical* one. By its nature the elitist perspective, with its image of small, relatively cohesive groups directing foreign policy on the basis of prescribed goals and interests, must emphasize a historical approach. This approach would stress the continuity of strategic elite interests over a period of time, and should therefore provide greater insight into the broad sweep of foreign policy than any other perspective. An analysis of foreign policy divorced from such a historical context provides little guidance in understanding trends in foreign policy outcomes. Not only does the historical background set the stage for action and place the issues within a recognizable framework, it conditions much of the responses as well. Moreover, the historical dimension provides the context in which the interests of major political, social, and economic forces are converted into the objectives of foreign policy. Such a perspective would be especially useful in providing new insights into the nature and content of the consensus underlying American foreign policy. It would help us identify the range of elite interests in American society, and would encourage us to ask why these interests and objectives are what they are. It would also direct our attention to the manner and extent to which foreign policy decisions are informed by the strategic elite goals and interests in society. Finally, and perhaps more important, it would offer us a critical insight into the relationship between these interests and stated national objectives in foreign policy.

REFERENCES AND BIBLIOGRAPHY

ALLISON, GRAHAM T., *Essence of Decision: Explaining the Cuban Missile Crisis.* Boston: Little, Brown, 1971.

The Politics of American Foreign Policy: The Social Context of Decisions

ALMOND, GABRIEL, *The American People and Foreign Policy.* New York: Praeger, 1960.

BACHRACH, PETER, and MORTON BARATZ, *Power and Poverty: Theory and Practice.* New York: Oxford University Press, 1970.

———, "Two Faces of Power," in *The Bias of Pluralism*, ed. William E. Connolly. New York: Atherton, 1969.

BARBER, JAMES D., *The Presidential Character.* Englewood Cliffs, N.J.: Prentice-Hall, 1972.

BARNET, RICHARD J., *Roots of War.* Baltimore: Penguin, 1973.

BERLE, A. A., *The 20th Century Capitalist Revolution.* New York: Harcourt, Brace, 1954.

DE RIVERA, JOSEPH H., *The Psychological Dimensions of Foreign Policy.* Columbus, Ohio: Charles E. Merrill, 1968.

DOMHOFF, G. WILLIAM, *The Higher Circles.* New York: Vintage Books, 1970.

DOMHOFF, G. WILLIAM, and HOYT B. BALLARD, *C. Wright Mills and The Power Elite.* Boston: Beacon Press, 1968. (See especially the essays by Lynd, Sweezy, and Rovere.)

DOUGHERTY, JAMES E., and ROBERT L. PFALTZGRAFF, JR., *Contending Theories of International Relations.* Philadelphia: Lippincott, 1971.

FRANKEL, JOSEPH, *The Making of Foreign Policy: An Analysis of Decision-Making.* New York: Oxford University Press, 1963.

GALBRAITH, JOHN KENNETH, *American Capitalism: The Concept of Countervailing Power.* Boston: Houghton Mifflin, 1952.

GILLAM, RICHARD, ed., *Power in Postwar America.* Boston: Little, Brown, 1971.

JANIS, IRVING L., *Victims of Groupthink: A Psychological Study of Foreign Policy Decisions and Fiascoes.* Boston: Houghton Mifflin, 1973.

KLINEBERG, OTTO, *The Human Dimension in International Relations.* New York: Holt, Rinehart & Winston, 1964.

LOWI, THEODORE J., "American Business, Public Policy, Case Studies and Political Theory," *World Politics*, July, 1964, pp. 677–715.

———, "Making Democracy Safe for the World: National Politics and Foreign Policy," in *Domestic Sources of Foreign Policy*, ed. James R. Rosenau. New York: Free Press, 1967.

MILLS, C. WRIGHT, *The Power Elite.* New York: Oxford University Press, 1956.

MORGENTHAU, HANS, *Politics Among Nations*, 4th ed. New York: Knopf, 1967.

OSGOOD, CHARLES E., *An Alternative to War or Surrender.* Urbana, Ill.: University of Illinois Press, 1962.

PARRY, GERAINT, *Political Elites.* New York: Praeger, 1969.

PERLMUTTER, AMOS, "The Presidential Political Center and Foreign Policy: A Critique of the Revisionist and Bureaucratic-Political Orientations," *World Politics*, October, 1974, pp. 87–106.

PREWITT, KENNITH, and ALAN STONE, *The Ruling Elites: Elite Theory, Power and American Democracy.* New York: Harper & Row, 1973.

RICCI, DAVID, *Community Power and Democratic Theory: The Logic of Political Analysis.* New York: Random House, 1971.

RIESMAN, DAVID, *The Lonely Crowd.* New Haven: Yale University Press, 1950.

ROBINSON, JAMES A., and RICHARD C. SNYDER, "Decision-Making in International Politics," in *International Behavior,* ed. Herbert C. Kelman. New York: Holt, Rinehart & Winston, 1965.

SCHLESINGER, ARTHUR, *The Imperial Presidency.* Boston: Houghton Mifflin, 1973.

SNYDER, RICHARD C., H. W. BRUCK, and BURTON SAPIN, eds., *Foreign Policy Decision-Making.* New York: Free Press, 1963.

SPROUT, HAROLD, and MARGARET SPROUT, *An Ecological Paradigm for the Study of International Politics.* Princeton, N.J.: Center for International Studies, 1968.

VERBA, SIDNEY, "Assumptions of Rationality and Nonrationality in Models of the International System," in *International Politics and Foreign Policy,* rev. ed., ed. James N. Rosenau. New York: Free Press, 1969.

WOLFERS, ARNOLD, "The Actors in International Politics," in *Theoretical Aspects of International Relations,* ed. W. T. R. Fox. Notre Dame, Ind.: University of Notre Dame Press, 1959.

ZIMMERMAN, WILLIAM, "Issue Area and Foreign Policy Process: A Research Note in Search of a General Theory," *American Political Science Review,* December, 1973, pp. 1204–12.

14

The Interplay
of Ideology and Interest

We are now in a position to examine the ways in which the interests of elites are linked with the objectives of American foreign policy in the post–World War II period, particularly those objectives that are justified in terms of a national interest. The concept of national interest has been perhaps the most pervasive and central idea in the literature on foreign policy, and it is of particular importance to us since it serves as the conduit by which elite interests are translated into national objectives. A look at some of the ways in which this concept has been used will clarify our argument. It has been used by various writers as an *explanation* of the motivating force behind a nation's external policies, as a *rationalization* of existing policies, and as a *guide to action* that helps us sort out "good" from "bad" policies.

One of the most systematic treatments of the ways in which this concept has been used by both scholars and practitioners in recent years can be found in an article written by James Rosenau (Rosenau, 1971, pp. 239–49). Viewing the vast and rich literature devoted to explanations of the role of national interest in the study of foreign policy in particular, and of international politics in general, Rosenau concludes that in spite of the diversity of views and methods, one can perceive two dominant schools of thought into which most treatments of the concept of national interest fall.

The first of these schools is identified as the *objectivist* school. The most fundamental assumption made by objectivists is the existence of a "real" and objectified national interest, independent of its perception by either scholars or policy makers. These are the basic interests upon which the survival and prosperity of a state depend, and they may be said to exist in much the same way as the "natural laws" of eighteenth-century philosophers. It is therefore the primary task of the practitioners of statecraft to discern what these interests are, and to shape specific policies that are compatible with them. The wisdom or foolishness of a particular policy, then, depends on whether it is linked in some positive way to such basic national interests, or whether it is dysfunctional to such interests. Men such as Hans Morgenthau, George Kennan, and Henry Kissinger are among the leading figures that Rosenau would identify with this school of thought (see Morgenthau, 1967; Kennan, 1954; Kissinger, 1974).

Just what these basic general interests are, and how they may be formulated in such a way that they provide a reliable guide to action for policy makers—this is the central problem that confronts objectivists. In answering this question, Morgenthau provides us with what has become a dominant paradigm within this school —the notion of "interest defined in terms of power." Power is defined in the conventional way by Morgenthau—the ability to control and influence the behavior of others in accordance with one's own ends. He then goes on to tell us that the amount of such power at a nation's command (its power capability) is the basic fact of life in international politics. All policies must take this into account first and foremost, and the most foolish of all policies is one that leads a nation to pursue goals that are beyond its power to achieve—the sin of overextension. Interestingly Morgenthau, who at least in the later stages of the Vietnam war might be counted among the severe critics of America's Vietnam policy, mounted his criticism exclusively from within this perspective. Unwilling to share the moral objections to the war stated by other critics, he denounced American policy in Vietnam primarily as an overextension and miscalculation of American power capabilities. The basic failure of American policy, according to Morgenthau, was simply that the United States, in pursuit of moralistic goals, ignored the realities of Chinese and Soviet power. In fact, a major proposition shared by almost all writers in this school is that the failures of American foreign policy throughout recent years have been a result of its obsession with moral and ideological goals, to the neglect of national interest (see Kennan, 1954). How the United States rose to its position of preeminence as the dominant nation in the international order in the face of such blundering and foolishness on the part of its policy makers is never explained, nor is the contradiction even acknowledged. William A. Williams and other revisionist historians have provided us with an alternate interpretation of the history of American foreign policy that stresses a spectacularly successful blending of the realistic pursuit of specific interests with statements of moral and ideological purpose that served to mobilize support for these interests (see Williams, 1959).

Be that as it may, objectivists are left with the problem of identifying precisely what the goals of American foreign policy—or for that matter, the policy of any nation—should be. Morgenthau provides us with an answer when he asserts that the basic goal of any foreign policy should be the maximization of a nation's power. It is the task of the policy maker to calculate coolly and rationally in any situation what policy is most likely to achieve this objective within the limitations and restraints imposed by his country's capabilities and the power of other nations. This model of the perfectly rational policy maker operating in an environment free of ideological compulsions and irrational political considerations, and able to coolly calculate his own and other nations' power capabilities, is the dream of all objectivists. It is in many ways the image of nineteenth-century diplomacy, especially as practiced by the British. It goes far in explaining the perspective within which Mr. Kissinger has been pursuing his policies of détente and adjustment to the power of both China and the USSR. It is precisely such fine and delicate adjustments leading to a stable balance of power (favorable, of course, to one's own nation) that the wise statesman pursues. Mr. Kissinger's angry and exasperated reaction to the intrusion of such considerations as the Soviet treatment of Jews is understandable in the light of this model.

There are, of course, serious problems with this model of the national interest, both as an explanatory concept and as a guide to action. Simply insisting on the national interest, even when it is formulated in this way, tells us nothing about how, in any specific situation, it is to be defined, and who is to define it. Power is too elusive a concept to be calculated with the accuracy demanded by such a model. As Quincy Wright (1964) demonstrated in his classic study of war, statesmen have miscalculated both their own and other nations' power capabilities more than fifty percent of the time. The only way of determining, then, whether the national interest is or is not being pursued is through hindsight—the success or failure of policies. Another problem with the objectivist model is that the assumption of almost perfect rationality on the part of statesmen simply does not, as we have already suggested, accord with the reality of modern politics, especially in democratic societies.

But perhaps the most serious objection of all is the extent to which the objectivist approach tends to elevate power to the status of an end in itself, and thereby render it completely useless as an analytic concept. Power, as defined even by the objectivists, is a *relationship* involving the ability of one party to make the other behave in a way compatible with the first party's goals. To speak about maximization of power, then, tells us nothing about what those goals or interests are. Of what use is it to be able to control and influence another nation's behavior if one has no conception of just what kind of behavior is wanted? Only a clear-cut analysis of interests and goals can provide such a conception. Power abstracted from interest and treated as an end rather than a means becomes meaningless, and diverts the policy maker and the scholar from the real task—a hard analysis of just what concrete interests the nation is, or should be, pursuing.

Partly as a reaction to such problems, and also to avoid what they considered the excessive value orientation of the objectivist school, the second school of thought—*the subjectivist*—arose. The subjectivists start with the assumption that the national interest is not "an objective truth that prevails whether or not it is perceived by the members of a nation, but it is rather a pluralistic set of subjective preferences that change whenever the requirements and aspirations of the nation's members change" (Rosenau, 1971, p. 242). The national interest, therefore, is not susceptible to objective measurement, even when it is defined in terms of power. The only way to discover what a nation needs and demands is to assume that these are, in the long run, reflected in the choices of the authoritative decision makers. A political system cannot, after all, continue to ignore the major needs and demands of its members for any considerable period of time. If it does, it will surely cease to exist. The logic of the political process, especially in pluralist, democratic societies, therefore forces the political leaders of a nation to be responsive to group demands. Thus, the national interest is whatever the authoritative decision makers say it is.

This approach side-steps very neatly the problem of conflict over values or the evaluation of any given policy. Revealing an inherent bias toward "what is," it tends to automatically ratify whatever decisions are made by the nation's official leaders, and to remove foreign policy from the realm of political debate. The concept of bipartisanship, which has been a major theme of American foreign policy for decades, is an indispensable component of the subjectivist approach.

The limitations of the subjectivist school are obvious. First, it provides us with no real method of identifying and quantifying the demands of all significant groups making up the nation. The problem of cumulating these interests, once they have been identified, is also ignored, as is the problem of assigning relative weights. Most subjectivists avoid these problems by relying on a procedural rather than a substantive definition of national interest. They simply assume that the nation's political process will perform this task of cumulating and synthesizing the many demands of subnational groups into something called the national interest. Whether the result is simply the sum of its parts, or something greater and qualitatively different, is never specified. The assumption is simply that the selection of the national decision makers is itself a result of the politics of bargaining and compromise, and that once these decision makers are in power, the logic of their situation makes it virtually impossible for them not to reflect the aspirations of the various groups in society. Their survival depends on it, and should they ignore this reality they will simply be removed from power by the political process.

It is obvious that whatever validity is contained in this image of the national interest, it is relevant only to the most open pluralist societies. Whether there exists a society that possesses a political process open enough to perform this cumulating and synthesizing function to the degree demanded by the model is open to question. After all, even in the United States one can point to many groups (blacks, the poor, migrant workers, and so on) that are excluded or very nearly excluded from any significant participation in the political process. In closed authoritarian societies, where many groups have no opportunity to articulate their needs and wants, the lack of relevance of the model is clear. The subjectivist model, therefore, possesses very limited applicability to an extremely small range of societies, if any at all. It rests on the assumption that the opinions of decision-making elites are shaped by the demands of the mass public, and there is considerable evidence that in almost all modern societies the reverse is more nearly true. We will have more to say about this later, for the present it will suffice to point out that the utility of the subjectivist approach is restricted so severely that this approach is almost useless as an analytic tool.

Where does all this leave us? Does it mean that the concept of national interest must be entirely abandoned in our analysis of foreign policy? Not necessarily. A fruitful approach, as we suggested earlier, joins a historical perspective to an elitist one. Stated simply, this approach asserts that the chief determinant of the national interest is the struggle among political, economic, and social forces within a nation. According to Barnet, "foreign policy is more an expression of our own society than a programmed response to what other nations do" (1973, p. 6). Analysts of this school stress two important elements in examining the national interest—its *historical nature* and its *specificity*. At any given moment in the history of a society, the interests pursued by a nation are a reflection of the internal distribution of power. Those groups that are favored the most by the existing power distribution are also those that have been most successful in penetrating and influencing the behavior of a state. Indeed, it is the object of all *political* activity to achieve precisely such influence. Control and influence over the state is the object of political power for two reasons. The first is that the state is the source of the authoritative and legitimizing "rules of the game" of politics, and such rules are, as we have seen, never neutral. They always give some groups an advantage and others a disadvantage, even when they are applied equally to all (as they almost never are).

A simple example will suffice. In boxing a classic confrontation is that between the slugger, slow of foot and brain and depending primarily on the power of his punch, and the clever, agile boxer, who relies chiefly on his ability to outmaneuver and outpoint his opponent. In such a confrontation, one simple alteration in the rules, equally binding on both contestants, can decide the matter. Simply decrease the size of the ring, and you have given the slugger an enormous advantage over the boxer. The rules or laws or authoritative decisions of the game of politics are of this nature. Having control over the apparatus of the state, therefore, means being able to manipulate or alter the rules of the game in favor of one or another group in society.

But more important to our discussion is the second reason why control over the state is the object of political competition. It is simply that such control carries with it the ability to translate the private, selfish interests of any group in society into the interests of the state. This very same set of interests then becomes the public interest, or, in the domain of foreign policy, the national interest, and is surrounded with all the authority and majesty that the state possesses. This, of course, enormously facilitates the task of mobilizing public support for such interests, and even of convincing the other members of society that in defending those interests they are in fact defending their own. The simple statement by an authoritative decision maker that a given policy is "in the national interest" is enough to invest it with a power to elicit positive responses on both the emotional and intellectual levels. At any given point in history, then, the national interests pursued by a nation or stated by its official leaders are simply the interests of the dominant groups or classes. It is this transmutation of private interests into national interests that is the essence of the elitist tradition. This transmutation was never stated more succinctly and lucidly than in the classic statement by former Secretary of Defense Charles Wilson that "what is good for General Motors is good for the United States." From an elitist perspective it follows that the national interest can never be understood fully unless it is viewed within these two important dimensions—the historical and the specific. In the first dimension, the national interest must be seen as the reflection of a historically specific distribution of power, a distribution that changes over time as groups fall from power and other groups with different interests replace them. In the second dimension, the national interest must be seen as the concrete interests of specific groups in society, rather than from some generalized ideological perspective. In the elitist view, all generalized and abstract statements of the national interest can be seen, on closer inspection, to be simply an ideological formulation of a more specific set of interests.

The classic and in many ways the best study of the national interest written from this perspective is Charles Beard's *The Idea of National Interest* (1934). In it he traces the evolution of the concept from the "dynastic interest" of seventeenth-century commercial elites. The specific content of the formulation changed in response to internal shifts in the distribution of power. The dynastic interest, operating within a mercantile system, focused on the enrichment of the royal treasury. The colonial scramble for gold, spices, and other easily convertible wealth, as well as the attempt to integrate the economic activities of the territorial state, were all subordinated to this overriding interest. As dynastic elites were replaced by the new bourgeois commercial elites, national objectives moved toward the search for markets and raw materials, and the phrase "national interest" replaced the older formulation of "raison d'état."

Whereas Beard focused mainly on Europe, revisionist historians such as William Appleman Williams (1959) provide a similar type of analysis for the evolution of American foreign policy. Thus, Washington's statement that the interest of the United States lay in the avoidance of "entangling alliances" is seen as simply reflecting Federalist desires to be rid of obligations to the new revolutionary French regime that were incurred during the American Revolution. Manifest Destiny is seen as reflecting the need of new and powerful railroad and mining interests to exploit virgin territory, and the open-door policy is congruent with the need of the emerging industrial elite to extend its economic activities outside the boundaries of the United States. Ideological principles, then, are not simply expedient rationalizations of material interests, but are functionally indispensable to the realization of these interests. They provide the moral content and purpose necessary to mobilize the kind of support that no display of naked self-interest can.

C. W. Mills extends this analysis into the twentieth century and the post–World War II era of the power elite, which is the period covered by our case studies, and the one with which we are most concerned. Certain questions about this period become critical for us:

1. What elites have been most successful in translating their interests into national policy?
2. What is the specific content of those interests?
3. What are the ideological formulations through which they are filtered?

In our view, the cases we have analyzed do support at least a tentative answer to these questions. In answer to the first, it seems quite clear to us that the consensus that underlies American foreign policy not only tends to favor elite interests in general—and especially, of course, those elite sectors represented in the presidential court—but it disproportionately benefits the interests of one segment of that elite—the corporate business community. To support our claim, we might note, first, that a disproportionate number of individuals in the key positions within the presidential court are invariably drawn from the world of business or the corporation.

Dulles had had considerable experience in corporate law before he was enlisted by Eisenhower. Acheson, Ball, Harriman, Dillon, and a host of other top members of the presidential court had significant corporate business experience before joining the inner circle. According to Gabriel Kolko, who investigated the 234 top foreign policy decision makers, "men who came from big business, investment, and corporate law held 59.6 per cent of the posts" (1969, p. 19). (See Table 6.)

Second, much of the substance of American foreign policy in general tends to be remarkably consistent with the general aims and interests of the business community. Whether one chooses to use Perlmutter's list of ideas that make up the consensus, or to propose some alternative or addition, such as anti-Communism or the preservation of America as a dominant power in the world economic and political system, as the chief motivating concept of American foreign policy (see Kolko, 1969, for even more specific assertions), it is clear that these are all basically congruent with the value system of business circles. In our investigations it would be difficult to point to a single decision that directly contravenes the interests of the business elite within the presidential court. In fact, it is only as we recognize the virtual congruence between the prevailing consensus and the interests of the presidential court's business elite that an interpretative framework for the diversity of our case studies becomes possible.

Of course, we are not claiming that the business elite's viewpoint prevails on every foreign policy decision before the presidential court. On occasions, the business position is not unified. Issues of international trade, arms control, and foreign aid, as we have seen, may divide it at least temporarily. Nor are we suggesting that in all instances the business elite has a clear perception of its long-run interests and the policies by which these interests may be furthered. It may let policy drift while it develops its position, or it may support a program that runs counter to its objective interests. But these situations are by far the exception rather than the rule. When major issues are at stake, or when its interests are clearly and incontrovertibly involved, or when the consensus is being challenged or threatened, the business elite proceeds with absolute unity of purpose and action.

TABLE 6 Number of key positions in government, 1944–60, held by individuals designated by nongovernment career origin and by a government career origin

Nongovernment and Career Government Category	No. of Individuals	% of Individuals	State Dept.	Defense Dept.	War Dept.	Treasury Dept.	Commerce Dept.	Navy Dept.	Army Dept.	Air Force Dept.	White House Staff	International Bank for Reconstruction and Development	Export-Import Bank	E.C.A.-M.S.A.-I.C.A.	Budget Bureau	C.I.A.	Japan and German Military Governments	Miscellaneous Government Departments	No. of Positions	% of Positions
¹Key Law Firms	45	19.2	16	12	12	7	1	15	8	8	2	1		4	2	5	3	31	127	18.7
²Banking and Investment Firms	42	17.9	19	7	3	8	7	8	4	1	4	7	4	8	3	1	4	30	118	17.4
³Industrial Corporations	39	16.7	9	5	1	2	12	1	4	9	3		1	9		1		31	88	13.0
⁴Public Utilities and Transportation Corporations	4	1.7						1		1		1			1				4	.6
⁵Miscellaneous Business and Commercial Corporations	24	10.3	8	5		3	1	8	2	2	5			12	6			15	67	9.9
TOTAL: 1–5	154	65.8	52	29	16	20	21	33	18	21	14	9	5	33	12	7	7	107	404	59.6
⁶Nonprofit, Public Service, and Universities	14	6.0	4		1	1	1		2	1	3			10	4	3	3	16	49	7.2
TOTAL: 1–6	168	71.8	56	29	17	21	22	33	20	22	17	9	5	43	16	10	10	123	453	66.8

TABLE 6 (Continued)

Nongovernment and Career Government Category	No. of Individuals	% of Individuals	State Dept.	Defense Dept.	War Dept.	Treasury Dept.	Commerce Dept.	Navy Dept.	Army Dept.	Air Force Dept.	White House Staff	International Bank for Reconstruction and Development	Export-Import Bank	E.C.A.–M.S.A.–I.C.A.	Budget Bureau	C.I.A.	Japan and German Military Governments	Miscellaneous Government Departments	No. of Positions	% of Positions
7 Career Officials—No Subsequent Nongovernment Position	26	11.1	26	1	1	4	2		2			3	7	10	4	1	1	43	104	15.5
8 Career Officials—Subsequent Nongovernment Position	20	8.5	7	4	1	2	2	3	2	2		5		4	4	1	4	10	51	7.5
9 Career Officials—Subsequent Nongovernment Position and Return to Government	14	6.0	12	5	1	1	1	4	1	2	2	8	1	9	2	1	1	19	60	8.8
TOTAL 7–9	60	25.6	45	10	3	7	5	7	5	2	2	8	8	23	10	3	5	72	215	31.8
UNIDENTIFIED	6	2.6	1		1	1					2	1	2	1	1			1	10	1.5
COMBINED TOTAL	234	99.9	102	39	20	29	27	40	25	24	21	18	15	67	27	13	15	196	678	100.1

Source: From Gabriel Kolko, *The Roots of American Foreign Policy* (Boston: Beacon Press, 1969), pp. 20–21. Copyright © 1969 by Gabriel Kolko. Reprinted by permission of Beacon Press.

Third, on a broad structural level the mutuality of business interests and foreign policy may well be a reflection of the extent to which the goals of the industrial system—the expansion of output, an increase in consumption, technological advance—have become the goals of the state. This coincidence of the industrial system and the state is perhaps the paramount feature of the contemporary world.

> The industrial system, in fact, is inextricably associated with the State. In notable respects, the mature corporation is an arm of the State. And the State, in important matters, is an instrument of the industrial system. . . . The relationship of the technostructure of the mature corporation to the State is symbiotic. The State is strongly concerned with the stability of the economy, with its expansion or growth, with education, with technical and scientific advance, and, most notably, with national defense. These are *the* national goals. . . . All have their counterpart in the needs and goals of the corporate technostructure. At each point the government has goals with which the technostructure can identify itself, or more plausibly, these goals reflect the adaptation of public goals to the goals of the techno-structure. . . . Therein lies the influence of a mature corporation—an influ-ence which makes purely pecuniary relationships pallid by comparison. (Galbraith, 1971, pp. 298–99, 311–12)

It should thus be no surprise that the national interest, especially as defined in the post–World War II years, virtually coincides with what is sometimes called "the American business creed" (see Bar-net, 1973, Chapter 6).

In answer to the second question, a comparison of the cases we examined in terms of the policy objectives pursued enables us to identify some specific elite interests. The efforts to preserve and expand access to sources of raw materials, markets, and investment opportunities are most obvious in such cases as the Marshall Plan, the Trade Expansion Act, and the Foreign Assistance Act. But even in cases where the economic dimension is not as evident (Vietnam, the Dominican intervention, the intervention in Leba-non), the policy chosen almost always has the effect of attempting to preserve American economic dominance in the world. (Table 7, p. 294, illustrates the remarkable growth of American economic power abroad during post—World War II years.)

This argument is reinforced by the recent work of several scholars. Gabriel Kolko, in *The Roots of American Foreign Policy*, focuses on the strategic role of resources. He argues that two facts have converged in recent American history to produce the basic thrust of American foreign policy. One is the increasing dependence of the American economy on continued access to strategic raw materials located outside the United States. The other is that a major portion of such resources is to be found in areas of the world that are being destabilized by fundamental forces of political, economic, and social change. Kolko supports his thesis by citing an impressive array of statistics, as well as statements by official policy makers, all of which are designed to document the absolute dependence of the United States on continued access to important raw materials. (In this regard, see Table 8, p. 295.)

Attempts to refute this thesis by pointing out that the total dollar amount of American importation of raw materials is insignificant compared to the total volume of American trade and GNP are countered by the fact that such raw materials are strategically located in the economy, and that key sectors of industry, such as electronics, communications, weapons manufacture, and aviation, are significantly dependent on them. It is not necessary, as well, to demonstrate that the United States has a large direct economic stake in areas of the world where it intervenes. The general posture of the United States is to take action to preserve its control over, and access to, the world's raw materials. Any victory of left-wing Marxist governments is seen as being likely to have a domino effect that could topple the entire structure of American economic dominance. Vietnam may therefore be considered a kind of "rational overhead charge" for the preservation of the American Empire, which is defended, as all empires are, at its outposts.

Kolko perhaps places too much weight on the role of resources, but the general outlines of his argument are by no means unconvincing. His analysis tends to provide a frame of reference that makes American policy in the postwar years hang together with a substantial degree of consistency and continuity. This, of course, runs counter to the prevailing image of postwar policy as a discrete series of confused and logically inconsistent acts. Kolko

The Politics of American Foreign Policy: The Social Context of Decisions

TABLE 7   U.S. direct investments abroad: book value at yearend, by geographic area and sector of activity (in millions of U.S. dollars)

	Year	Total	Mining & Smelting	Petroleum	Manufacturing
World total	1950	11,788	1,129	3,390	3,831
	1957	25,394	2,634	8,991	7,898
	1960	31,865	2,997	10,810	11,051
	1965	49,474	3,931	15,298	19,339
	1970[1]	78,090	6,137	21,790	32,231
Canada	1950	3,579	334	418	1,897
	1957	8,769	996	2,154	3,512
	1960	11,179	1,325	2,664	4,827
	1965	15,318	1,851	3,356	6,872
	1970	22,801	3,014	4,809	10,050
Other Western Hemisphere	1950[2]	4,576	628	1,416	781
	1957	8,052	1,238	3,060	1,675
	1960	8,365	1,319	3,122	1,521
	1965	10,886	1,474	3,546	2,945
	1970	14,683	2,037	3,929	4,604
Europe	1950	1,733	21	424	933
	1957	4,151	50	1,184	2,077
	1960	6,691	49	1,763	3,804
	1965	13,985	54	3,427	7,606
	1970	24,471	71	5,487	13,704
United Kingdom	1950	847	3	123	542
	1965	5,123	2	1,093	3,306
	1970	8,015	1	1,852	4,988
EEC	1950	637	+	210	313
	1965	6,304	16	1,624	3,725
	1970	11,695	15	2,525	7,126
Japan	1950	19	..	+	+
	1960	254	..	125	91
	1965	675	..	321	275
	1970	1,491	..	540	753

TABLE 7 *(Continued)*

	Year	Total	Mining & Smelting	Petroleum	Manufac- turing
Australia, New Zealand,	1950	366	+	+	+
South Africa	1960	1,195	79	373	602
	1970	4,348	572	909	2,241

[1]Preliminary data.
[2]Excluding European dependencies.
+ Included in totals, but not itemized.
Data from *Survey of Current Business*, October 1971, August 1964, Sept. 1960, Aug. 1957, Jan. 1951.
Source: David P. Calles and Benjamin M. Rowland, *America and the World Political Economy: Atlantic Dreams and National Realities* (Bloomington: Indiana University Press, 1973), pp. 167–68.

TABLE 8 **Present and projected importance of the underdeveloped world to the U.S. economy and its global corporations**

A. **Increasing U.S. dependence on imports of strategic materials**

	% Imported from All Foreign Sources				% Imported from Underdeveloped Countries
	1950	1970	1985	2000	1971
Bauxite	64	85	96	98	95
Chromium	n.a.	100	100	100	25
Copper	31	17	34	56	44
Iron	8	30	55	67	32
Lead	39	31	61	67	32
Manganese	88	95	100	100	57
Nickel	94	90	88	89	71
Potassium	13	42	47	61	n.a.
Sulfur	2	15	28	52	31
Tin	77	98	100	100	94
Tungsten	37	50	87	97	37
Vanadium	24	21	32	58	40
Zinc	38	59	73	84	21

The Politics of American Foreign Policy: The Social Context of Decisions

B. Competition with other advanced nations for the natural resources of the underdeveloped world

	% of Total (1971) World Output of Strategic Materials		
	Produced by	Consumed by	
Strategic	Underdeveloped	All Advanced	
Material	Nations	Nations	U.S.A.
Antimony	54.1	59.8	19.5
Bauxite	55.6	75.5	24.6
Copper	41.0	75.23	24.8
Fluorspar	46.4	80.7	26.3
Graphite	67.3	69.4	22.6
Lead	26.3	72.8	23.5
Manganese	41.5	33.7	11.0
Tin	80.5	83.8	28.5

C. Increasing dependency on imported energy sources U.S.A./other advanced industrial nations (as a percentage of total domestic consumption)

	1960	1965	1970	1971
Total Energy				
U.S.A.	6.2	10.55	8.4	10.2
West Germany	7.9	44.5	58.9	60.6
Japan	46.6	74.9	94.5	98.5
Oil				
U.S.A.	16.3	21.5	21.5	24.0
West Germany	83.8	90.4	94.4	94.7
Japan	100.0	98.2	100.0	100.0
Natural Gas				
U.S.A.	1.2	2.79	3.5	3.8
West Germany	0.0	29.3	22.7	29.3
Japan	0.0	0.0	32.3	34.5
Coal and other solid fuels				
U.S.A.	0.0	0.0	0.0	0.0
West Germany	6.5	7.6	8.8	7.7
Japan	13.3	26.5	56.3	58.7

Source: From Global Reach: The Power of the Multinational Corporations, pp. 126-27. Copyright © 1974, by Richard L. Barnet and Ronald E. Muller. Reprinted by permission of Simon & Schuster, Inc.

paints a success story rather than the usual depressing picture of the abject failure of American foreign policy that academic critics tend to portray. Interestingly, Kolko, a left-wing critic, shatters another prevailing left-wing image—the notion of a military-industrial complex in which the military has played the dominant role in shaping American policy. He points out that it was "civilian liberal leadership" that involved us in Vietnam as well as in other postwar interventions. In general, the military has been content to serve the ends determined by the politico-economic sector of the elite, and to receive its rewards in terms of prestige, status, and perhaps ultimate acceptance into the ranks of the political and economic elites.

Robert Heilbroner (1967) carries this argument a bit further. America has, he suggests, consistently intervened in favor of traditional elites and against revolutionary modernizing elites throughout the developing world. It has done so because the logic of modernization and the enormous mobilizing effort needed to accomplish it make it virtually certain that such modernizing revolution will be led by Marxist-oriented elites who would adopt positions, such as the nationalization of resources, that are a danger to both the "American way of life" and American economic well-being. It is certain, at least, that a general success for such revolutionary regimes throughout the world would threaten American control over and access to resources, as well as American markets. America has thus become the foremost defender of the status quo, maintaining a consistent counterrevolutionary posture in its postwar foreign policy. A recent article by Tad Szulc (1974) indicates the extent to which this interventionist posture has continued to the present. Szulc describes how the supersecret, highly centralized "40 Committee," led by Secretary of State Kissinger, directed the successful effort to "destabilize" the Allende regime in Chile. He also describes the role played by previous versions of the committee in similar ventures during previous administrations. This counterrevolutionary thrust of postwar American foreign policy has been underlined by recent evidence turned up in the hearings of congressional committees investigating both the "covert activities" of American intelligence agencies and the political activities of American corporations, both here and abroad (see U.S. Senate, 1973).

We think it is important to point out that this view of the "roots" of American foreign policy is not the exclusive property of left-oriented critics of American policy. Conservative writers such as George Liska, for instance, would agree that the overall objective of American policy is, and should be, the maintenance of America's imperial position in the world. In a somewhat emotional concluding paragraph to his study of "Imperial America," Liska writes:

> The function defining great nations—and constituting their manifest destiny—has always been, first, to consolidate a viable habitat to the outermost natural and morally sanctionable limits; and, secondly, having done so and outgrown the adolescent oscillations in moods between exuberance and seclusion, to contribute in their maturity to the construction and consolidation of a wider matrix of order. Such order serves more than one purpose. It is the stage for self-affirmation in the time of strength and vigor; it is the creator's support in moments of failing and, for a time, in his eventual decline in strength relative to others. And, last but not least, it is a feat to be remembered, and a model to be imitated, after the imperial creator has left the world of action for the realm of history. (1967, p. 113)

What is more, the content of this imperial position, it is quite clear, is dominated by the need for continued access to the important regions of the world, a need that can be interpreted only in economic terms. In writing about the Vietnam war, Liska says:

> The Vietnamese war will eventually have to be justified and understood instead as one of the less agreeable manifestations of the American world role. This role implies the necessity to define—by force if necessary—the terms on which regional balances of power are evolved and American access to individual regions is secured. . . . (Author's Preface, paragraph 5)

Liska's disagreement with the left is to be found not so much in his analysis as in his value preferences.

Now that we have identified some of the basic interests pursued by American elites in the post–1945 period, we can turn to our third and last question: the ideological formulations through which these interests are filtered. The most prominent element in these formulations has been a pervasive and continuing ideology of anti-Communism and its concomitant strategies of containment and counterrevolutionary intervention. The belief that American foreign policy must adopt a posture of continuing resistance to the spread of Communism wherever it occurs, or threatens to occur, has shaped all of our foreign policy decisions, determining the range of options and defining the choices. This is borne out in striking fashion by our case studies. There is not a single decision, from the Marshall Plan, foreign aid, and trade expansion, to the Cuban missile crisis and the Lebanese and Dominican interventions, that was not justified by raising the banner of anti-Communism. In fact, one can safely say that virtually every important American foreign policy decision in the postwar period has occurred in response to some perceived or apparent Communist threat.

The degree of consensus on this ideology is also remarkable. Excluding the extreme left, virtually all portions of the political spectrum have accepted anti-Communism as the major parameter of American foreign policy. In his opposition to the Bay of Pigs invasion, for instance, even so persistent a critic of American policy as Senator William Fulbright was careful to point out that he too perceived the basic Communist threat; he differed only on the means by which to counter it. In the Cuban missile crisis it was clear that such options as the simple acceptance of the right of Cuba as a sovereign nation to determine its own defense posture were quickly excluded by the acknowledgment of the Communist threat. The entire history of American postwar intervention under the Truman Doctrine, the Eisenhower Doctrine, and the Nixon Doctrine provides us with further documentation of this principle. In each case, intervention was justified under the broad banner of anti-Communism, combined with more specific arguments based on strategic and economic necessity. Recent empirical investigations substantiate this line of argument. Barnet (1973, Chapters 6, 7), after demonstrating the preponderance of men with business orientations and backgrounds in key foreign policy positions, shows the extent to which the anti-Communist credo has coincided with the *Weltanschauung* of business elites. John C. Donovan has argued that an expanding body of empirical data (for example, *The Pentagon Papers*) "indicates that the struggle within the innermost circle [of foreign-policy makers] did not involve significant disagreement over the *ends* of U.S. national security policy during the 1960's" (1972, p. 20).

At the beginning of this chapter we indicated that we would

try to show how the interests of elites are linked with the objectives and goals of American foreign policy. It now appears that in the postwar years there has existed in the highest circles of decision making a remarkable degree of unanimity regarding ends, and that members of the economic elite have exercised a disproportionate degree of influence in the determination of those ends, so that their foreign policy preferences have prevailed for almost three decades.

It is clear, then, that in order to make some sense out of the surface disorder of foreign policy, it is not sufficient to simply identify, or even analyze, the external stimuli, the personalities of the actors, or their institutional roles in individual decisions. Decision making is, as we have seen, "a social process imbedded in the stream of social processes" (Bauer et al., 1972, p. 479). Even when the unit of analysis is the foreign policy decision, an effort must be made to study a range of such decisions in their social context and within a comparative framework. It is only when this is done that we can adequately answer the fundamental questions: Who makes foreign policy, how is it made, and for whose benefit is it made?

REFERENCES AND BIBLIOGRAPHY

BARNET, RICHARD J., *Roots of War*. Baltimore: Penguin, 1973.

BAUER, RAYMOND A., ITHIEL DE SOLA POOL, and LEWIS A. DEXTER, *American Business and Public Policy*. Chicago: Aldine-Atherton, 1972.

BEARD, CHARLES A., *The Idea of National Interest: An Analytical Study in American Foreign Policy*. New York: MacMillan, 1934.

BERKOWITZ, MORTON, and P. G. BOCK, *American National Security*. New York: Free Press, 1965.

DONOVAN, JOHN C., *The Cold Warriors: A Policy-Making Elite*. Lexington, Mass.: Health, 1972.

GALBRAITH, JOHN KENNETH, *The New Industrial State*, 2nd ed. Boston: Houghton Mifflin, 1971.

HEILBRONER, ROBERT L., "Counterrevolutionary America," *Commentary*, April, 1967, pp. 31–38.

HOROWITZ, DAVID, ed., *Corporations and the Cold War*. New York: Monthly Review Press, 1969.

KENNAN, GEORGE F., *The Realities of American Foreign Policy*. Princeton, N.J.: Princeton University Press, 1954.

KISSINGER, HENRY A., *American Foreign Policy*, expanded ed. New York: Norton, 1974.

KOLKO, GABRIEL, *The Roots of American Foreign Policy*. Boston: Beacon Press, 1969.

LISKA, GEORGE, *Imperial America: The International Politics of Primacy*. Baltimore: Johns Hopkins, 1967.

MILLS, C. WRIGHT, *The Power Elite*. New York: Oxford University Press, 1956.

MORGENTHAU, HANS, *Politics Among Nations*, 4th ed. New York: Knopf, 1967.

ROSENAU, JAMES, N., *The Scientific Study of Politics*. New York: Free Press, 1971.

SZULC, TAD, "How Kissinger Runs Our 'Other Government,' " *New York Magazine*, September 30, 1974, pp. 59–66.

U.S., Senate, Committee on Foreign Relations, Subcommittee on Multinational Corporations. *Hearings on Multinational Corporations and United States Foreign Policy*, Parts 1 and 2, 93rd Cong., 1st sess., 1973.

WILLIAMS, WILLIAM APPELMAN, *The Tragedy of American Diplomacy*. Cleveland: World Publishing, 1959.

WRIGHT, QUINCY, *A Study of War*. Chicago: University of Chicago Press, 1964.

Index